D1478914

In Search of Ogopogo

SACRED CREATURE OF THE OKANAGAN WATERS

Arlene Gaal

hancock

house

ISBN 0-88839-482-9
Copyright © 2001 Arlene Gaal

Cataloging in Publication Data
  Gaal, Arlene B., (date)
  In search of Ogopogo

  ISBN 0-88839-482-9

  1. Ogopogo I. Title.
  QL89.2.O34G33 2001   001.944   C00-911220-0

Cover design: Caleb Doubtfire
Back cover photograph: David Gaal

We acknowledge the financial support of the Government of Canada through the Book Publishing Industry Development Program for our publishing activities.

Published simultaneously in Canada and the United States by

HANCOCK HOUSE PUBLISHERS LTD.
19313 Zero Avenue, Surrey, B.C. V3S 9R9

HANCOCK HOUSE PUBLISHERS
1431 Harrison Avenue, Blaine, WA 98230-5005

(604) 538-1114   Fax (604) 538-2262
(800) 938-1114   Fax (800) 983-2262
Web Site: www.hancockhouse.com   *email:* sales@hancockhouse.com

Contents

To my grandsons:

*Jordan, Colton and Joshua whose youthful influences
and probing minds help sustain the very existence
of future generations!*

Year of the Dragon (2000)

The dragon is ubiquitous throughout Asia, appearing in architecture, fashion, art, literature and mythology. It serves as the symbol for the capital city of Hanoi as the Vietnamese believe they have descended from the union of a dragon and a fairy. The dragon, whose totemic symbol was a crocodile or snake, was said to rule the coastal peoples while the fairy in the form of a bird, governed the mountain tribes.

Western mythology portrays dragons as malevolent creatures that breathe fire and barbecue hapless bystanders while going around capturing princesses and getting subdued by gallant knights. In Vietnam, the dragon is the symbol of a benevolent animal. When the black dragon fetches water, it means sunshine; when the white dragon fetches water, it portends rain.

It is believed that the great dragon myths and legends originated 2,000 years ago in southeast Asia. The creature's original form was most likely that of a crocodile or large sea snake—aquatic animals that were abundant in hot, wet, rice-growing cultures.

The dragon is a powerful symbol in Chinese mythology, worn only by the king to symbolize power. Even though mythology states that no one has ever seen a dragon, mountains are said to resemble the hunched backs of dragons and rivers are equated with dragons serpentlike bodies. The Chinese refer to mountains as mountain dragons and rivers as water dragons. The Year of the Dragon, which began February 2, 2000, is believed to bring strength and good luck to all.

About the Author

Arlene Gaal was born and raised in a coal-mining town in southeastern British Columbia; she is a teacher by profession and author/journalist by choice. In 1968 she and her husband Joe and three children moved to Kelowna, a city located on Okanagan Lake in central British Columbia and home to the famous Ogopogo. To her, it was Canada's Hawaii because of the exquisite scenery and comfortable climate.

A curiosity-seeker at heart, Arlene soon began tracking the many sightings of the creature in Okanagan Lake. Her search led her to the first film footage taken of the animal, the Folden film, which she purchased. Her first book, *Beneath the Depths*, was launched in Kelowna in 1976. Soon after that, Alan Landsburg Productions from Los Angeles, arrived to shoot the very first program about Okanagan Lake, *In Search of Ogopogo,* and Gaal worked alongside the crew as a consultant. This was the beginning of a continuing relationship with television crews from around the world and interviews with major newspapers, including the *New York Times*, *London Daily Mail* and *Chicago Tribune.*

Arlene Gaal became the reporting station for sightings of Ogopogo, and as the years progressed the accumulated data would easily fill a moderate-sized room. Not only did she document the sightings, but she made certain that any film, video or still photos taken did not go astray as they were filed for historical preservation. By 1984 it became apparent that it was time for another book, and Hancock House Publishers released *Ogopogo, The Million Dollar Monster* written by Gaal.

Interest in the unknown is never without controversy and the Chaplin video footage presented one of the more difficult periods in Ogopogo research. The television program, *Unsolved Mysteries* paid $30,000 for the material as critics offered their explanations for the video. In 1990 and 1991, Nippon Television from Tokyo, Japan, requested Arlene Gaals' presence as a consultant for two productions shot on Okanagan Lake. Helicopters, Deep Rover submersibles and a remote operating vehicle (ROV) were part of an intensive search for the elusive creature. Nippon crews did not go home disappointed as video footage and sonar readings captured what could only be explained as Ogopogo. Gaal was present for both productions.

In 1999, crews worked with Gaal on numerous programs: two separate crews arrived from Germany; Fortean Television from London aired a production in February, 1998, and crews from Los Angeles, including Sachnoff-Lipman Entertainment aired a documentary on Ogopogo for the Learning Channel in the latter part of 1998. Gaal was also in consultation with script writer Barry Authors and producer Kim Todd regarding a year 2000 motion picture to be filmed on Ogopogo. Arlene Gaal moves into the millennium with *In Search of Ogopogo: Sacred Creature of the Okanagan Waters* as her greatest achievement yet. New photos, film footage and untold stories are featured in the book, with Ogopogo once again front row center.

Arlene Gaal was awarded a lifetime honorary membership to the B.C. Cryptozoology Society and continues her hands-on interest, whenever opportunity arises. She still lives and works in Kelowna, B.C. with her daughter Laurie and three grandchildren. Husband Joe died suddenly December 25, 1986, and her oldest son Joey was murdered while a guest at Ocean View Hotel in Pattaya, Thailand, April 30, 1989. Son David lives with his wife Miyuki in Fukuoka, Japan. Gaal continues to write a weekly column for the *Kelowna Daily Courier* as she has done for the past twenty-four years and is presently completing a book on her son's murder investigation.

Acknowledgments

To the many witnesses who provided detailed accounts, photos, film footage and videotapes, making this book possible; to the *Kelowna Daily Courier* for its continued reporting of events; the Capital News, CHBC Television and radio stations in Kelowna, Vernon and Penticton for opening doors to contacts; to Calib Doubtfire for doing a great job of the cover image of Ogopogo; and, to everyone whose interest and confidence allows Ogopogo research entry into a science of its own.

—Arlene Gaal

Witnesses and friends of Ogopogo are invited to write to Arlene Gaal at the following email address:

GaalA1035@aol.com

First Word

I am a skeptic when it comes to the unexplained. I do not know what it was I saw, however I know what it was not. It was not a boat, a log a sequence of waves or a school of fish. It is my opinion that many people have probably seen it and not been aware of what they were really seeing. All too often we tune out our observational skills and make an assumption to something logical. I am a converted Ogopogo believer.

—Phyllis Frew, Kelowna teacher, May 19, 1987 sighting.

Writing this third book on Ogopogo has been a revelation. As I approached it, I did so with an open mind realizing that it takes a brave soul to step forward in this age of skepticism and ridicule to report seeing something out of the ordinary. Perhaps it takes an even braver soul to write about it and face the judges. Most of the evidence in this volume has been accumulated from 1984 to the present time, with some reflection on history and parallel animals.

My first book, *Beneath the Depths*, was published in 1976, and was followed by *Ogopogo: The True Story of the Okanagan Lake Million Dollar Monster* in 1986 and each has its place. In *In Search of Ogopogo: Sacred Creature of the Water* we are much closer to finding an answer to these mysterious creatures who rise from the depths. They have been presented in biblical text, written up in nautical journals and sought out by monster hunters from Loch Ness to Okanagan Lake. Working with the more recent pictures and videotapes was exciting and of course rewarding, as the burden of proof unfolded.

In this visual age, with compact videocameras and the more recent digital camera, people are prepared for that great photographic experience. Okanagan Lake is one of Canada's most picturesque lakes and perhaps even one of the best in the world. To visit its shores without a camera may rouse an individual to the same level of stress as the lottery enthusiast who said "no" to the Extra, should N'ha-a-itk/Ogopogo make an appearance. For most, the opportunity comes around only once.

Our entrance into this era of visual consciousness has allowed this book to be one of the most convincing ever written and provides fruit for the believers and food for the skeptics. Credit goes to the individuals whose questioning minds caused them to document, photograph or videotape what it was they were seeing. As I prepared the photographic evidence, there was an excitement and zeal not experienced with the last two books, as the Zaiser photos, DeMara footage and others give the world its first real glimpse of this majestic animal. It is real and very much alive, contrary to popular belief.

The enormous size of this animal and the evidence of a family of such creatures raises many questions and taunts our awareness to a consideration of science fiction. A close encounter could indeed prove disastrous in a threatening scenario. There is, however, some solace in the knowledge that the animals have never presented a real threat and appear to be both docile in nature and cognitive of territorial rights as they maneuver in and around the many swimmers and boaters of Okanagan Lake.

As we move into the twenty-first century, sightings of Ogopogo continue. N'ha-a-itk has dispelled myth for almost three centuries, frightening the natives, alarming early settlers and mesmerizing hundreds of clear-headed individuals, as its majestic body rises from the depths at times and places convenient only unto itself. Unidentified swimming animals of unusual size and description are often seen in freshwater lakes and oceans around the world pushing creationists and evolutionists alike to attempt to explain the how and why of their existence. One interested enthusiast stated, "I'd still like to believe that there are some animals that haven't been touched by man."

Enjoy the book, for in time there will be another.

—Arlene Gaal

In the Beginning

Whether it be Japan's Nippon Television, England's Yorkshire Television or David Frank, producer of the Fox network program called *Sightings*, Ogopogo appears to be a phenomenon that stirs endless interest. Naitaka or N'ha-a-itk, as he/she was referred to by the local Native people, has been discussed, written about and photographed since the mid-1800s. Indian legends abound, stories of close encounters are analyzed and skeptics, certain that it is simply all nonsense, make up the audience of today's Ogopogo script.

Why then, if something is as elusive as an unidentified lake monster, would there be such an intense interest and demand for information? Science accepts only data that can measure up to its standards. We, of course, would have to be prepared to provide a carcass or tissue sample for proper DNA analysis to meet these expectations. On the other hand, there are those who choose to believe because they have indeed seen, and others who choose to believe because the existence of unidentified species being uncovered and identified provides a strong link from the unknown to the known. Either way, whether skeptic or believer, this book will leave you with information and questions that are deserving of further pursuit.

In 1872, while scanning the lake in search of her husband John, expecting his return from his journey across Okanagan Lake, Mrs. Susan Allison was the first settler who reported seeing an unusual animal swimming against the waves. Afraid that her husband had met his demise in the jaws of N'ha-a-itk, she perhaps could be credited for opening the door to Ogopogo reporting. Very familiar with Okanagan Lake, she knew full well that this creature was something she could not readily identify, making its presence all the more foreboding.

John Allison, being a stalwart soul, listened to his wife's tale and laughed it off while he jokingly accused her of taking a nip or two from the wine barrel. However, his safe return from across Okanagan Lake through an intense storm, created a respect for the power of nature's wrath, whether it be monster or otherwise, and made him appreciative of the pleasures of home.

Susan Allison (who died in 1928) spent much of her lifetime studying Indian folklore and even contributed articles to London journals. Her writings told of a kindly old Indian who once lived by the lake and who was killed by an evil wanderer. As punishment, the Gods turned the killer into a giant lake serpent so he would spend eternity at the scene of the crime.

Long before the white man arrived, the Indians told tales of a lake monster they called N'ha-a-itk, a creature both revered and feared by the local Natives. So strong was this reverence and fear, that the wise man about to enter into communion with the unknown would procure a small animal to be used as a sacrifice, should they encounter the wrath of the beast. It was considered foolish to do otherwise. All too often a storm would spring up and out of the lashing waves the demon would appear and attempt to claim another life. To appease the serpent and ensure a safe return, the small animal would be thrown overboard.

One story told of a popular chief named Timbasket who failed to heed the warnings of his elders. Chief Timbasket and family, while visiting the Okanagan, were very skeptical of N'ha-a-itk as they watched the village tribesmen prepare for the trip down the lake. The canoes to accompany the honored guest were marked with a special symbol and a live dog was prepared for sacrifice. It was decreed that all canoes must travel within a certain distance from the shore and every precaution was taken to avoid rousing the fearsome beast. The chief, however, was not frightened by superstition, nor would he agree to steer a roundabout course simply to keep away from Squally Point. As he paddled his canoe close to shore, waves suddenly appeared, and in a flurry of lashing water, the chief and his family disappeared. The Indians were familiar with the antics of the lake monster who often lashed its tail in anger, churning up the waters to ward off the approaching enemy. Foolish Chief Timbasket was never seen again. Some say his canoe disappeared in the middle of the lake, other stories tell of his canoe being discovered washed up on shore near Squally Point, the home of N'ha-a-itk, or Ogopogo.

According to all who knew and believed, this young Brave succumbed to the jaws of the ferocious one.

The story of John McDougall and his horses often surfaces in conversations about N'ha-a-itk. This well-known Metis, who always crossed the lake in his canoe with his horses in tow, suddenly noticed his horses being pulled under. Realizing the danger, John grabbed his sheath knife, cut the tow rope and paddled off feeling very distraught as his horses slowly disappeared beneath the depths of Okanagan Lake.

With the arrival of the first settlers, stories of a large unknown animal in Okanagan Lake continued. Concerns arose and many settlers took turns patrolling the lakeshore, musket in hand, to protect their families from an impending Ogopogo attack.

When the British Columbia government announced that a ferry would run between Kelowna and Westbank in the summer of 1926, it was stated that "the ship would be armed with devices designed to repel attacks from Ogopogo."

The story caught the attention of some big game hunters from around the province and Washington State who began staking out the lake awaiting opportunity to shoot this unusual creature. Much to their disappointment, the animal did not comply and remained beneath the depths of Okanagan Lake. The hype, of course, soon died down.

Frank Buckland, in his book *Ogopogo's Vigil*, wrote: "From time out of mind this legendary creature has viewed with bulging, 'picis-zooid' eyes, the hills, benches, and flats surrounding Great Okanagan Lake. A mysterious something makes its appearance, usually in the warm summer and early autumn, to excite the credulity of those who look upon it.

"Long ago, the elusive monster was known as N'ha-a-itk, Sacred Creature of the Water. It was not until some years later that it was referred to as the Lake Demon."

The evidence of an unusual animal observed by the Native culture can be seen in the many pictographs found in the rock face and on bluffs that border Okanagan Lake. Although interpretation may be deemed questionable, there is no doubting the resemblance to some form of aquatic species. One in particular shows an animal upright with a long neck, flippers, reptilian head with raised ears. Other pictographs in the Gellatly Bay area portray similar creatures, an obvious early artistic depiction of something other than fish, that were either observed or perhaps remembered from stories told to them by the elders.

Ogopogo, or N'ha-a-itk, is a subject of controversy among tribal members. Much like in our culture, there are those who believe and others who stand firm and deny its very existence. The skeptic is deserving of the same respect as the believer.

Okanagan Lake extends from Vernon in the north to Penticton in the south, some eighty miles (129 km), with depths varying from a few feet to nearly 1,000 feet (305 m) near Okanagan Center. Reported sightings of this Okanagan USO (Unidentified Swimming Object), occur in almost every area of Okanagan Lake and descriptions are invariably similar. A large animal from twenty to seventy feet (6–21 m) in length, darkish green or brown in color moving or undulating through the water with two or more equidistant protrusions.

A sighting of Ogopogo is as rare as a lottery win, but seeing the animal with the head out of the water is even more unusual. Those lucky enough to see the head have described it as being reptilian or serpentine in shape. Others allude to protrusions or horns on its head, a description that rarely if ever crossed my desk during many years of research. It could possibly be a physical characteristic similar to a periscope, that can raise and lower according to its oxygen requirements. Another theory is that we may be observing the animals in various stages of development, which can account for the differences. Ridges on its back have been reported and an identifiable fin was photographed by Mike Paskal in 1990. The Riegers, while out fishing in the north end of the lake, talk of seeing an animal of at least twenty ton (18 t) having front appendages with a distinct join at the elbow and strong back legs similar to those seen on a dinosaur. They described a swooshing sound as it propelled itself through the water pushing with its strong back legs. It was apparently feeding, as its neck moved back and forth beneath the surface where a school of fish was spotted.

Ogopogo has been observed moving at incredible speeds through Okanagan Lake while creating impressive waves. Others have witnessed the creature thrashing about in one spot much like the sighting filmed by Japan's Nippon Television near Peachland in 1990, an event I was able to witness. At times the animal is seen gliding slowly over the lake's surface, oblivious to anything around it. As it surfaces and submerges, it can be likened to a submarine with massive waves rolling off its back.

This amazing lake creature is unlike any known species, but does indeed bear striking similarities to Nessie in Loch Ness, Champ in Lake Champlain, Issie in Lake Ikeda, Japan, and the many other aquatic animals reportedly seen in hundreds of lakes around the world. If ever the world grew tired of its present probes into space or if money was in abundance, just think of what man might uncover in planned excursions beneath the depths of each of these lakes. Jacques Cousteau was my mentor and the recent loss of this great explorer ended my dream to have him participate along with his mini sub in the greatest expedition ever for these unknown animals of Okanagan Lake. His son now carries the legacy of his father's expeditions.

Imagine being thrust back to a time to witness your very own Jurassic Park in an era some 200 million years ago when dinosaurs roamed the earth. It is said that summer existed for millions of years allowing palm trees to grow in Alaska and fig trees in Greenland. Perhaps it is here that these unusual aquatic animals now being reported in hundreds of freshwater lakes throughout the world could trace their history.

As dinosaurs ruled on land, distinctly related reptiles swam in the seas. The *Tylosaurus*, *Plesiosaurus* and *Mosasaurus* may have been the forerunners to creatures now being reported in lake systems around the world. To assume that they survived the Ice Age in the same structural form as their predecessors may be presumptous but not entirely impossible. It may be more reasonable to assume that the above reptiles evolved in accordance to the environment in which they now live. How else could they have survived for so long?

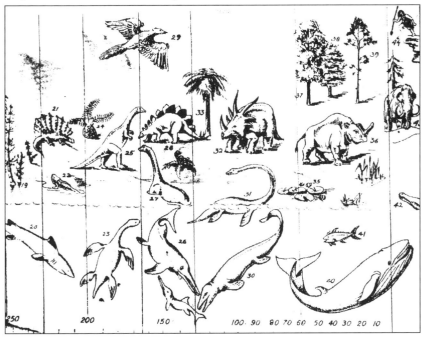

A program produced in 1999 by Omni Productions, called *The River Giants*, in which I had the pleasure of participating, revealed some interesting facts. In order to provide fertile soil conditions to allow for farming, Sumas Lake near Chilliwack, British Columbia, was drained, fill was provided and farms were built. What was somewhat unbelievable is the fact that as the farmers plowed their fields even after five years, they often came across large prehistoric sturgeon buried beneath the mud. Amazingly, these animals, which should have been dead, were very much alive, and were reintroduced to the nearest body of water. What conditions were present to allow for this amazing resurrection? Is there some characteristic that has allowed for the perpetuation and existence of prehistoric species that the sturgeon was privy to? Could this condition have existed in the Mesozoic era at the time when the *Pleisiosuarus* began its reign in the Triasic period, or when the *Ichthyosaurus* swam about in Jurassic times or as the *Mosasaur* and *Elasmosaurus* entered the Cretaceous age, allowing also for the perpetuation of these species in our time?

To be realistic, the answer to these questions should be an emphatic "No." However, not to contemplate it as being a possibility would be an error in judgement, considering the many reported sightings today of animals resembling reptiles who lived during the Mesozoic age. Descriptions of these creatures cannot be discounted nor can the photos, film footage or videotape accounts showing creatures of enormous size that do not conform to the normal inhabitants of the lake systems in which they now live.

It is a rare interview in which I am not asked, "What exactly do you believe is being seen in Okanagan Lake?" To this I generally take a deep breath and reply: "First of all, I am not a scientist, but a researcher or historian with some fellow reporters coining the phrase Ogopologist, to which I take kindly as it does not commit me to any known science and therefore is free of assumption. No one can presently state without eliciting some doubt just what these aquatic creatures found swimming in hundreds of lakes around the world really are. We can speculate, provide intellectual examinations and state that they have similarities to... or bear a resemblance to..., but until an actual carcass is found and properly examined or a species captured, it is open season for any and all hypotheses. Until such time, the mystery continues."

The second question that almost always follows is: "Has anyone ever been harmed by the creature?" Once again, there is always the temptation to go with the dramatic to stir up the listening audience. However, my usual truthful response is: "Not to my knowledge." Unusual holes have suddenly appeared in the bows of boats and bodies of some unfortunate drowning victims have never been recovered, but rational explanations for the mysterious happenings take precedence to an encounter with Ogopogo. It should be remembered that this animal is much like any other living creature; if provoked or threatened in any way, it will react to protect itself or its young.

Lake History

Okanagan Lake is a "fjord lake." Geologists state that the steep-walled, elongated, deep-water basin has all the same characteristics as a coastal fjord.

Recent seismic tests conducted by a team from the University of Toronto indicate the Okanagan Basin is one of the most impressive surface geological features in North America.

Nicolas Eyles, Henry T. Mullins and Albert Hines found the bedrock under the sediment in the lake at 2,133 feet (650 m) below sea level. They observed a steeply sloping V-shaped bedrock valley along most of the Okanagan Basin.

They state: "The average elevation of the surrounding plateau into which the basin is cut is 1500 meters above sea level indicating a total relief of over 2000 meters. We emphasize that this relief exceeds that of the Grand Canyon of Arizona (1600 m.) where the Colorado River cuts across the Kabib Plateau."

The sediment of the bottom of the lake forms three layers. The first layer is thought to be ice moraine, left by retreating ice. The second layer was deposited while huge Glacial Lake Penticton existed, covering an area from Okanagan Falls to Enderby. The third layer was laid down after the glacial lake era; it is sediment brought down by the streams feeding the lake.

Kelowna-based geologist, Dr. Murray Roed does not agree with the current belief that Okanagan Lake gets all its water from these surface streams. He believes there is a huge source of groundwater also feeding the lake.

"There is a very high oxygen content in the water even at great depths," he states, "and there is no way that it all comes from surface runoff." To say that the surface runoff accounts for all the water going into the lake is unrealistic according to Roed who believes that at least

17

half the water feeding the lake comes from underground springs and simple groundwater leaching through the hundreds of fractures in the rock all around the basin (Kelowna *Daily Courier*, February 16, 1992).

The latest geological theory among Canadian scientists Dr. Randy Parrish of Ottawa and Dr. Dirk Templeton-Kluit of Vancouver, suggests that the Okanagan Valley was actually part of the west coast of North America, 1.7 billion years ago. Recent studies report that Okanagan Lake straddles a huge fault line at least twelve and a half miles (20 km) deep and extending well into the middle of the earth's crust, representing an earlier torn edge of the continent.

At one time the three layers were all stacked on top of the other. Then the bottom layer uplifted, forcing the two top layers to separate. One layer quite literally went west and the other east forming part of the Coastal Range and Cordillera, including the Coastal and Rocky Mountains.

Dr. Murray Roed is excited about this theory, saying it helps to explain a lot of the valley's landmarks. "Okanagan Mountain Park is probably the oldest existing rock in the area and lies across the lake from Mount Boucherie, which, along with Knox Mountain, represent more recent volcanic activity."

Ice-age scouring alone does not account for the amazing depth of Okanagan Lake. The bedrock floor of the lake sits at 2,100 feet (640 m) below sea-level. The water level measured at its greatest depths is1,200 feet (360 m) or more.

Roed stated that the Grand Canyon can't hold a candle to the way this valley looked at one point during the Jurassic age, when dinosaurs roamed the earth. The distance between the highest point in the Kelowna area, Little White Mountain, and the lowest points, the bottom of the lake, is 6,562 feet (2,000 m). That 2,000-meter difference in this valley was more dramatic 170 million years ago with great rifts and huge volcanoes side by side. After the upheaval and following at least two ice ages, an immense lake covered much of the valley from Enderby to Okanagan Falls and was known as Glacial Lake Penticton. Perhaps it was at this time that the prehistoric-like creatures that we now refer to as Ogopogo or N'ha-a-itk took up permanent residence in the massive lake system.

As the last of the ice damming the glacial lake at Okanagan Falls melted, a huge outrush of water swept out of the Kelowna Basin and carved out many of the hollows and spaces that we see today.

Toward the end of the age of reptiles, the great seas that flooded much of the land returned to their old basins and perhaps there is truth in the theory that the swimming reptiles such as the *Elasmosaurus, Mesosaur* and even the *Tylosaurus* survived, making the many reported sightings of a prehistoric-like creature in Okanagan Lake, Skaha Lake, Lake Kalamalka and Shuswap Lake much closer to reality than many would care to imagine.

The creatures of the lakes could very well have possessed biological survival traits far greater than even the Sardis Lake sturgeon, allowing them continued existence. The on-again, off-again sturgeon debate is a theory that does not appear to "hold much water," where Okanagan Lake is concerned, according to some believers.

Cal Bevan, a well-known diver who not only lived on the lake in Bevan's Barge with his family for many years, but also spent countless hours in the depths of Okanagan Lake, was very much attuned to the different species. He offered an open $5,000 reward in the early 1980s to anyone who was able to catch a sturgeon while fishing the waters of Okanagan Lake. To this day no one has claimed the money. A few years later, a local radio station and sports store offered a $10,000 prize to anyone catching the elusive sturgeon in Okanagan Lake.

"The Okey-dokey Lake Monster Derby, sponsored by CKIQ and Harvs Outdoor Sports in Kelowna is being held in an attempt to prove that Ogopogo is indeed a sturgeon." Chris Gibson, CKIQ director of promotions and national sales states that "when Okanagan Lake Bridge was being built, local divers reported sightings of monstrous creatures in the lake, namely sturgeon."

Although Gibson hasn't been successful in finding someone who has caught a sturgeon from Okanagan Lake, he is "positive the prehistoric-looking fish do live there." In twenty years of research and investigating sightings, there has never been one single sturgeon caught in Okanagan Lake. I do, however, reserve the right to be corrected, as it is a known fact that sturgeon thrive in freshwater lakes.

Considering the great depth of Okanagan Lake and the fact that sturgeon are bottom feeders, if they do indeed inhabit the lake, they would rarely, if ever, need to come to the surface. Ogopogo, on the other hand, not only breaks water but enjoys swimming at high speeds through the lake with head held high. Sturgeon, as we know, remain underwater while swimming and do not have the classic neck of the Ogopogo. Upon request from Tokyo's Nippon Television who planned an expedition to Okanagan Lake, I obtained a species list from the Department of Fisheries. It mentioned common fish, such as kokanee, ling cod, trout and others, but clearly states that to their knowledge sturgeon were never reported in Okanagan Lake.

Searches

To say that there has been a real scientific search of Okanagan Lake for the elusive Ogopogo, similar to that which has taken place in Loch Ness over the years, would not be quite true. But to say that there has never been interest expressed in finding out what really lives beneath the depths of Okanagan Lake would be just as inaccurate. Since the publication of my first book, *Beneath the Depths*, in 1976, hardly a week has passed by without some form of inquiry about Ogopogo from film producers, television networks, reporters, television news teams as well as from serious searchers. All of this really began in 1977 when Landsburg Productions made a decision to produce the television special *In Search of Ogopogo* on the shores of Okanagan Lake. I was a novice and very new to the game of television and agreed to work with producer Nick Webster and the team as a consultant, receiving the grand sum of $350 for the complete week. At that time the money did not seem to matter, it was the excitement and thrill of being a part of Hollywood.

Landsburg Productions went into this in a big way; the First Nations People cooperated, erecting teepees, telling stories around a camp fire, offering a prayer to Manitou to appease the lake serpent, while locals agreed to reenact the roles of settlers patrolling Okanagan Lake to protect their families against an Ogopogo attack.

The late Mary Moon was a co-consultant as she too had just completed a book on Ogopogo. I grew to know Mary well during that week, and admired her tenacity and straightforwardness. (She died mysteriously a few years later while investigating the files of Nazi war criminal Klaus Barbie, whom she suspected was somehow being protected by the CIA in his trek to Bolivia.)

Halfway through the shoot, with Ogopogo fever high in Kelowna, producer Nick Webster was entrapped by what appeared to be an Ogopogo just off the beach of Gyro Park. The excitement registered in his voice as he threw rocks at the creature, yelling for the crew to start filming. I calmly went to the trunk of my car and took out a pair of binoculars, smiling as I clearly made out the white-wall tires that had been purposely set up in the lake. Needless to say, it was a great prop for our local actors who were about to reenact the scene involving the settlers patrolling the lakeshore.

A few years ago I was asked to list the number of film crews that had come to Kelowna in search of an Ogopogo story. I soon realized that I never really did do a count, as there was always a crew of some sort either here for a shoot or waiting on the sidelines for an opportunity to tell their version of the story. Taking some time to seriously consider the question I had counted almost forty crews consisting of a producer/director, cameraman and soundman. My house had been transformed into a movie studio setting so many times that I did indeed lose count. My neighbors became accustomed to seeing interviews conducted on the front or back lawn, and in time the initial excitement died down. Most producers, other than the Japanese, generally arranged for a support crew from Vancouver, appropriately dubbed Hollywood North, and traveled to Kelowna as a team.

I was just beginning an interview with Fortean Television from London when the twinkle in their soundman's eye caught my attention. The crew had already been in the house for an hour and the flurry of setting up kept all else at bay. Suddenly I blurted out, as our eyes continued to focus: "Weren't you here earlier this year?" His moustache twitched as he laughingly replied. "I wondered how long it would take for you to recognize me." Patrick, whose last name I never learned, returned again May 17, 2000, with the crew from *EXTRA* to film a segment on the "two-million-dollar reward."

Personal interviews with newspapers, including the *New York Times*, *London Daily Mail*, *The Chicago Tribune* and *Seattle Times* caught international attention, bringing *Inside Edition*'s Rick Kirkam and *Unsolved Mysteries*' John Cosgrove to Kelowna. Needless to say, the publicity was great for the city of Kelowna.

Remembering Jack

"You mean to say you're going to sit there and have me believe that there's a monster in Okanagan Lake? Convince me! Convince me!" The voice was that of Jack Webster, prominent talk show host for CJOR in Vancouver and his thick Scottish brogue had me spellbound.

It was at that moment in 1976 while being threatened by the CJOR microphone and staring into the visage of the all-powerful Webster, that I realized that I had some gall. I had dared to write a book about the Okanagan Lake monster, Ogopogo, and this was to be my first actual interview. I had been forewarned and realized that I must now atone for my deed.

To my surprise the show was a great success and Jack Webster, elated by the response, continued the show into the next hour. He was far from terrible as rumored, but was instead a most admirable gentleman to be placed high on my list of greats. We met again a few years later, when I was a guest on CBC's *Front Page Challenge* alongside Janet Leigh. Jack was one of the panelists, joining Pierre Berton and Allan Fotheringham. Jack soon steered the subject to Ogopogo, and in his Scottish accent, called: "Arlene, Arlene, Arlene!" I was thrilled that he had remembered and more so when he took a strong stance as a believer and challenged Fotheringham's and Berton's chiding remarks, "If I have seen UFOs why can there not be Ogopogos?" When Jack Webster died in 1998, I felt that I had lost a friend.

Japanese Interest

In early 1990 communications began coming in from Tokyo. Nippon Television was considering Ogopogo as a project for their series on the world's greatest phenomena. Having planned a visit to Japan in mid-March of that year to visit my son David and his wife Miyuki, the director of the series, Michihito Ogawa, agreed to fly from Tokyo to Fukuoka to discuss the proposal. I went armed with the recent *Unsolved Mysteries* video, which included a copy of the Folden film. Mr. Ogawa was polite and quite responsive. When I returned to Canada, I received positive confirmation of their intent with a written request for me to act as consultant on a proposed search for Ogopogo in mid-July. Heading the team would be producer Hidetsugu Honda. Nippon expected the very best and I was prepared to do what I could.

By early July, almost everything was in place—houseboat secured, motor boats lined up, helicopter service made available and witnesses prepared to cooperate. The media hype in the valley as well as other parts of British Columbia began to pick up. Most of all, the weather was ideal and the time of year for Ogopogo sightings could not have been better. The team arrived on cue and took up residence at the Capri Hotel. Mrs. Ono was hired to prepare the *bento* (lunch boxes for the crew) and members of the Okanagan Similkimeen Film Association had offered their assistance. Now all that was needed to make this adventure work for the Japanese would be an appearance by Ogopogo.

The lake was mysteriously calm with mist hanging in the distance. Divers positioned themselves, stopping momentarily on the ramp of the Shelter Bay Houseboat for one last equipment check before descending to the depths of Okanagan Lake.

Underwater cameras were readied and expectations high. Would they record an underwater sighting of the elusive lake creature, Ogopogo? Producer Hidetsugu Honda, a skilled diver himself, led the way. He was followed by Sarama and John, two local Kelowna divers who had been hired to assist. The setting was Rattlesnake Island and Squally Point, home of N'ha-a-itk. Nippon Television was in the second day of a serious search for Ogopogo. A huge splash indicated the divers were in the water. A camera crew set out behind them in a boat manned by Mike Guzzi, news director of Kelowna's radio station CKIQ. I stayed aboard the houseboat, attempting to keep an eye on the divers as well as the two sonar units positioned on either side.

Every so often the unit on my right would signal an alarm, indicating something in the water. It didn't take long to learn to distinguish between schools of fish and the surface and bottom of the lake. I spent a great deal of time observing the sonar readings, as I knew full well the importance of not missing anything unusual.

In certain areas the lake appeared to have two bottoms; one was an underwater peninsula and below that was the real lake bottom. I continued to monitor the readings and as we were nearing Squally Point, Rattlesnake Island area, I was captivated by what appeared on sonar. There was a 4.5 to 6 meter-wide long tunnel leading to unknown depths in the surrounding area of what has always been described as Ogopogo's home. Was this an entry tunnel? Was it a volcanic tunnel formation that allowed the animals to enter our water system and travel back and forth to an unknown home? Would this be a possible explanation for not ever finding the bones or dead carcasses of these elusive animals? When they intuitively knew the end of their life was near, did they retreat from whence they came? I wondered how many of these volcanic tunnels might exist in our eighty-mile-long lake system (129 km). They were identifiable by sonar and may provide answers to why the animals are spotted more often in some areas of the massive lake system than in others. This would be a challenge to other searchers.

Just as Gordon Ficke, a production assistant, came over to where I sat observing the sonar, a large object suddenly appeared on the screen at about the sixty-six-foot mark (20 m), moved across and then disappeared. "Did you see that?" he asked. Quite stunned, I nodded yes. "What do you think it was?" I asked. "Whatever it was, it was about twenty feet long," he replied.

Later that day, I learned that Mike Guzzi had reproduced a printout from his sonograph indicating an object of the same size and at the same depth. It was interesting to note that neither of us began screaming what might be expected "Ogopogo!" Experience produces a guarded optimism as credibility was, and still is, important to any seasoned researcher.

As I contemplated the events, my mind flashed back to the day before. After a deluge of reporters and cameraman, Lyndon, our houseboat captain, finally set out from Shelter Bay Marina. The plan was to have the main craft escorted by smaller boats, some with sonar, others acting as surface spotters.

For the first half hour, the six-man Japanese crew were taken in by the beauty and majesty of Okanagan Lake, while attempting to assimilate all the media excitement generated by their presence. Finally, the serious intent of our reasons for being there took over. As we neared the Bear Creek area on the west side of Okanagan Lake, I left the main houseboat and settled in on Mike Guzzi's craft with Masayuki Tamacki, writer and reporter from Tokyo, to observe the sonar equipment. I asked a lot of questions and soon began to understand how to read the sonograph units. Mike pointed out the surface and lake bottom. There were very few fish in sight.

We moved out into deeper water. Still no fish. As we hit the 500-foot (152 m) depth, Mr. Tamacki suddenly asked, "What's that?"

I moved over to have a look. Mike Guzzi indicated that the reading was coming from the 350-foot (107 m) depth mark and whatever it was looked to be at least thirty feet (9 m) long.

He moved the boat slowly out of the range of the sonar reading and then returned to the same spot. It was still showing a reading. There were indications of air bubble activity around it. The object began moving slowly across the screen and then remained stationary. Reporter John Daly and a crew from BCTV had just moved up beside us for an interview and of course they immediately began filming the LCD readout on the sonar monitor as well. This made the experience all the more authentic as we could never be accused of manufacturing a situation for the sake of gaining publicity. This was a real, live happening, and BCTV as well as Nippon Television had the exclusive.

"I've fished this area many times, and I've never seen anything like this come up on the screen," Mike Guzzi stated. By this time I was somewhat stunned as my eyes continued to monitor the screen. I don't recall showing any real excitement, but did get caught up in Masayuki Tamaki's enthused response. The realization of what had just happened and the magnitude of the event had not really registered. I knew it was no fish, but was something very much alive. It took at least fifteen minutes before I would attest to the probability of it being an Ogopogo species. The readout showed an object that appeared to have body proportions, smaller at its head section, a neck and a protuberant body structure with what appeared to be a tail attached. If my memory serves me correctly, there were also side appendages.

The excitement of the early afternoon soon subsided and we continued on with the search.

After a Chamber of Commerce reception later that day, the crew and I headed out along Highway 97 to Peachland as they wanted some film footage of Rattlesnake Island from land. We were using two vehicles, my car and a van. As we neared Peachland, we realized the crew had suddenly dropped from view. They were not ahead of us, so, thinking they might have taken a wrong turn, I immediately began to backtrack.

In a few minutes I spotted the crew and cameraman moving swiftly toward the lake. They had noticed a disturbance in the water and from the bluff off of Buchanan Road I could clearly see something churning up the water. The object broke water in an almost rectangular-shaped surface area. It began moving quickly toward shore, then it did something quite unexpected. The USO turned two complete circles, creating a wake with each turn, and just as suddenly it disappeared, leaving the lake as mirror-calm as it had been before its appearance.

We were all able to observe solid protrusions coming out of the water as it moved. All of this was, of course, being captured on camera by the

Nippon Television crew. This time, however, it was difficult to hide my feelings as I realized that unless someone could offer a better explanation, we had all been privy to a visit by a member or members of the N'ha-a-itk/Ogopogo family.

What was even more important was that Shinji, our camerman, had sprung immediately into action, and the event was preserved on film. A preview of the tape reconfirmed the reality of what had happened.

Gan Hanada, an interpreter for Nippon Television, who had come to Kelowna from Los Angeles to join the search, later commented on the incident: "I just considered this another assignment, and really believed it was something like a fairy tale. Now I know different."

The seven days soon came to an end. The fifteen-hour days had generated a great deal of excitement. Although the crew had lost an expensive underwater camera during the shoot at Rattlesnake Island, the film footage compensated for the loss.

It was a week of excitement for Kelowna that had taken me at least four months to organize after my initial contact with Michihito Ogawa while in Japan that previous March. But as I looked back on the experience I would not hesitate to do it all again.

Good-byes were said, and there was a promise of a planned return for an even more intense search of Okanagan Lake—this time with sophisticated equipment to conduct a concentrated search for the legendary Ogopogo.

The return of Nippon Television just eight months after the July, 1990, expeditions once again stirred the interest of the community as well as outside media. One would assume that once the *World's Greatest Phenonema* on Ogopogo aired in late August for some 80 million Japanese, the interest would wane. Not so!

Ogopogo apparently left a lasting impression not only with the Japanese audience, but with the advertisers and management of Nippon Television as well. This, of course, resulted in the decision to return to Kelowna for a more extensive search while utilizing the latest and best technology available.

News release: NIPPON TV TOKYO UMA OGOPOGO SEARCH The investigation will run from February 28 to March 10, 1991 for a period of 11 days. NTV requests that Arlene Gaal be in charge of all coordinating matters concerning NTVs Ogopogo Search in Canada.

Signed: Michihito Ogawa, Nippon T.V. Tokyo.

Once again, fax requests and communications began to fly between Michihito Ogawa and me. His first request was for a submarine, something not readily available nor easy to procure on short notice. However, the wheels were put in motion and contact with Murray Spiers of Can-Dive in Vancouver, British Columbia, brought word that they had two submarines of interest: the *Aquarius* and *Deep Rover*. After consulting with the director of UMA (Unidentified Mystery Animal) Search for Ogopogo, Mr. Ogawa, the decision was made to use *Deep Rover*.

The team arrived in Kelowna February 28, amid snow and sleet. Due to the inclement weather, a trial run of the 200-pound (91 kg) remote-controlled camera was conducted in the swimming pool of the Capri Hotel . Team members included CKIQ news director Mike Guzzi along with Don Defty and Gordon Ficke of the Okanagan Similkimeen Video Film Association, and everyone was given a team jacket boldly displaying UMA 91. The biggest problem was securing a proper boat to house the remote control camera and, of course, the winter weather conditions did not help. This was just not Ogopogo's favorite time of year nor mine, for that matter.

Mike Guzzi and Alfred Addison manned the sonar boats, braving the waves that at times were higher than Okanagan Lake Bridge. "There were times when we took some serious risks, but you don't really recognize it at the time, it's when you get home and think about the day's events that you realize some of the dangers," said Guzzi.

Few people were aware that the inventor of the 200-pound (91 kg) remote-controlled camera, Haruo Makinaga, was part of the Japanese team. He explained that the camera could be lowered to any depth in Okanagan Lake and could be remotely guided while filming beneath the surface. At one point it hit its greatest depth at 656 feet (200 m) near Okanagan Centre, sending back come fascinating footage and clarifying the presence of mysis shrimp, krill and other smaller aquatic life.

Two other members of the UMA team, Hiroaki Morika and Hideyuki Wandi, the soundman and cameraman, were credited with having climbed Mount Everest, a feat many dream of but rarely accomplish. So, hanging out of the side of a moving helicopter with the door removed while filming action on Okanagan Lake was no big deal, for they had mastered all fear of heights.

Adding to the prestige of the Japanese team was Professor Sakuji Yoshimura, Egyptologist of the Waseda University of Tokyo. He was most anxious to get a glimpse of Ogopogo and was extremely excited when told he could pilot *Deep Rover*. "I'm not afraid. I trust this machine," he said, as photographers snapped photos of him holding the robotic arms of the submersible.

"Most scientists will believe only what they see. But in cases of unusual phenomena, when there is a great deal of evidence pointing to its existence, I believe their role should be to examine the data that has been gathered and investigate before drawing up a conclusion," stated Professor Yoshimura.

The UMA expedition was not as fruitful as Nippon's 1990 summer project, but if nothing else, it did show that under ideal conditions and at the right time of the year a search of this magnitude could be carried out smoothly. Helicopters flying overhead, *Deep Rover* submarine below, sonar boats on the surface, along with a remote-controlled camera gliding along the surface and divers ready for back-up were all a part of this operation.

When the final curtain came down, the director, Hidetsuga Honda, seemed satisfied with the results, but no doubt disappointed that Ogopogo and the elements were uncooperative with the team and their project. However, there was still the evidence from the expedition just eight months prior, and Honda-san was not about to make this his final effort. He had still another project in mind, but again he would have to convince his superiors. Nippon left with promise of return. The footage from the 1991 UMA expedition, would be aired in a program produced by Nippon Television in Tokyo called *The World's Supernatural Phenomena* that March. Japan was paving the way with leading technology in its search for unknown animals and other unexplained occurrences throughout the world.

Past and Present Interests: Voyageur Expeditions '85

On July 21, 1985, Dave Faubert and Rick Bain announced the formation of Ogopogo Voyageur Expeditions '85.

"Our goal is to search the depths of Okanagan Lake between Penticton and Vernon to prove positively the existence of Ogopogo, the legendary serpent-like creature of the lake. We plan to search the lake with five of the most up-to-date sonar units, capable of outlining fish of any size to a depth of 2000 feet. The sonar is capable of not only finding Ogopogo, but will also be able to track it. When spotted, our boat will be ready to drop our team of divers and cameraman. If the creature is below 150 feet, our submersible submarine will go into action and will be lowered to the exact desired depth to capture it on film. The submersible is capable of diving to a depth of 2000 feet. The one-half-hour documentary produced from the expedition would make this our most exciting expedition yet."

Both men came with exceptional credentials. Rick Bain was a scuba diving guide in Freeport, Bahamas, from 1967 to 1972. He was part of the expedition to search for Kampenfelt Kelly in Lake Simcoe, Ontario, in 1978. When Voyageur Expeditions was formed in 1984, Rick was working as a mechanical contractor in Vancouver, British Columbia.

In 1974, Dave Faubert was part of a journey to Nepal to search for the Yeti of the great Himalayan Mountains. In 1976, following a journey across Afghanistan, he traveled to Australia to explore the Great Barrier Reef along its treacherous coastal Cape York Peninsula. While exploring the underwater world, he learned the fundamentals of commercial diving. He, too, lived in Vancouver and worked as a contractor.

Faubert and Bain went into this with serious intentions. Expedition members besides themselves included, Dr. Lindsey, Director of Zoology at UBC Paul LeBlond, department of Oceanography at UBC; Stephani Hewlett, staff biologist at the Vancouver Aquarium; Arlene Gaal, author and advisor; Michelle Gervais, president of Underwater Recovery Specialists; Janice Boyd, marine biologist; John Saslow, underwater technologist; Marv Coburn, camerman; Bar Hodgson, production advisor.

Dale Alsager, a zoologist with Canadian Bio-Scientific Consultants Ltd. of Kelowna joined Voyageur Expeditions '85 search for Ogopogo on April 3 and agreed to oversee an expanded scientific investigation into the existence and origins of Ogopogo.

In an interview with the *Kelowna Daily Courier*, Alsager stated that they would use an unmanned submersible to collect scientific data near the bottom of the lake. As well, chemical and radioactivity residue analysis would be done on the specimens and rock samples collected from selected areas, to determine mineral content. He stated he has long had an interest in the existence of Ogopogo and believes the animal exists. Ogopogo may be a remnant of the prehistoric *Plesiosaur*, a large smooth-skinned animal that lived in water. Fossil records show an apparent die-off of most prehistoric animals between 100 million and 160 million years ago, said Alsager.

Zoologists believe something rather catastrophic happened to cause the extinction. It is possible that a few may have survived by retreating to holes in the deepest inland lakes. Ogopogo, perhaps, is a close relative to the plesiosaur. The search for Ogopogo will also be tied into other scientific research which could boost the final cost to $200,000. The entire expedition could last up to two months based on the availability of the submersible to study lake sediments and pollution levels."

As the months passed, funding became the biggest issue. A planned one-hour documentary of the search added to the cost and by late summer only $30,000 was realized.

Faubert and Bains plan for Voyageur Expeditions was a serious venture. Hats were made, logos cut, and a team of experts to oversee the event was in place. The use of a sonar net to sweep Okanagan Lake involved forty to fifty people and although the team leaders said they would be back in early June or July of 1986, nothing materialized. It was clear it was not about to happen.

Some months later, Canal Flats inventor Hank Pronk, called me to say he was coming to the Okanagan to conduct an underwater search for Ogopogo with his submersible robot. Hank and his brother Sjac were to arrive in Peachland with a submersible robot less than a meter in length, to videotape any underwater action the robot could detect. Plans were to lower it from the boat so that it would be capable of "walking" along the bottom or through the water to relay information back to the computer and television monitor housed on the boat. The computer was equipped with a digitizer, and anything unusual that was spotted could be photographed, enhanced and printed out immediately.

"I'm going deep because nobody else has gone deep enough and sitting on the surface hasn't worked for anybody", he said.

Pronk claims that he has taken the world of underwater robotics a step further as his model can detect metal and pick up objects as well as play music to the creatures of the deep, something he hopes will woo Ogopogo into camera range.

The project was completely financed by Pronk, who had to secure bank financing to carry it out. "I've got a million dollar robot, and I guess I'll continue the search until I'm broke."

Hank Pronk's plans were a scaled down version of Voyageur Expedition. As always, I was waiting for that great photo that I had talked about for years. Pronk's plans were short-lived when his robot failed almost at the beginning of his search. Needless to say, I was personally disappointed at having two searches so close together fall through.

An interesting letter arrived March 13, 1987, from Terrrance R. Mitchell of Bellingham, Washington. It stated:

> I used to be the chairman of the board of Quadterra International an expedition that did not materialize as a result of insufficient funding. On the other hand, I think I will attempt to catch Ogopogo this summer. In fact, I am going to organize a small select group to participate in the venture. Of particular interest to you would be the fact that there is a way to get the creature to surface. In 1972 we tested a device at Okanagan that drew Ogopogo to the area of Monster Island. Sadly we were not equipped for underwater photography or Ogopogo would no longer be a legend. We did however, film the surface turbulence and jumping fish inherent with the presence of all such creatures.
>
> In case you are curious, Ogopogo is a very large winged fish similar to a Manta Ray. My research indicates that a mature one will measure 80 feet from wing tip to wing tip. Weight150 tons. Sometimes I wonder how the people around the lake are going to feel when they find out their legend can swallow a small cabin cruiser. Its mouth alone is some 30 feet wide and 8 feet high. This is why the fish jump when he is near the surface.

Like Quadterra International, Terrance Mitchell failed to arrive for any form of expedition. Mitchell's perception of the animal was somewhat farfetched; it is huge, but not of the dimensions he proposed. As for it being a large, winged fish measuring eighty feet (24 m) from wing tip to wing tip, with a thirty-foot (9 m) mouth that could swallow a small cabin cruiser, this description would delight any Hollywood producer

Following a Dream

In 1995, a young man with vision, enthusiasm and drive arrived in Kelowna. Alan Gillette decided to launch an expedition of his own. California-born and raised, he felt it would be a real challenge to go out and search for the unexplained. Lake monsters caught his fancy and Ogopogo became his prime target for almost five months.

He arrived in Kelowna in May of 1995 with $8,000 in his pocket, camping gear and a dream to prove or disprove the existence of the denizen of the deep. Alan had no sophisticated equipment, but he did have a video camera and was looking to find a boat to equip with sonar. Once everything was in place and Alan had touched base with me on where to best focus his search, he began a solo vigil of Okanagan Lake in a twelve-foot (3.5 m) fishing boat.

In the beginning, Alan would arrive at my house with some exciting event and videotape of something unusual he had seen that day and we would discuss it. I recall his story about an eerie sound that he was picking up in the center of the lake. The lake was mirror calm, the day quite warm and he was out in very deep water with no boats in sight. Suddenly there was this weird sound coming from the far end of his boat. He turned on his video recorder, and somewhat apprehensively, continued to listen. Later that day, I heard the playback and admitted it was a sound I couldn't readily identify. For the next few days Alan continued to monitor the sound, which would always come when he was alone in open water and utterly defenseless, should it be Ogopogo. Near the end of the week, he returned, somewhat sheepish and apologetic, for he had discovered that the unusual sound was a loon that was in an underwater dive, searching for fish.

As Alan's vigil was coming to an end, I wrote this clip for *The Daily Courier*:

Alan Gillette heads back to California as he winds down his search of Okanagan Lake in a scientific effort to prove or disprove the existence of our beastie. After logging some 500 hours in his 12-foot boat, armed with a video camera and fish finder, he leaves with no conclusive evidence and some interesting but questionable videotape that is deserving of further enhancement. Over the months Alan has kept in touch, and had queries on times and places to frequent and reports of his quest. Naturally there was always that anticipation of getting that one great photo or footage which could help solve the missing pieces in the Ogopogo file.

Alan sums it up by saying: "What ensued was in many ways more extraordinary than I could have imagined. Coincidences happened that have since caused me to wonder if I am leading an enchanted life. There are so many memories, the summer of 1995 was uncanny.

"On the morning of June 12, 1995 I was cruising the waters of Okanagan Lake taking depth readings of the bottom. A characteristic of this lake is that for about the first 500 yards out from shore, the water is rarely more than 30 feet deep. Beyond 500 yards, however, there is a steep drop-off to depths of 500 feet or more.

"At about 10 a.m., I was directly over one of these drop-offs, which I could easily see on my Lowrance Sonar. Then about 10 feet under my boat I received a reading of something lying in the water at a 45-degree angle which from my screen measured at least 20 feet in length. I have some experience with what a big school of fish looks like on my sonar, and this was nothing like it. What I saw on my screen was long and elliptical in shape and furthermore, I could see the various densities of the body.

"This would have been fascinating except for the chill factor. I'm pretty hardened, but this kind of spooked me. It hadn't helped that I had been interviewing fishermen and others who had seen the monster. My boat was only 10 feet long and a somewhat flimsy one at that. I circled around the area just to check that I wasn't seeing a submerged log or some other debris. I traced the area for 15 minutes, but whatever was there had gone."

Alan Gillette dared to follow his dream, something that our early explorers dared to do without fear or favor, and in his own right deserves, what Kelowna failed to provide, The Order of the Ogopogo.

Ogopogo Museum and Exhibition Center

I had always maintained that Kelowna and the Okanagan in general had not capitalized as strongly as they could on Ogopogo. Loch Ness, of course, had seen the writing on the wall and took every opportunity to publicize Nessie to the fullest extent and thus reap revenues no doubt in the millions of dollars. Ogopogo, on the other hand, had gained its notoriety through the media and had become a world-wide phenomenon. There was, no doubt, a vested interest established by the presence of Ogopogo in Okanagan Lake.

So when I was approached by Chris and Jerry Lee who wanted to discuss a marketing plan, I was prepared to listen. They came armed with a written mission statement which read: "Our mission is to give the Okanagan's best known being the recognition it deserves by creating a comprehensive, dedicated Ogopogo Exhibition Centre, a genuine information center concerning Ogopogo, its history, its sightings and its mythical presence in Okanagan Lake."

This, of course, caught my attention. I could envisage its potential, and realized it was long overdue. I did not have the money and had no idea where it would come from, but the possibilities were endless.

The Ogopogo Museum and Exhibition Center would provide a visitor experience designed to educate and entertain. The visitor would be self-guided through a series of display areas, and a video production would be available for viewing at regular intervals in a cavelike theater environment. A small gift shop would offer a variety of gifts such as

33

books, posters and souvenirs. All products would be tasteful and feature an original logo and artwork.

Chris and Jerry had indeed done their homework. The report included a marketing plan and the methodology of achieving the goal. Location was important and the former restaurant in City Park, the Grand Okanagan Convention Center and the property on Abbott Street adjacent to City Park were singled out as possible sites.

I was impressed, and agreed to meet with them again. My home was a museum unto itself as far as Ogopogo data and memorabilia, which of course could not take the place of a public exhibition. They could not go ahead with the proposal without the needed artifacts and I was certainly open to discussion. Our meetings were going along well, but there was always the question of just where the dollars would come from as the cost would be in the hundreds of thousands. There was also the need to protect my research material, which after some twenty years of gathering had become quite valuable. It was suggested that I give daily lectures on Ogopogo with a question and answer follow up.

I gave this some serious thought and put together a proposal that would not only reflect my experience, but one that would include some form of return for the use of all my material. A third book was in the works, and releasing anything that had not as yet been published was just not good business. I liked the plan, and they had the skills to make it happen. I waited for some form of reply. It did not come. The Ogopogo Museum and Exhibition Center became just another file.

Andy Schwabb was more serious about his plan. He believed in what he was doing and worked to make it happen. His first goal was to restore one of the old ferry boats and make Ogopogo its central attraction. In 1999 he took over the *Fintry Queen*, a popular paddle boat that attracted tourists who enjoyed a leisurely lake cruise. Once again, Ogopogo was included in his long-range objective, I would be a guest lecturer on a daily two-hour cruise and at the same time have an opportunity to get out on the lake more often than I had been able to do for the past years. Completing the book would be the first priority. Until this was done, I suggested that Andy place a telescope and sonar unit on board with a constant print-out and a screen that would project any image that may be captured. Making the tourists aware of Ogopogo would be easy, and books and souvenirs in the gift shop would enhance the presence of the Okanagan's best kept secret.

The year 2000 would see a revival of interest and a rivalry to com-pete for Ogopogo's attention like none other. The Japanese began calling in early March and were talking about filming a segment for an unusual animals production in the coming months. The April 5, 2000, announcement of a $25 million family feature film on Ogopogo to be filmed in Manitoba by Winnipeg's Original Pictures Inc., caught Kelowna by surprise. Negotiations began immediately with London-based scriptwriter Barry Authors. Authors stated that he was "keen on exploring Okanagan locations and would consider shooting a few scenes here, even though he is committed to filming the bulk of his independent family drama in Manitoba." The millennium and Ogopogo were certainly off to an interesting beginning.

A resolution April 11, 2000, from Peachland Town Council declaring Peachland "OGOPOGO'S OFFICIAL RESIDENCE," caught the rest of the Okanagan by surprise. The proclamation reads:

> Whereas, after exhaustive studies, meticulous research and a review of laws, customs, precedents, conventions, traditions, international treaties and common sense have determined with absolute certainty that the waters of Okanagan Lake, within the vicinity of Peachland, are the non-disputable home of Ogopogo, the legendary lake creature.
>
> Therefore, let it be known from this day forth that Peachland is the home of Ogopogo. Other Okanagan Communities, which share lakefront frontage, should correctly acknowledge that Ogopogo may occasionally visit their waters, but the creature's place of domicile is within the waters of Peachland.

April 29, 2000, would see Penticton Chamber of Commerce announce a $2-million reward to "anyone safely capturing the mythical Okanagan Lake Monster or providing scientific proof that he exists." The contest would run from September 1, 2000, to September 1, 2001, with the prize money underwritten by Lloyds of London.

Top-secret discussions for the first serious search of Okanagan Lake from July 15 to September 1, 2000, for Ogopogo were finalized as Primal Productions of Winnipeg issued a press release May 5, 2000. "The latest sonar scans, divers, high-powered boats and aerial equipment had been secured. A computerized grid of Okanagan Lake would be set up based on the Chronology of Sightings from this book as areas, frequency of sightings, and weather conditions would be charted to determine a proper search pattern." I had agreed to act as consultant for the expedition. It would be an exciting summer and one that would raise the hopes of Ogopogo believers world-wide.

Hunting Ogopogo a dream

BY RON SEYMOUR
The Daily Courier

CHRISTOPHER STANFORD/The Daily Courier
American Alan Gillette quit his computer programming job and will be spending a lot of time on his 10 foot boat this summer looking for the elusive Ogo-

A young American computer programmer who quit his job to come look for Ogopogo says he's just chasing a boyhood dream.

Alan Gillette, 25, said Friday he has always been fascinated by tales of myths and monsters - so he set out to investigate one first-hand.

"I was living a very normal, nine-to-five life and I just started realizing I needed an adventure," the St. Louis resident said. "Life is too short to be stuck doing something you don't really want to do."

Gillette first heard about Okanagan Lake's legendary sea serpent a year ago, while watching a quasi-scientific program on unexplained phenomena.

"I told my friend I'd like to go look for this creature. And he said, 'Well, why don't you?'" Gillette recalled. "It seemed like a good idea."

So Gillette saved up $8,000 and started making plans to spend the summer on Okanagan Lake, trying to find firm evidence of the reclusive reptile.

He arrived in Kelowna earlier this month, after being briefly detained at the border by Canada Customs officials who raised a few eyebrows when he told them

the purpose of his visit.

"I probably shouldn't have been so brutally honest," Gillette laughs. "They kept me there for about 45 minutes while they checked me out."

Armed with a fish finder and video camera, Gillette spends about 10 hours a day cruising Okanagan Lake in his small rented boat.

"I'm sitting and waiting and looking at the lake the whole time," he says. "I guess it's a test of patience. That's what it's going to take if I'm going to see anything."

So far, he says, he hasn't. No inky black shapes cresting placid [...] no three-humped apparitions, certainly no [...]

pogo. Although his search may not be the highest tech or have the biggest budget Kelowna has seen, he spends 10 hours a day on the lake.

"I'm a confirmed fence-sitter," he says when asked if, based on what he's heard or read so far, he believes in Ogopogo.

"I have a positive attitude, but it doesn't cloud my judgment. I won't believe there's something there until I've seen it with my own eyes."

Gillette, who has a math and physics university degree, hopes to make a mini-documentary of his Ogopogo expedition.

He dreams of a career travelling the globe in search of other exotic creatures. But he expects to be back at work this fall, maybe in California's robotics industry. "Right now," he says, "I'm just having a lot of fun being a would-be adventurer."

Cousteau finds lake under Saguenay River

QUEBEC (CP) — A unique salt-water lake with frigid, arctic-like water has been discovered under Quebec's Saguenay River, French oceanographer Jacques Cousteau said Tuesday.

"What we found was a little Arctic Ocean under a river," he told a news conference called to progress report on a film [...] making on the St. [...] River in collabora- [...] the National Film [...] Canada.

[...]'s son, Jean-Michel, [...]iver is deep — 180 [...]ut only the top 12 or [...]e fresh water emp- [...] the St. Lawrence.

called a geological dam.

The river is a fiord, bounded on either side by spectacular cliffs. Jean-Michel said to get to the lake he followed one of the cliffs down under the water in a diving saucer.

Going through the fresh water was like going through "Coca-Cola and then through chocolate," he said. Visibility was about a metre and the water temperature varied between 10 and 13 degrees Celsius.

Suddenly, visibility increased to eight to 10 metres and the water temperature dropped to one degree Celsius.

"The water was nearly clear and supercharged with [...]

JACQUES COUSTEAU

Ogopogo searchers eye a 'gold mine'

By BRIAN DRISCOLL
Courier Staff

Ogopogo may have a $1 million price tag on its head, but a scientific expedition searching for the legendary sea monster is after a different kind of gold mine.

At a press conference in Kelowna today, expedition leader Rick Bain said that, win or

Voyageur Expedition 85's springboard to future expeditions, notably one planned for Japan in the fall.

But the commercial potential of the search for the legend of Okanagan Lake underlies a serious venture by a committed group of scientists, technicians and com-

Kelowna Mayor [...] Hammill and o[...] private and governm[...] officials this week, t[...] members are makin[...] exploratory dive into lake Saturday.

During the next [...] months, Bain will [...] searching for more [...] a sea monster. $40,000 budget ne[...] sponsorship he [...]

Inside scoop on Ogo excites TV reporter

By ROB GEREIN
Staff Writer

Arlene Gaal was in her glory Friday.

The Rutland home of the uncontested Ogopogo expert was awash in the lights, cameras, and action of the U.S. television tabloid news program *Inside Edition*, which had a reporter and a two-man crew in town to film an eight-minute segment on the legendary lake creature.

"Today's going to very busy," Gaal said excitedly.

After being interviewed by Rick Kirkham, senior correspondent for the New York-based program, Gaal, Kirkham and crew left on a three-hour fact-finding tour of Okanagan Lake.

The four were to be joined on a houseboat by Ogopogo eyewitnesses, hoping our freshwater friend would surface for the cameras.

Kirkham planned to pull on a wet suit some time ... lake tour and try to meet Ogopogo face to ...

an lake monster would sell during February sweeps week.

"We're here to get a story that will get ... ing — that's very important to us. Ther ... lions of people watching this. They wo ... me here with five days notice if it wasn't ... said Kirkham, who arrived in Kelown ... night after getting married in Las Vega ... end.

Inside Edition won the race to get ... story, as its chief competitor, *Hard Cop* ... contact with Gaal for the past few mor ... an Ogopogo exclusive.

And, as is usually the case in Am ... sion, particularly during ratings perio ... object.

Kirkham said the Ogopogo story ... get, just "whatever it takes to get a go ... "I've gone through $50,000 in ... working on a story, *Inside Edi* ... $250,000 on stories. If there's a ...

TV crew to search for famous creature

By MAUDIE WHELAN
Staff Writer

Nicholas Webster, television producer and director of such TV greats as *Bonanza*, *Mannix* and *The Waltons*, is in Kelowna to do a documentary on the mysterious Ogopogo.

Much has been written and surmised about the supposed creature, and Webster and his co-producer Dyann Rivkin along ...

base material for the script along with Vancouver's author Mary Moon's book, Ogopogo.

Webster said at a Tuesday press conference that the program, In Search Of, is not a scientific research project but does follow the curious and the unexplained events that occur all over the world.

"We don't claim to answer the question but we ... p the interest ... se an answer ...

that the crew as scientific as

... of the venture, ... r plans to use ... cumented by a ... man. Ed Fletc- ... de his search of ... eature late last

Rivkin said she believes the Indian legends and hopes to bring out the beauty of the Indian culture in the television production. Members of the Indian Band of Westbank have already been contacted and co-operation has been assured.

Bill Derrickson told the Progress Tuesday the program should do the Okanagan a lot of good and indications are that Bill Derrickson's father, William E. Derrickson will be one of the characters featured in the film.

Diving will be done through the Bevan's Barge Scuba School and on Saturday producer Webster hopes to interview members of the general public for their opinions on the Okanagan celebrity. This ... will take place, near the

Filmmakers zero in on Ogopogo

Move over Loch Ness monster, make way Abominable Snowman. Here comes Ogopogo.

The elusive Okanagan Lake serpent is about to take its place on the world's stage.

Two Swiss filmmakers, one of five francophone teams roaming the world to document the most interesting stories they find, are aiming their cameras at the Ogopogo legend.

Alexandre Bochatay and Alain Margot were in Kelowna this week to research and begin filming a five-to-seven minute documentary. They met with Arlene Gaal, author of two books about Ogopogo and

advisor to the upcoming Voyageur Expeditions '85 search for the serpent.

The five documentary teams — from Canada, France, Belgium, Monaco and Switzerland — are in competition for a $10,000 prize. Each must produce one documentary and a crew at a new loca-tion. The contest began five months ago in ...

the contest is a challenge to each team's ingenuity. They arrive unknown and clamour to uncover an intriguing story.

Bochatay and Margot arrived in B.C. from China, where they made three documentaries. Their first film here was made in Fort Nelson and concerned a ...

Wednesday anti-climatic for Ogopogo filming crew

By J.P. SQUIRE

Daly was interviewing Gaal in the middle of the ... opposite Bear Creek Provincial Park when ... owner Mike Guzzi twice spotted a 10-metre ... ct swimming through the water at a depth of ... metres.

... houseboat carrying the Japanese crew and ... r media were nearby, but nothing surfaced.

... bout 5:45 p.m. Tuesday, the crew and Gaal ... e descending a hill into the ...

Ogopogo? No go

Rocky start for Japanese TV team's monster hu...

By Lyn Cockburn
Staff Reporter

KELOWNA — The gods are with Ogopogo — so far.

But a bit of bad luck almost sank Day One of the biggest expedition to search for the legendary monster of Okanagan Lake.

The Nippon TV expedition ran into its first problem at the Okanagan Lake Bridge yesterday. A barge carrying the crew's mini-submarine and a crane to lower it into the lake wouldn't fit under.

So the barge was pumped part-full of water, for ballast, and it squeezed under with an inch or two to spare. It headed for Rattlesnake Island, 15 kilometres south, where Ogopogo has often been spotted.

But the other half of the convoy, a houseboat which is home to the 15-member expedition, was doed in the water, its engine belching oil.

And the two divers who were to search the underwater caves off Rattlesnake Island were aboard the stranded houseboat.

But that wasn't enough for expedition member Prof. Sakuji Yoshimura, an archeology professor at Tokyo's Waseda University.

"I'd rather find a live animal than a dead tomb," the Egyptologist had said on Friday after a glass or two of Okanagan wine.

Then he suggested the expedition should capture Ogopogo — and give it a big kiss.

But, yesterday, as snow and sleet blew across the barge, the only thing Yoshimura was cuddling up to was Can-Dive's Deep Rover submersible — for publicity pictures.

"I am not afraid," he said. "I trust this machine."

The expedition's footage is for the program The World's Supernatural Phenomena to be shown March 28 in Japan.

Expedition leader Michihito Ozawa refused to divulge the cost

Ogopogo Topic Of 'White Paper' As Chamber Seeks Evidence

A concentrated "search" for Ogopogo is planned by the Kelowna Chamber of Commerce.

And if the chamber can gather enough information about the friendly Okanagan Lake monster a "white paper" will be prepared.

A statement presented to the chamber's executive meeting Thursday afternoon by Frank Addison said:

"A group of local citizens is interested in acquiring as much data as possible on our friendly water "beastie" — commonly known as Ogopogo.

"Interest has been aroused with the recent showing of movies taken by Art Folden of Chase and it is felt there are many other instances of sightings that have gone unreported, probably because people thought they might be ridiculed.

"The immediate objective of the group is to ask anyone who has ever made a sighting — or think they have — to drop a note to: Ogopogo, Box 398, Kelowna, giving the details as accurately as possible. Important information would include:

• Approximate date of sighting
• Area of lake where sighting made
• Weather conditions at time (clear, cloudy, wind direction)
• Condition of lake (rough or calm)
• Behaviour of Ogo and direction of travel
• Witnesses to sighting

"It is hoped enough information will be gathered, to enable an assessment to be made of Ogopogo's habits, to see if there are any common denominators such as lake area and time of year. When sufficient information has been gathered — the results will be released in a 'white Paper'.

"The comittee, which will operate as a sub-committee of the visitor and convention committee of the Kelowna Chamber of Commerce, feels a great deal of interest can be created which will benefit the community. However, to be successful, the support of all people in the area is essential.

"The committee has already discussed many suggestions from Ogopogo excursion to an Ogopogo Society to a liaison with the Loch Ness Society—and many more."

The one-minute color film of "something in the lake" was shown to about two dozen people Feb. 4 at a press conference organized by the chamber. The film quality was not good, but definitely showed something in the lake about a half mile south of the Peachland, about a half mile south of home of Ogopogo viewpoint.

Whatever was in the movie surfaced and submerged three times and moved at speeds varying from slow to fairly quickly, for an object of its size, at least 50 feet long.

If nothing else the film touched off renewed interest in Ogopogo.

There is no record of how ...

The Province

Lake Search Technology

Attempts to prove or disprove the existence of a large aquatic animal have been more often talked about than acted upon. Interest was there but not the necessary technology. The sonar units used during the 1990 and 1991 search for Ogopogo were useful and did indeed capture visuals of something very large swimming beneath the depths of Okanagan Lake that did not resemble known fish species. There was a strong need for a Dr. Robert Rines figure complete with the technology and drive that prompted the taking of the famous photos at Loch Ness in 1972, using image-scanning sonar techniques and MIT cameras, two useful techniques that allowed that team to see and photograph the body of an animal with a large attached flipper. The 1980 expedition to Loch Ness also allowed Rines and Wykoff to take an interesting photo of the front part of the body. This picture has been well scrutinized and has stood the test of time.

Okanagan Lake has "hot spots." Over the years I have tracked these areas and know for a certainty that if an intensive lake watch was carried out during peak sighting periods with the proper equipment, conclusive proof would result. For persons like myself who strongly believe in the existence of something very extraordinary making its home in Okanagan Lake, a lack of funds, scientific interest and time has unfortunately put dreams on hold.

Andrew Bennett, a resident of Westbank, became a believer after he heard close family members tell of their encounters with Ogopogo. Andrews grandfather, W. A. C. Bennett, and his uncle, Bill Bennett were both former premiers of British Columbia and on one occasion, W. A. C. admitted that he believed in Ogopogo.

Geoffrey Tozer, son-in-law of the late W. A. C. Bennett, was never hesitant to speak of his encounter on Okanagan Lake in 1936 when he was a thirteen-year-old. While W. A. C. listened and nodded in agreement, Tozer told his story to Tony Healey, an Aussie who visited Kelowna on his trek around the world to search for unknown animal species.

Geoff and his fifteen-year-old friend, Andy Aikman, were no strangers to Okanagan Lake. Both were sea cadets and both had spent every possible hour since pre-school days swimming and boating on the lake in the summer and skating in the winter. It was mid-August and the boys had heard a rumor that Mr. Crighton of Okanagan Mission had been catching sturgeon a few miles south of Cedar Creek, so they decided to check it out. They took Andy's old spread trapper's canoe and planned to camp for a few days to see if they could latch on to a sturgeon. The day was very hot, and the lake perfectly calm as they headed out. Groups of gulls, nestled in the water, waited for kokanee, as the boys neared the mouth of Mission Creek heading for the campsite at Cedar Creek.

Geoffrey Tozer reported:

> I was rowing when Andy, who sat in the stern, hooked a fish. I shipped the oars, reeled in my line and netted the fish for him. We were both excited at actually catching a fish and had no thoughts of Ogopogo or anything else. This activity took about two minutes and during this time we drifted to within twenty yards of a large group of seagulls. Suddenly they all started to screech in terror and took off from the surface as straight as a gull can go. Following them was the head and neck (or body) of a large creature! When the gulls reached the height of about fourteen feet, the creature grabbed one of the gulls in its mouth and disappeared below the surface leaving only a few ripples on the glassy surface. It started all the other gulls within hundreds of yards flying and screaming. O. L. Jones. who had a summer cabin nearby, came running from the cabin with his children, to see what the noise was all about. Andy and I were scared to death and gave up our great fishing expedition right then and there. We spent the night as far up the lake as possible on the Jones beach and headed for home the next morning. When asked the size of the creature, I remember saying that it was as big around as a telephone pole and the color was dark and fishlike and it had a head like a cow.

Forty-seven years later on August 29th, 1983, Frank Penner was also fishing near the mouth of Mission Creek. He was stunned when he saw a 50- to 60-foot (15–18 m) snakelike object at least 10 to 12 feet (3–3.75 m)

39

wide, with a blunt head, break water. The animal was dark in color and propelled itself by snaking and coiling. Just 250 yards (229 m) from the creature, Frank states, "I believe what I saw!"

In the summer of 1973, the Bennetts and Richies were heading north on Okanagan Lake past Poplar Point at 30 mph (48 kmph). It was around 11:00 P.M. In the headlight, they saw a large object about four feet (1.25 m) high, and thinking it to be an overturned boat, they circled back. Whatever was there had vanished. Kevin Bennett was waterskiing and waited for the boat to pick him up. When it did, he was told that something very large had been heading toward him.

These stories made Andrew Bennett a firm believer. His interest led him to the pictographs along Gellatly Bay, which he photographed and recently placed on his Sunny Okanagan web site. Currently, he is talking about preserving the pictographs to prevent further erosion. Andrew e-mailed me in 1998 and stated: "The pictograph is interesting. It is only 2 inches (5 cm). The neck is almost completely gone, just a speck left but the peeling away left the neck outline. Several of these paintings have been retouched by the natives which may explain why the body and flipper show but the neck is only visible after looking at the photograph. The striking thing about it to me are the waves above, the body underneath with possibly four flippers and the neck that sweeps down and up as if poised to strike."

Andrew asked the Westbank First Nation office to consider a study of the pictographs, "as I would show them where they all are, if they were interested." He felt they were important enough to establish an historical link and an opportunity for the First Nation People to take pride in the work of their ancestors.

As his interest grew, he talked to persons from the Vancouver Aquarium about placing a hydrophone in Okanagan Lake for a few months on the chance that if he picked up any unusual sounds they would be the first to have opportunity at analysis. They agreed and he soon had it in place. Andrew would return faithfully to check the tape and replace it when needed. There was an unusual sound recorded, but the analysis was inconclusive. Andrew wrote: "I will mail you the tape of the hydro phone recording from my web site. I have about a dozen tapes. Sometimes there is silence and then there are times with lots of background noise. Very hard to prove anything. Looked at the sound waves on my computer, but they were not good enough. A spectrometer of some sort is necessary to tell if it is anything. John Ford at the Vancouver

Aquarium listened to the tape, and thought that the sound was something non-living but I wasn't certain if he had found the area of the tape that I was referring to."

Over the years Andrew and I have had discussions about placing strobe cameras at a central point on both sides of Okanagan Lake Bridge. But in March 2000, when CHBC announced its Bridge Cam Project, which gives a fabulous view of the bridge and surrounding lake, it was learned that the Department of Highways has six such cameras mounted on the Okanagan Lake Bridge Tower and that the Kelowna television station was utilizing three of them. Quite naturally, my attention turned to the potential to videotape Ogopogo. The bridge, being a viable spot for sightings, offered a great opportunity, as the animal appears to make a point of swimming under the bridge on a regular basis, either north to south or south to north. Fishermen wanting to be assured of a good catch would often stake out the bridge. Perhaps Ogopogo discovered their secret.

When the bridge was under construction in the mid-1950s, divers who helped build it told stories of large aquatic animals they were not able to identify, swimming close by. It frightened some into quitting, while others would discount it as being nothing but a large ling cod or lake sturgeon. The latter theory was more comfortable to live with as the divers still had a job to do.

Okanagan Lake Bridge was completed in 1958 joining the mainland to the Central Okanagan and provided a link from Vernon in the north to Penticton in the south. It was classified as "monster proof" and shortly after, the Okanagan Lake ferry was officially retired. Whatever it was the divers saw continues to remain a topic of conversation even today.

When the lake ferries were first put into operation in the mid-1920s, the government made plans to arm them against an Ogopogo attack, more likely than not as a reassurance for the passengers. The thought of lake monster versus lake ferry in a bloody confrontation was perhaps considered; although the animal was sighted from time to time, no one was ever in real danger.

On September 4, 1976, Lloyd Wong and Ed Wong along with their cousin Colin were fishing on the south side of the bridge, when suddenly the head of what appeared to be a very large prehistoric-like animal surfaced. The men in the boat froze. A nearby camera was not even given a second thought, for they had no idea what this creature was capable of doing. Almost as quickly as the head and part of the shoulder surfaced it

41

submerged, leaving a massive wake that rocked the boat. Shaken and in shock, the fishermen brought their trip to an abrupt end.

The Kelowna anglers were all professionals. Ed Wong was a music technologist, his brother Lloyd, a sociology professor at Okanagan University College. Colin, chose not to reveal his last name nor his profession. Although there was no picture, they did produce a very convincing sketch of an animal that would bring most of us to our knees should we ever encounter it. I knew the family personally and realized that they had more to lose than to gain by going public. The Wongs have never retracted their story.

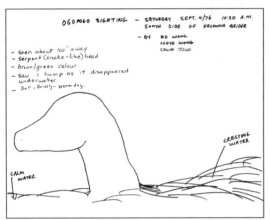

My own first experience with Ogopogo occurred on the west side of Okanagan Lake Bridge, October 24, 1978. I had gone to check out a sighting by Bill Steciuk that took place a few days earlier. As he crossed the bridge on his way to work in Kelowna, Bill had observed the animal swimming in a southeasterly direction. The lake was very calm, and the temperature ideal. Everything about the lake that day was captivating. Just as I was preparing to leave to go home to cook supper, my whole being was placed on alert.

I was seeing something that I really could not believe; a dark shadow was moving below the water near the bridge just a few hundred yards away. It broke water and all I could see were massive waves rolling off its back. It reminded me of a submarine surfacing in a 1940s war movie. My car door was open and my Nikon was on the seat. I grabbed the camera, ran toward the lakeshore and began taking as many shots as I could. When the activity subsided, I sat back down in my car, still too stunned to believe that anything out of the ordinary had actually happened. Looking at my camera and then at Okanagan Lake that had now returned

Sketch by Bill Steciuk depicting his sighting of Ocotber 17, 1978.

to its shimmering self, I had no idea what might or might not be on that roll of film.

That evening, I handed the film to my son Joe to develop as he was the *Daily Courier*'s photographer. I did not expect to really see much, as I was unable to photograph the most dramatic portion of the experience. What I did see was rather amazing. On the surface of a very calm lake something long and dark was moving through the water. It had to be all of forty to fifty feet (12–15.25 m) long. I also noticed that the camera had picked up the waves that had moved toward the shoreline, where only a few minutes before, the surface had been calm. There was not a boat in sight.

In 1989, the B.C. Cryptozoologist Club arrived in the Okanagan to search for Ogopogo. The group, which included Jim Clark and his son, along with John Kirk Sr. and John Jr., were about to set out on a serious search of the lake. They had come armed with an underwater remote camera and other viewing equipment. Although Ken Chaplin had not revealed the location of his July sighting, the cryptozoology team knew the lake well and had plans to search areas that they felt held the greatest potential.

Peach Orchard Beach, Summerland sighting, July 30, 1989. The following are witness sketches of the sighting:

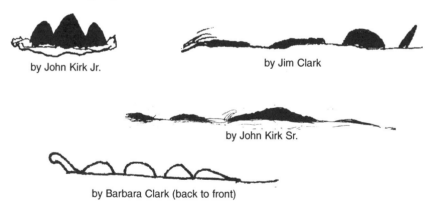

by John Kirk Jr.

by Jim Clark

by John Kirk Sr.

by Barbara Clark (back to front)

Several sightings of the animal were recorded and some videotape taken. All four members of the investigating team were stationed at various points on Peach Orchard Beach in Summerland, when at 3:55 P.M. a large patch of white water materialized at the southern end of the beach, and it was clear that a large animal was swimming in a northerly direc-

43

tion against the prevailing wind and slight swell. Using a Bushnell 40X telescope, Kirk Sr. was able to confirm that this was the classic Ogopogo others had talked about. Both Clarks were able to see the object clearly through binoculars. Kirk's telescope allowed him to see that the animal's skin was whalelike and that there appeared to be random calcium type deposits under the skin, resembling barnacles. All team members agreed that the animal was between thirty to thirty-five feet (9–11 m) in length and almost three feet (1 m) out of the water at its peak.

By 1989 John Kirk had become what I now call a dedicated convert. Once you have experienced a sighting of Ogopogo, nothing can sway your belief. For John, this was to be his calling after he saw and video-taped Ogopogo from Mission Hills Winery May 19, 1987, in the presence of his former wife, six-year-old son John, and family friend Phyllis Frew from Kelowna.

John Kirk Sr. was standing on a slope overlooking Okanagan Lake in 1987 when he spotted a creature with a twelve-foot (3.5 m) long neck, a tiny head and faint humps, sticking out of the water. Kirk, who had been filming the sunset through a videocamera, zoomed in with his telephoto lens. Later analysis showed the creature to be about fifty-nine feet (18 m) long. He called me later that evening, and I visited the Frew household and was able to confirm that John definitely captured an animate object moving through the water.

Although teams of divers had entered the lake for recreation dives or technical reasons, Ogopogo was never part of the plan. However a few years after the Japanese visit, I received a call from a gentleman who had been doing some work in the lake near Rattlesnake Island. He described it as being a government project and he had been working the area for a few weeks. He first asked, "Do you know that the Japanese have a team of divers out here?" I knew nothing of it but thought it interesting. I knew that Nippon Television from Tokyo had lost a very expensive underwater camera during the 1990 shoot, and thought perhaps they had come back to retrieve it and had said nothing to avoid embarrassment. But there was also the chance that they may have returned to see if they could capture any further footage to use for upcoming programs.

The caller then went on to say that when one of the divers was busy below, the crew on top saw a large animal swimming directly above. They quickly sent a message to the diver, to turn off the lights immediately and look up. He saw a large black object come into view and pass by. When he surfaced, the crew told him they had just seen Ogopogo.

Bruce Shepherd, from the B.C. Fisheries, has stated that his crew had related some scary experiences. On one occasion they went out into the lake to measure the depth with a tow rope. As the rope was being lowered, it struck something solid, which was puzzling, as they were nowhere near the bottom. Then, just as suddenly, the rope continued to make its way to the depths below, completing the task. Whatever it was that blocked the rope's descent had moved on. Speculation and questions spurred conversation among the workers for some time.

On October 22, 1999, I was busy working on this book when the telephone rang. The person identified himself as Tom, one of the crew who worked on the seventy-two-foot (22 m) *Okanagan Princess* cruise ship. He told me that the boat was equipped with sonar and that they were interested in getting the proper underwater camera and whatever else was needed to photograph Ogopogo. Tom also had an Ogopogo experience to share. In August of 1998, they were out on a cruise when the sonar picked up a large body of an animal at least sixty feet (18 m) long just sixteen feet (5 m) below the boat, showing flippers and a long tail. "Our screen identifies the known marine life but the outline of this animal made my mouth drop." Tom discussed it with the captain who was somewhat skeptical until it happened again in the same area, and the same month a year later in August, 1999. The creature appeared to be identical in body features but this time was only eight feet (2.5 m) below the vessel. They had no printer, so all they could do was observe the outline on the screen.

I immediately suggested they keep a still camera as well as a video-camera close by in the event of a similar happening. Tom spoke of underwater camera equipment and whatever else he would need to get a good picture of the animal. I knew about the equipment that Dr. Robert Rines had used in Loch Ness and although I had no idea of the cost, suggested the Edgerton strobe camera. Tom and the crew of the *Okanagan Princess* had no doubt that the animal, for reasons of its own, often frequented this area of the lake. Next time they would be prepared.

The Folden Film Revisited

I have never, ever, stopped believing in the potential of the Folden Film and have been its strongest advocate since my search led to its resurrection and purchase just prior to the writing of *Beneath the Depths* in 1976. The potential this film holds in unlocking the mystery of lake monsters world-wide has never really been appreciated by the scientific community even though it has been seen by millions of people in Europe, Great Britain, Asia and North America. Here is a reminder of what was filmed that eventful day.

It was a beautiful August day in 1968 and Okanagan Lake was glassycalm as Art Folden and his family were making their way back home to Chase after a visit with family in Kelowna. They were only twenty-five minutes into their journey, traveling along Highway 97 south of Peachland, relaxed at the serenity and mood of the lake, when Art spotted something moving through the water. This large and unusual object immediately had the attention of his wife and children, and Art thought it best to pull over.

As Art grabbed his 8-millimeter movie camera from the back seat, he could determine that the object was about 300 yards from shore. Excitement rose in the voices of his wife and children as Art Folden blurted out: "It's the Ogopogo!" He had a great vantage point, standing above the lakeshore on a bluff overlooking the object, and as he began filming, the animal submerged and resurfaced. Art, fearful that his film would run out, opted to stop the camera each time the animal disappeared.

The creature then took off at high speed, pushing water furiously in what appeared to be an attempt to evade any further human observations. Being a private person, Art Folden told few people about his experience.

He did, however, have enough courage to show the footage to family and friends whenever the opportunity arose. It wasn't until 1970 that his brother-in-law Dennis McGregor convinced Art that others may be interested in his find. It was previewed by the mayor of Kelowna along with interested city councilors, wildlife experts, newspaper publishers and reporters.

When dealing with an unknown entity, few people have the courage to stand up and be counted for fear of ridicule and this group was no different. Although those viewing the footage were polite and acknowledged the fact that something unusual was certainly visible in Okanagan Lake, something very large indeed, no one would really utter the magic word needed to verify the sighting. Some called it a log, others a wave and then there were the perhaps and maybes.

Roy Atherton, city editor of the *Kelowna Daily Courier*, did agree that something definitely submerged and surfaced three times while moving at a slow cruise prior to taking off at high speed churning up white waves while leaving a heavy wake.

Even *Kelowna Daily Courier* publisher, R. P. MacLean, who later became a strong advocate of Ogopogo, would not openly commit and concluded his editorial on the subject by writing: "Doubters will undoubtedly tear the film to pieces; for my part being a sympathetic believer, I choose to reserve judgment, to be neutral. And the classic definition of being neutral is being afraid of one side and ashamed of the other."

Mayor Hilbert Roth of Kelowna, William Stevenson, manager of the Chamber of Commerce and Jim Treadgold, an *Outdoors Weekly* columnist all gave it a thumbs up and were convinced that it was indeed the mysterious creature Ogopogo.

The Folden film returned with Art to his home in Chase. Although disappointed by the reaction, he never stopped believing in what he had seen and filmed in Okanagan Lake. He left a copy of the film with his brother-in-law Dennis McGregor who never missed an opportunity to comment whenever the subject took center stage. It was in the McGregor home that I first had opportunity to view it. I found myself in awe at what I was seeing, as there was no doubt in my mind about what Art Folden had filmed. It was a rare find. I began asking questions and within days, I had a personal conversation with Art Folden.

After some negotiating, Art agreed to sell me the footage and I immediately applied for copyright. The general public was given its first true glimpse of Ogopogo in my book *Beneath the Depths* in 1976 after Wayne

47

Duchart of Photography West in Kelowna reproduced some of the better stills from the footage. Doubters and believers alike had opportunity to express their views. Where I could see an actual outline of the shape of the creature, others saw just a blob or large shadow one that surfaced, submerged and took off at high speed.

When I read the accounts today, the realization remains that no matter how strong the proof, there will always be those who choose not to believe. Fair enough. I would also be the first to admit that skeptics are important as they help to maintain a healthy balance between truth and untruth. However, I have given this analogy many times that, one could take the animal out of the water and place it directly in front of certain people and they will almost always explain it as being something other than what it appears to be.

Whenever producers, reporters and interested people, asked for my opinion on the many proofs of the existence of this great beastie of Okanagan Lake, no matter what else had materialized in my twenty-six years of research, I always came back to the Folden film. Quite often, on camera, I would issue a challenge to NASA offering the footage to them for analysis. Very often I invited Jacques Cousteau, along with his submarine, to Okanagan Lake to conduct the type of search that only he was capable of. I was naturally saddened by the passing of this great man of science and now invite his son, whom I believe has also exhibited great promise as a descender of the deep. NASA, of course, has missed a great opportunity.

William K. Floyd of Westbank, B.C., sent me this written encounter.

Record of a Strange and Unusual Creature in Okanagan Lake October 27, 1986. (I say strange and unusual in that the creature was strange to me, being different than anything I had ever seen before and unusual in that it did not conform to any descriptions I had ever read in the newspaper accounts of the so-called Ogopogo in Okanagan Lake.) This was a creature obviously alive and healthy. This record is typed by my own hand from handwritten notes I made immediately after the sighting.

I was returning to Kelowna from Penticton. Since the lake was glassy smooth and the late afternoon light was especially beautiful on the cliffs and mountains at lakeside, I stopped and walked to a cliff (steep slope high above the lake) to enjoy the scene in few moments of quietness.

I was on the west side of the lake between Summerland and Peachland, B.C. just south of the Okanagan Lake Provincial Park. Both the sky and the lake water had a special clarity about them that day.

I had stopped just after 4 p.m., walked to the cliff edge, looked out at the cliffs on the east shore, then looked down at the waters color near the west shore directly below me and immediately saw the creature. It was about 15 to 20 yards from the west shoreline and was barely under the surface of the water. I was looking down on it and it did not appear to break the surface at anytime during the sighting, although later it gained speed and displaced water making a V shape of a wave pattern as it moved.

The creature seemed stationary for about 5 seconds, then started to move west to east very slowly. It was a creature with a long neck and its tail seemed only slightly smaller in diameter than its neck. (I could see no head and I suspect only a portion of its tail, as it seemed the tail was tapering down in the water deeper than the neck)

The body of the creature was very wide. While watching it I estimated the body width to be 8 to 10 feet wide and I thought, 'No that doesnt seem rational.' So I looked to compare it with the shore and I still came up with the same estimate of body width. I estimated the body length to be about 12 feet; this does not count the length of the tail and neck. The neck alone seemed longer than the length of the body. I saw no humps.

After about one minute of extremely slow swimming, (barely moving) it accelerated very rapidly (still west to east) and its acceleration was amazingly graceful to be so fast. It quickly gained speed comparable to a speedboat pulling a water skier at a fast clip and it went out of sight as it got further out into the lake. (William K. Floyd)

Reading William Floyd's account created an immediate flashback to the frames in the Folden film and the descriptions of Art Folden's experience. The similarities to Art Folden's film shot in 1968 and the Floyd sighting eighteen years later are uncanny. Both experiences took place in relatively the same area of Okanagan Lake between Summerland and Peachland. Folden and Floyd saw the creature from the bluff above the lake in a rare opportunity to look directly down at the animal below. A most advantageous position for the study of any lake creature. Art Folden had a camera, but William Floyd had the gift of observation and his quick decision to make notes immediately after, provides us with a verbal visual account. Both animals remained stationary and both moved from a slow graceful swim to a highly accelerated speed, displacing water as it moved.

William Floyd's introductory paragraph tells me he had not read about nor could he relate to Art Folden's 1968 film footage, stating that his experience "did not conform to any descriptions I had ever read in newspaper accounts." William K. Floyd believed that the animal he was describing was something that no one had ever reported.

The description of the animal, including its neck, long tail and very wide body are almost identical to the frames photographer Wayne Ducahrt enlarged from the 8 mm Folden film. William Floyd's description of the animal moving quickly through the water at high speed, displacing water as it swims is identical to what we see in the Folden film as it moves out of camera view in a second frame enhanced by Duchart. Art Folden did capture a reptilian head, front appendage and long tail, according to frame enlargement.

Although the classic sighting is of a multihumped creature slithering through the water in a snakelike manner, there are few who have had opportunity to view it from the position that Folden and Floyd did. In my professional opinion, the animal most often seen in Okanagan Lake does indeed have a wide and whalelike structured body with appendages, reptilian head and long tail. In almost thirty years of evidencegathering no one has ever described a beard or horns as is often talked about in earlier accounts.

Observations of the animal swimming in the distance or on direct eye level give the impression of it being multihumped, but this is merely an animal undulating as it swims with head, neck and shoulders out of the water in simultaneous motion.

On October 3, 1979, Rene and Bruce Flowerdew and Rene's father, Bruce Tisseure from Vancouver were driving around Okanagan Lake. It was 4:15 P.M.; the lake conditions were calm and the temperature bordered 70 degrees Fahrenheit (21°C). Just before Peachland they stopped near Ogopogo Lookout when they spotted a large, long, dark object in the lake below. It seemed to be basking in the sun just below the surface about 300 yards (274 m) from shore.

The head or what looked like a head was visible and the body was described as being very wide and at least fifty feet (15.25 m) long. It was a dark brownish green in color. Ducks were swimming close by and the animal pulled toward them, turned sharply as though it may have grabbed one and then taken off at high speed toward Peachland.

The Folden sighting, the William K. Lloyd encounter and the experience by the Flowerdew family all took place within a few miles of each other. All of the witnesses were looking down on the lake and the animal was within 300 yards of the shoreline. What is seen on the Folden film and the description of the wide body by both William Lloyd and the Flowerdews reinforces the fact that the body is more whalelike than snakelike.

Going into the year 2000, I began to wonder about the effect of the millennium. So much was being revealed to me, as sections of the new book began to take shape. Ogopogo has always held a certain mystique and as the millennium begins, there has been more interest in Ogopogo than in all the years I have researched and written about it.

Kerry Voth, a fellow crypto-seeker appeared on my e-mail inquiring about the Folden film. I always take the time to reply to any messages and I sent him a short note answering some of his questions. Kerry's next mail message had me all but sitting upright in my chair. He introduced himself as being a postal worker from Calgary, Alberta, who spent his free hours doing photo enhancement and reconstruction work.

I have a long-standing interest in unusual photos and films of supposed lake monsters. For my own entertainment I often do my own photo-analysis of photos and films as I own and can run most of the necessary equipment. I could do a clarification and restoration job on the Folden film frame by frame and this would give us a first-ever close up look at what Mr. Folden saw in the water so long ago. This is the same process recently used to clarify the JFK assassination film (Zapruder film).

To demonstrate what I mean by all of this, I've downloaded the still from the Folden film and performed a rough analysis of it. A ton of new information came out of my analysis. I was most surprised to find that a large portion of the object is out of the water. It isn't just a shadow after all. It has humps and it is a dark lawn-green color with a brown back. It appears to be coming out of the water at a rolling angle and has two protrusions sticking out of the side of it. As you can see from the light-blasted sharpened image, a lot of detail hides in the film. It's hard to believe that it's even the same picture. The computer only enhances what is already present, it does not retouch the photo. This is basically the same work that was done on the infamous Rines photos of Nessie underwater. If I could get a first generation video of this film, I would be happy to do a blowup restoration and size analysis of the object and this would give us a ton of info. The film seems quite clear and we might be able to see if it is an animate object, the size, shape and description and how it maneuvers through the water.

I am sending my report to you in a separate e-mail along with photos of the frame analysis, edge enhancement, color contouring etc.

Being somewhat of a novice at computers, it took me a few days to open the file. When I did, I found myself mesmerized and talking to my computer. Kerry had done a superb job. I could not take my eyes off what I was seeing, and knew his analysis must be included in this book. Kerry Voth and I would begin a working relationship. So many videos, film clips, and photos had been taken over the past years. It would take an expert to do justice to them. He had gained my vote of confidence, and a complete analysis of the Folden film would be the first priority.

The Thal Film

As with the Folden film, I chose to name the footage using the last name of the person who filmed the experience. It was August 11, 1980. The summer had been hot, so I was not surprised when I received word that some interesting footage had been shot just off Blue Bird Bay Resort near the Mission in downtown Kelowna. But the message also stated that there was a large group of tourists on hand to bear witness to what had transpired. Hopping into my car, I drove down to the resort and met with some very excited people. Each had their own version of what had happened that afternoon. I was able to take a group photo, finding that all of the observers were tourists. Some had known about Ogopogo, but the majority had not. They provided me with this signed written account.

> As we were sitting on the beachfront of the Bluebird Bay Resort Motel at about 4 p.m. August 11, we saw this object about 100 yards off shore moving horizontal to our view in a direction away from the bridge at about 25 miles per hour. It was about 60 feet long, dark green in color. It would submerge, turn, and reappear, going in the opposite direction, still horizontal to our view. Whatever we were seeing, made about four passes in exactly the same manner and was in view for about 45 minutes.

It was signed by Noel, Angie, Ethel, Stephen, and Michael Mellross, all of Calgary, Alberta; Kathleen, Allan and Mark Johnson, also from Calgary; Pamela, Katherine and Craig Meir, of Calgary; Alyson Miller of Edmonton; Nadine Deshayes of Sherwood Park, Alberta; Bordon Schari of Calgary; Jami and Shana Watson of Victoria, British Columbia; and the Wosk family of Vancouver. Larry Thal, who had taken some 8-millimeter film footage had already returned to his home in Vancouver, and you can only imagine how badly I wanted to talk to him about what he may have filmed.

Allen Johnson, a Calgary resident and the first to spot the monster, gave this personal account. "I'm fairly sensible - I'm an engineer and whatever it was, it was darn big. It was a peculiar green shape and I'll tell you it gave you a funny sensation in your stomach when you saw it." Johnson, originally from England says he was always skeptical of Ogopogo's cousin, the Loch Ness Monster in Scotland. But he's convinced he saw something other than a log or a wave from a boat.

"I'd never heard of this Ogopogo monster thing. When I pointed it out on the beach, they all started yelling, Ogopogo, Ogopogo. I didn't know what they were talking about."

He said that there were about fifty people on the beach at the time and they could all clearly see the round humps traveling through the water.

"I've been in the navy for seven years and I've seen some peculiar shapes, I'll tell you. I've seen fish from various parts of the world...but I've never seen anything like this in my life."

Johnson says the other people on the beach were as amazed as he was, standing up and yelling.

"To come here on vacation and see this thing on the water, was quite a thrill, let me tell you. It's something I'll not forget for as long as I live."

After completing the on-site interviews, I drove home and telephoned Larry Thal. After some discussion, he agreed to sell me the rights of the film and provide me with a written account as well. He wrote:

My family and I were visiting friends at the Bluebird Bay Resort Motel in Kelowna. While sunbathing on the beach, our attention was directed to the lake, where we viewed something going back and forth. At first it was believed to be the waves from the boat that was towing a water skier, but when the boat disappeared, the waves continued to go back and forth. It continued for some time and was an unbelievable sight. Everyone on the beach was standing up and looking in amazement at it and wondering what it might be. As I started to go toward the cabin, I turned toward the lake and decided to shoot, as I found it intriguing. A few minutes later it disappeared.

I shot the film using Kodachrome 40 movie film, Type A, Cassette Super 8 cartridge 50 ft/pi 15m-KMA 46 AP. The movie camera was an Eumig Movie Camera Vienette 3, 1.8 x 9.-27 lens zoom reflex.

The Thal film runs around eight to ten seconds. What I would not have given for the complete forty-five minutes of the animal's performance. The film showed persons on the beach as well as members of the Thal family. The film clearly shows a large animate object at least 50 to 60 feet (15–18 m) in length moving swiftly in a southerly direction, creating a massive frontal wake. Black protrusions reveal a back, center and front section clearly moving through the water in a simultaneous motion. Each protrusion appeared to be two feet (.6 m) or more out of the water with an estimated length from three to five feet (.9–1.5 m) each. A great deal of splashing and wave action surrounds each section as it lifts out of the water. I received the impression of a thrusting shoulder movement, particularly when observing the front section.

A few years later, a friend who had some sophisticated equipment offered to transfer both film footages to VHS. Two things resulted with the Thal film. First of all, the creature appears to have large appendages that flip out of the water rather quickly as it swims. But what was even more exciting was the presence of a head. One frame clearly shows a prehistoric-like image, similar to the sketch drawn by the Wong family during their 1976 bridge sighting. The next frame really caught my attention. The mouth opens as the jaws do indeed separate. Nothing like this had ever been nor has since been captured on film.

The day after the Thal film was taken, Edith and Orm Pasquill, both well respected seniors, were fishing across the lake from the Bluebird Bay Resort at about 3:30 P.M. They both spotted a turbulence in the water just fifty feet (15.25 m) away from their twelve-foot (3.5 m) fishing boat. Edith was in awe as she observed three humps break water, each ten feet (3 m) from end to end. The body was dark green in color, but there was no visible head or tail. During its ten-minute debut, the animal submerged and surfaced several times.

As I view the Thal film and the large dark appendage that moves out of the water, I immediately relate to another experience I had in 1990. I had been invited out on a boat by George Copeland and his wife, a young couple who were talking about conducting tours of Okanagan Lake. We left Shelter Bay, crossed under the bridge where it is always a bit turbulent, and headed north. I stood on the stern of the boat looking back toward the bridge, when I was stunned by the presence of this large appendage that flipped out of the water in front of me. It was black in color, at least three feet (.9 m) wide and had to be all of six feet (1.8 m) high. The event happened so quickly I did not have a chance to even alert the others who were busy at the front end of the boat attending to an oil leak. There was no chance to use a camera and I was the only eye witness to this almost science fictionlike experience. Somewhat shaken, my concentration moved to the problems plaguing the boat. Fearing a spark from the engines would cause a fire, we returned to shore.

The head, the size of the appendages and the length of this animal, is something that is not supposed to exist in the list of known aquatic species. Yet both the Thal Film and Folden film provide evidence that there is indeed an unknown, very large animal that continues to make its home in Okanagan Lake. As I write this in the year 2000, evidence continues to corroborate what so many hundreds of eye witnesses report.

The Boiselle Video

In 1982 we moved from the 8-millimeter film age to the age of video. Eugene Boiselle of Kelowna can lay claim to the first video footage shot of Ogopogo while he and his son were up on Knox Mountain at the second lookout. From this area you not only have a fabulous view of the lake, but also a bird's-eye view of the valley including the city of Kelowna. Their attention was drawn to some unexplained activity in what had been an extremely calm lake. It was about 1,500 feet (457 m) away and they stood at about 800 feet (244 m) above the lake surface. While watching for two or three minutes, they turned the video camera on for a brief two or three seconds.

Here is Eugene's audio account: "Looking back to the north again toward Vernon, here's that peculiar spot again. I can't quite make out what it is, but the water seems to be boiling in one small area. It could be a school of fish?" His voice was questioning, but very calm, as though he were concentrating on the object, but not really believing it to be anything to jump up and down about.

Eugene remained curious enough to call me and offered to bring the tape over for me to see. I took the opportunity to get his account on audio tape.

I have a picture of an unusual disturbance on the lake. It was taken Sunday, the fifth of September from the viewpoint on Knox Mountain Park, the one just below the summit. I watched the spot in the lake for several minutes, I took a few clips with the videocamera and really didn't pay much attention to it until I saw it on my own TV. I saw something there that I didn't see through the little viewfinder in the camera. It was a beautiful sunny day, and the lake was very calm. The disturbed part seemed to be near some contrails, little white lines in the lake that were very long. My son and I both saw it at about the same time.

When looking at the videotape, what's unusual is that the black object seems to rise from the lake. From that distance it would be out of the

55

water at least four feet (1.2 m). The trail looked like it stretched for miles. I don't know if it had anything to do with what was foaming up on the lake.

As I viewed the tape once again on September 14, my curiosity focused on the spot where there was foamy wavelike action that was definitely being created by something below the surface. Throughout this boiling turbulence, first one solid black object appears to surface and move very quickly to the right, leaving a large foamy trail behind, and then a back section appears behind this trail. As it moves, it appears to be going around in a circle or perhaps moving ahead ever so slightly. The object was definitely animate; there were no boats around, and the rest of the lake around the churning is perfectly calm as described by Boiselle prior to his sighting.

The trail was most likely created by the portion of the animal below the surface. If one were on the lake when this happened it would best be described as a wave, but from some 800 feet (244 m) above, looking straight down, it would be seen as a contrail.

A Kelowna broadcast journalist for CKIQ Radio, Yvonne Svennson, took an interesting photo in 1984 from Westside Road. Something was churning up a perfectly calm lake close to the spot where the Boiselle video was shot. The water appears to be almost boiling in an area at least 100 feet (30.5 m) long and all of thirty feet (9 m) or more wide. It appears, vanishes, re-appears, bobs up and down and continues this process for a good hour. Yvonne took some pictures and then she and her friend Sharon Ross drove back across the bridge to the east side of the lake to get a better view, but by then the lake had returned to normal. Whatever had been there had vanished.

Earlier that same year, on April 5, my son Joe, who was a photojournalist for the *Kelowna Daily Courier* and sports reporter Mike Levin were up on Knox Mountain Lookout, when they noticed a large dark object creating a commotion in the lake below. A section would rise out of the water, splash the surface and then submerge. Once again, confirmation for the Boiselle video of 1980.

The Kirk Video

On May 19, 1987, John Kirk along with his wife, six-year-old son and Kelowna resident Phyllis Frew were witness to Ogopogo surfacing from a vantage point on Mission Hill. John had his videocamera and began taping as soon as his son first noticed something unusual.

"It was the weirdest thing I ever saw in my life," stated John Kirk. "It was moving at high speed and looked like the picture in the book."

At first they thought it was a boat, but upon closer examination it appeared to be the mythical monster swimming head up.

"The object looked like it had a reptilian-type head. I tracked it with the videocamera and it veered to the left and headed toward shore. I thought, my God, this thing is going to walk out on dry land."

Kirk estimated that the object was a thousand yards (914 m) out from shore and left a 500- to 600-yard (457–549 m) wake behind it. His video shows a black moving object at first, later replaced by an almost stationary object displaying several black humps out of the water, but with no discernable head. The forty to forty-five foot (12–14 m) object slowly came to the surface, undulating as though it were catching its breath.

A telephone call from an excited John Kirk a few hours after he had taken the video, had me in the car and out to the Frew residence. The Kirks arrived in the Okanagan from Hong Kong, intending to stop for only a day before continuing on to Toronto, but the fascination with Ogopogo kept them in Kelowna longer than anticipated.

As I viewed the tape I could see a coiled up snakelike object with three or four solid black protrusions. It definitely was not a boat. Parts of the tape revealed similarities to the Boisselle video taken in 1982. Eugene Boisselle also viewed the animal from a vantage point above the lake.

Analysis of the video, using digital methods of enlargement has shown an animate object very similar to the Loch Ness Monster. Professional editors and analysts in Toronto agree the video shows a three-dimensional animate object of unknown species, according to Kirk.

ABC FILM

Producer David Frank, cameraman Michael Tabor and soundman Victor Nelli Jr. had no thoughts of going back to Los Angeles with anything other than eyewitness accounts when they arrived in Kelowna to shoot a segment for *Secrets and Mysteries*, in July of 1987. At about 2:00 P.M. Gerry Fredericks, manager of the Kelowna Chamber of Commerce agreed to accompany the team out on the lake to obtain some stock footage.

As they moved along at cruising speed, cameraman Michael Tabor, alerted to something to the side, turned around to film a long object floating in the water. Gerry Fredericks described it as like a snake with humps. It just hung out there for three or four minutes, about thirty-three to fifty-six feet (10–17 m) long. It came about six inches (15 cm) out of the water.

Tim Harper of the *Toronto Star* watched the film at CHBC local television station and reports conclusively there was something in the water. Frederick scoffs at any suggestion the film might have been of a log.

The Simmons Video

Dr. Rod Simmons and his wife along with Ed Liggett and his wife were boating near Peachland in August of 1990 when suddenly something broke water in a fairly calm lake some distance away. There were no boats in sight and the object was creating excessive waves and thrashing as it moved through the water. Rod Simmons grabbed his videocamera and began filming. The excitement and amazement portrayed by the group is documented in their voices as they observe this obviously unexpected event.

As I view the videotape it first appears to be one very long animal moving through the water with obvious large black protrusions out of the lake and large waves and whitecaps, creating an almost boiling action between some of the front protrusions. As the animal takes off at high speed, yells of "Look at it go," can be heard. It's at this point that I somehow feel that the animal is not alone. There may be a smaller one following behind as it appears somewhat removed from its fifty- to seventy-foot (15–21 m) companion. Dark "somethings," no doubt appendages, flip up as the animal moves at quite a fast speed.

The Bart Video

If nothing else, it could be classified as a day not like any other for the Bart family. Ewalt and Jackie had just moved to their Kelowna home in Casa Loma from Nikomis, Saskatchewan, and joining them for a visit were their son Ken, his wife Janet and grandson Devin of Regina.

When it was suggested they take the boat out, everyone agreed, for this would be the first time on Okanagan Lake for everyone. It was June 18, 1992, and the weather was unusually warm for the time of year, but ideal for boating.

After a light supper on board his nineteen-footer (6 m) that was cruising near Rattlesnake Island, Ken couldn't resist picking up his camcorder to capture the spectacular scenery, for in a few short days he would be back home in Regina. They had just gone through the passage around Rattlesnake Island, often referred to as Ogopogo's home, and were headed south around Squally Point. It was 5:45 P.M. Soothing music from the boat stereo hovered over the calm lake. Suddenly the feeling of peace and relaxation was broken by the sound of Ken's voice.

"What's that over there?" he queried, as he turned with his camera. All eyes moved to a distant, but very large, wave that appeared out of nowhere. Putting the camera in full zoom, Ken couldn't believe what he was seeing. "Devin, look at the fish jumping over there," he called to his young son.

Janet's stunned voice interjected with, "It's Ogopogo."

"Lets race him Dad," yelled Devin excitedly.

In a few minutes it was gone. The Barts, somewhat surprised at seeing something so large, really didn't give too much thought to just what it might have been, that is, until they got home and played it back in the presence of a neighbor, Doug Turner.

To Doug it looked too large to be your average fish, and after reviewing the tape he suggested that they give me a call to see if I would be interested in viewing it. It didn't take much convincing and I drove out to Casa Loma.

After watching it a fair number of times while taking notes, I was certain that it was not a fish or even a school of fish. What I observed was a very large animate object breaking water, creating a frothy rolling wave around sections of what appears to be a dark body. It submerges and reappears throughout the video and in two spots there is at least twenty feet (6 m) or more of the animal visible.

For some reason, although moving and thrashing about continuously in one spot, it doesn't appear to be going anywhere. Examining it more closely in slow motion, it seems to go around in a circular motion almost like it was chasing its tail, or perhaps feeding off a school of fish. A frame-by-frame analysis showed black protrusions flipping up, being either an appendage or perhaps the head or neck.

The Bart video has similarities to the1980 Thal film and the 1990 Simmons video filmed close to the same area across from Eddy Haymours Castle in Peachland.

Ken Bart, who works for Bennett-Dunlop Ford in Regina jokingly told his friends at work before he left, "I'll bring back Ogopogo," but never really believed it could happen.

His mother Jackie, actually thought she was seeing a group of logs bobbing up and down.

Young Devin is sure he saw something, but is not certain what it was. But there is no doubt he would have something to tell his friends when he returned to London, England.

The Rossmiller Video

On July 26 , 1993, at 11:42 A.M. an unusual disturbance in Okanagan Lake was observed by Stella and Carl Friedel of Westbank, and her cousin Patricia Rossmiller of Colfax, Washington and Stella's sister, Evelyn Montreuil, of Coeur D'Alene, Idaho, as they stood on the beach opposite the Chinese Laundry in Peachland.

Patricia Rossmiller was filming with her camcorder when they saw something jumping out of the water, just north of Rattlesnake Island. "It leaps two or three times and then swims north in the familiar three part weaving," states Stella Friedel. "Is it one or three animals?"

Looking closely as the videotape begins, a very large black object flips up out of the water and is reflected by the sun's rays. There is a definite unidentified object on the tape moving at a set speed in a defined direction.

The Mieras Video

The summer of 1995 produced still more interesting video, as Jack Mieras, his son Jeff and friend Patrick Morgan observed something in the water as they were standing on the beach at Strathcona Park. Okanagan Lake Bridge is visible in the background, and cars as well as long transport trucks can be seen going both ways. These vehicles provide a very good means of determining the size of the object that was seen moving along amid the waves.

Jack Mieras states, "At first I thought it was black plastic bags, but changed my mind when I saw water spouting up and water moving around the body. It made me think, that this is something that's alive. It had to be a live object as you don't normally see a log spouting up water. I could also see white stripes on it."

His young son Jeff commented, "I saw it go down, come back up for about a minute and then go down again. It looked like a whale." Patrick Morgan who was observing it through the view finder on the video camera was amazed at how much better it looked on the screen.

As I looked at the videotape, you could see without too much difficulty that two portions of the animal were visible, the back portion was quite large and somewhat bulbous. As I compared this section with a car on the bridge, it had to be all of twenty feet (6 m) in length, the front part was about six or seven feet (1.8–2.1 m). The back portion was at least three feet (.9 m) above water, and the other perhaps two feet (.6 m).

May 28, 1979, Arlene Gaal's second sighting of Ogopogo took place off Kinsmen Beach in Kelowna. Note what appears to be a wake coming off what could be its head.

Photo: Arlene Gaal

The DeMara Video

In late July of 1992, I received a call from Denise DeMara, a family name I recognized immediately, not only for the downtown family business, DeMara Insurance, but for an Ogopogo connection that immediately flashed through my mind. Denise's husband Monty had reported a sighting July 8, 1951, while out fishing with his friend, Bill Fisher and both stated at the time that the animal came within thirty-five feet (10.5 m) of their boat.

Denise, in her demure, calm way proceeded to tell me that her son Paul had captured something unusual on videotape July 24 while they were eating dinner at Denise's lake property one mile south of Okanagan Lake Resort at approximately 7:15 P.M. She asked if I would like to see it and I enthusiastically agreed to be there within the hour.

I lost count of the number of times we viewed the tape. Each time there was something more to see. While Denise and Paul were excited about the first part of the tape, my attention focused on an area that appeared to show an animal swimming through the water with three sections of the body clearly visible at various times. Head, body and back sections surfaced at intervals as the animal made its way through the lake. Paul had captured some great footage, and other than preserving it on videotape for his own use, he never attempted to exploit it in any way. When it was shown on *Inside Edition*, *Pacific Northwest Afternoon*, as well as the 1999 program called *Strange Science*, it was a result of my enthusiastic comments while talking to producers.

Here is Paul DeMara's written account:

> Reason for being in Kelowna, working vacation. Location of the sighting approximately one mile south of Okanagan Lake Resort on the west side of Okanagan Lake, on deck at Denise DeMara's camp.

Video equipment used: Cannon VME2 8mm Camcorder with Sony Metal MP 120 videotape.

First Sighting: While eating dinner 7 people including myself observed an anomaly in the water directly in front of our lake property at approximately 7:15 p.m. on Friday, July 25, 1992. The anomaly appeared to be approximately 500 to 1000 feet in front of our dock and possibly 30 to 50 feet long.

I was surprised by what I observed because during all the time I had spent in Kelowna I had never seen anything which resembled what I saw that evening. I proceeded to get my binoculars and tried to observe what was making the disturbance in the water. After about one minute the object had created various levels of water disturbances. None of the seven people seemed to be able to identify what was causing the disturbance but it was suggested that it looked like something or some things were traveling just below the surface of the water at a fairly good speed, estimated at 5 miles per hour. None of us indicated the presence of a head, tail, or any other body part that we could identify.

The surface of the water did appear to have what looked like waves being generated from something just below the surface. These waves remained more or less constant until a boat and water skier approached from the east. Even with the help of binoculars I could not tell what was causing the movement of this water disturbance.

After about one minute I grabbed my videotape recorder and I began to video the anomaly moving north toward Okanagan Lake resort. The object did appear to be bobbing just below the water through the viewfinder but could not make out even with the camera what was causing it. A few seconds after starting to tape I observed a boat with a water skier approaching the water anomaly. The boat turned and the water skier appeared to cross over the location of the object and then fell. I jokingly commented that, 'this person was going to get eaten alive. This all occurred in a period of 3 to 5 minutes'.

As Paul DeMara provided me with a copy of the tape, I had opportunity to record my own observations. If ever we were to believe that there is more than one Ogopogo living in Okanagan Lake, viewing this tape certainly adds credence to the thought. I observed a series of objects with solid portions breaking water as though competing in a race. They swam parallel to one another, each in a different position but moving in a definite direction. The two leaders, seem to be larger, judging by the size of the protrusions out of the water. The two nearest the camera are further back and appear to be smaller as is the one on the far right. I counted seven that broke water, as can be seen in the photograph. I also did a size comparison with the downed water skier and feel that the larger protrusions were out of the water at least three or four feet (.9–1.2 m).

What tends to increase the drama is the appearance of the boat towing the unidentified water skier who seems oblivious to the surrounding events until he skis over the back of the smaller object. Just as suddenly, he can be seen turning his upper body and head in the direction of the larger object when he loses his balance and falls into the lake. The animal remains visible as the person frantically swims toward the tow boat.

I obtained a still from the videotape and it shows the series of protrusions moving through the lake and each appears to have a distinct pattern of turbulence, as waves appear to roll over each section. I believe the water skier fell because the driver of the boat clearly saw the animals ahead and made a complete U turn, causing the skier to lose his balance.

Second Sighting
Paul continues:

After watching the object disappear, we scanned the lake and about five minutes later observed a similar anomaly two to three thousand feet in front of our property to the east. It resembled the first disturbance except that it looked more like only one object was creating the disturbance. The direction of travel appeared to be southbound. The duration of this was about three minutes.

Paul DeMara is quite right, as there is only one animal visible, but this part of the tape is most interesting as the animal appears to be swimming at a comfortable speed, propelling itself most likely by its back appendages, and as it forges ahead, sections of the body appear. In one frame you can see all three sections out of the water and its head is angled upwards, similar to what we see in the Chaplin videos. On the side of the creature at a greater distance from the camera, water is being churned up near the front end. I will make reference to this later on as there are some important elements to consider. Parts of this second sighting should be enhanced and perhaps more interesting facts will be revealed. Judging from the shore line, the animal had to be at least thirty feet or more from front to back. It was somewhat eerie, but helpful, to see most of the animal out of the water, for the only visuals similar to this were from witness sketches. Two stills were obtained of this portion of the video and two sections of the body along with a head and neck are visible. Very exciting material, to say the least.

Third Sighting
Paul DeMara writes:

> After several more minutes I also sighted and videotaped something that appeared to be a similar anomaly three to four thousand feet to the north of the camp property. Due to the distance it did not tape well and was similar to the other two, some sort of underwater object moving through the water creating unusual anomalies on the surface. We watched this for 5 to 8 minutes. Later that evening, a few boats went by but they did not create anything similar to what I had videotaped. I watched the water of Okanagan Lake for three days and was not able to see anything that resembled what we had seen Friday night.

In this last taping, again Paul filmed what appears to be the same animal as is seen in the second sighting but at quite a distance. You can just make out the solid dark sections out of the water as it it swims horizontally, heading toward shore. This part of the tape, as with the second sighting, really held my attention, as there is no doubt that the head, neck and part of the body have surfaced. This was verified by the still prints I managed to acquire from the video.

With Paul was his wife Kathy, Ken Fraser and his wife Donna, owners of Sound In Motion in Kelowna, Daryl Banks and his girlfriend Tracy Robinson both of Coquitlam, B.C, and his mother Denise DeMara whom he described as a businesswoman living in Kelowna along with one of Paul and Kathy's children, whose voice we hear in the video asking questions.

Paul is a manager in Cantel West's main office in Burnaby, B.C. and was born and raised in Kelowna before moving to Vancouver in 1980. The DeMara's have never sought publicity for their tape but when producers from *Inside Edition, Pacific Northwest* in Seattle and *Strange Science, Bizarre Phenomena* met with me, I pointed out the importance of this tape and the program enabled the general public to see some of what was filmed.

The area where this tape was shot is near Okanagan Center, known to be the deepest part of Okanagan Lake, at about 1,000 feet (305 m) or more.

In 1979, not far from the DeMara sighting, Frank and Jim Rieger spotted an animal "at least twenty ton," according to Frank, that had visible front and back appendages. Rick Trembley of Vancouver, while working at Okanagan Lake resort, told everyone he had just seen a whale in Okanagan Lake. Quickly reminded that there were no whales in the lake, he realized that he had experienced a sighting of Ogopogo.

Having spent over two hours with Paul and his mother Denise, I can honestly say that they are both very solid citizens. Denise spoke of her late husband, Monte, a very prominent and well-respected businessman and his 1951 Ogopogo experience near Rattlesnake Island.

The Berry Video

Two years later, on March 15, 1994, I received a call from Kevin R. Berry, a resident of Winfield. He had taken some footage in Okanagan Lake near Okanagan Center, in the vicinity of the DeMara footage shoot and asked if I would be interested in seeing it. Invitations to view footage assumed to be Ogopogo are rare and provide a good opportunity to do comparisons.

The tape was shot on a sunny warm day on an absolutely smooth-surfaced lake. Two pine trees similar to those seen in the Folden film, dominate the foreground. To the right of the first pine tree two very clear objects are visible, heading in a northwesterly direction, each creating a solid V-wake.

At first, each protuberance appears almost identical in size, but as the videotape progresses, the animals make a slight turn at which point one animal heads left and the other continues right. The creature on the left surfaces a bit more and an almost bulbous body seems to emerge, then submerges. By this time the animal that had continued on to the right is lost from view, mainly due to the sun's reflections on the water.

The last part of the tape is somewhat lost due to the sunlight, but one can still make out what appears to be a large disturbance in two areas of the lake, and amid all of this there are definitely two animate objects bobbing in and out from view. From the angle, it is apparent that Kevin moved in closer in order to shoot this last part of the video.

The Berry video has distinct similarities to the 1990 tape taken by Paul DeMara. The DeMara tape shows at least three creatures or more swimming together with one animal taking the lead but paced on either side by two smaller animals a few feet back, each showing a dark section out of the water with a long wake trailing behind. The Berry tape shows more of the animal's body out of the water with two definite independent animals visible, who then part company, moving through the lake at a similar speed to that in the DeMara video.

With permission from Kevin, I obtained a still photo from the videotape, showing the two animals moving through the mirror-calm lake. The date, March 15, 1994 is clearly imprinted.

Kevin Berry, married with two children, is also a professional musician. His creation of "The Ogopogo Rap" has caught the attention of many producers who have been delighted to include it as part of the music of choice for their Ogopogo documentaries. Kevin will soon produce his first children's CD to include "The Ogopogo Rap."

March 9, 2000, Kevin Berry records the first sighting for the year 2000 on video. It is appropriately placed in the final chapter of this book.

The Chaplin Saga

It was July of 1989, and I was still quite traumatized by the mysterious death of my son Joe, who as a photojournalist covering the war in Afghanistan, was found dead at Ocean View Hotel in Pattaya, Thailand, April 30. So it was that my first connection with the Chaplin family came at a time when my body and mind desperately needed respite, something that would temporarily interrupt the bondage of dealing with death.

It was midmorning when the telephone rang. The voice on the other end did not identify itself, but instead posed a series of questions regarding Ogopogo: "What proof was there of the existence of Ogopogo? Had anyone ever photographed or videotaped the creature? Do I believe that such an animal exists? How important is it to respect the anonymity of an Ogopogo sighting?"

By this time I realized something unusual must have happened on the lake. "You have something don't you?"

The voice on the other end responded, "Maybe." Then added, "If I do, how can I be sure that you can be trusted not to disclose or go public with what I tell you?"

I was really being given the third degree. Generally it would be me firing the questions, but not this time. I gave the caller my utmost assurance, which is all that I could do.

There was silence, then there was a firm response. "I want you to see something that I shot on videotape and I would like your opinion."

I agreed. However I did have to know who I was dealing with. "May I have your name?"

"It's just Ken. My father lives here in Rutland on MacIntosh Road and he told me about you. I'll bring him along."

Assured that he was no ax murderer, I felt a bit more at ease about having a stranger enter my home where I had only my Maltese poodle for protection.

Thirty minutes later, a tall, lanky person carrying a black case, accompanied by an older gentlemen, came walking down the road. I looked for a car but could see none in either direction. I realized that this person really did not want to be identified. They walked down the driveway to the front door. As I opened the door, he introduced himself as Ken Chaplin, his seventy-year-old father Clem was by his side. Ken immediately took charge of my video machine, expertly hooked up the camera and turned it on. I watched the TV screen with curiosity, uncertain of what I was about to see.

On the screen a large animal surfaced, swimming in a set direction. It then very suddenly arched its head, slapped its tail with a sharp whiplike motion and then submerged, leaving a sizable wake. All I could say at that moment was "Wow!" I was admittedly excited. But I needed to know more.

Ken Chaplin explained: "A week ago, I got this call from my dad. He and Mom were camping at Bear Creek when they saw this large eel-like head poke out of the water and swim out toward the lake. He described it as being something the like of which he had never seen before and asked me to come down and bring my camera to check it out. Well Dad had never appeared so insistent, and I knew I would have a few days off so I decided to come down, knowing I wanted to test out a new boat I had just bought. We went out on the lake, taking a family friend, Horst Simpson and this thing appeared and I videotaped just what you saw."

Clem Chaplin proceeded to tell me that it seems to appear like clockwork at a specific time and that they had seen it more than once. Ken showed footage of an animal surfacing, swimming in a set direction and submerging without the sharp tail slap.

I agreed to maintain confidentiality, but stressed the need to go out and see for myself. A few days later, early in the evening, Ken and his father picked me up and we headed for Bear Creek. I had my camera, with no real expectations of seeing anything, but this was Okanagan Lake and I knew the full potential of Ogopogo appearances in July. The lake was beautifully calm and the temperature ideal.

The road was narrow and winding around the log booms, and I had never been that comfortable driving it. The only plus was the fabulous view one had of the lake. Bear Creek is a provincial campground and is rarely empty. Bees, however, have always presented a hidden danger and they were everywhere.

It was around 8:10 P.M. The sun had not as yet set. I followed the Chaplins walking through the campground to Bear Creek. Clem said that the animal surfaced at around 8:30. Checking my watch once again, I readied my Nikon camera.

At precisely 8:30 P.M., to my amazement, I observed something dark surface in the creek and followed it with my eyes as it headed out toward the lake. I began snapping pictures and Ken Chaplin had his videocamera rolling as he leaped over the logs to follow as the creature made a turn toward the log booms. Little comment was made afterwards, as I think I was a bit stunned at the thought of the animal being so cooperative and on cue.

I had my photos developed but for some mysterious reason, Ken Chaplin never disclosed that experience nor showed any of that footage. In fact, he was rather upset when I allowed CHBC to show the pictures on television a few days later. This made me just a bit uneasy and uncomfortable, as my reputation as an expert researcher on Ogopogo was well entrenched, and I had never hidden anything from the media and was not about to start.

What has always remained a mystery to me is that my photos show the head of this animal as it moved quite quickly though the water and its back portion showing it to be at least fifteen to twenty feet (4.5–6m) in length. So when cries of "beaver" began to come from wildlife experts who viewed the Chaplin footage, I found it difficult to believe as my photos showed a much longer animal, making it almost impossible to be a beaver.

Ken went the distance, contacting media everywhere. *National Geographic's* Paul Gasek came to Kelowna and took a copy of the video back with him to have it analyzed, television crews from as far away as Mexico arrived, and Ken Chaplin even hit the pages of *Time* magazine as well as the *National Enquirer*. Naturally he wanted to be paid, and he set a price for the use of the photos. John Cosgrove from *Unsolved Mysteries* flew up from California and we met with him at Horst Simpson's home in the Mission. Ken had struck a lucrative deal. *Unsolved Mysteries* had agreed to pay him $30,000 U.S. for the exclusive first-time rights of the footage.

I, on the other hand, meekly mentioned the Folden film, which was certainly given second billing. John Cosgrove wanted to use the Folden film as well as the Thal film and I agreed, at a cost of only $350. I never felt a need to exploit or capitalize on Ogopogo. I do realize now that had I asked for $2,000 U.S. they would not have refused.

A few weeks before *Unsolved Mysteries* scheduled their shoot, Robin Dorian, a producer from *A Current Affair* arrived from New York and wanted to film a segment. Ken was put through the paces as they shot and re-shot his run with the videocamera. By early November, John Cosgrove's team from *Unsolved Mysteries* was readied. Dr. Roy Mackal from the University of Chicago had been secured and was to arrive for the first part of the production. Dr. Mackal, a renowned crytozoologist, was to give his opinion on the possibility of Ogopogo's existence and I, of course, as a consultant, had opportunity to comment on the history of the animal and give an opinion on the Chaplin video. As Ken's father was close to eighty, his sister Marilyn agreed to help out. A stand-in was used for Ken's Dad and Ken, of course, played himself.

I often think back to that six-month period of my life and the time spent to either prove or disprove the Chaplin video. Knowing Clem and Joyce Chaplin as I had over those months, I knew they would not intentionally bait and trap anyone, nor could I believe that Ken was pulling a hoax. Clem and Joyce Chaplin have since passed on as has Horst Simpson.

Ex-guide Spots Creature in Lake

Retired big-game guide Ernie Giroux says he has seen Ogopogo and it sure isn't a beaver or an oversize otter.

"It was about fifteen feet (4.5 m) long and swam real graceful and fast," he said in a telephone interview from his Kelowna home. "It had a round head like a football and about two feet of the head and body stuck up out of the water."

Giroux and his wife Margaret said they saw the creature by the light of a full moon September 15, 1989, when they were walking beside Okanagan Lake near the mouth of Bear Creek, the same spot where former car-salesman Ken Chaplin took his video of a creature in the lake in July 20 and where I snapped my pictures while in the company of Ken and Clem Chaplin July 22, 1989.

The Girouxs said they decided to talk about their sighting after reading newspaper reports that wildlife experts categorized the creature in Chaplin's video as most likely a large river otter or beaver.

Ive seen a lot of animals swimming in the wild and what we saw that night was definitely not a beaver, said Giroux, age sixty-six, a retired big game guide from Fernie, British Columbia.

Giroux said he and his wife camped for two weeks in their motorhome at the Bear Creek campground in September and sighted the creature while walking beside the lake about 9:00 P.M. September 15.

"It looked black in the moonlight and slithered through the water like a snake," said Margaret Giroux. "We were so surprised. It swam in one direction, dove down, disappeared and came up again and swam back in the opposite direction. We could hardly believe what we were seeing."

The description of what they saw is very similar to the description given by Chaplin and his parents of what they saw in the lake several times in July.

As I reviewed other sightings of Ogopogo, there were definite reports of the animal hitting the water quite sharply with its tail. These occurrences took place in areas where the lake was from 300 to 500 feet deep.

In September of 1968 Peter Pearson sees a fifty- to sixty-foot object lashing the water, creating a loud noise near Lakeview Heights on Kelowna's west side.

This article ran in the *Kelowna Daily Courier* March 15, 1996, Penticton:

> A spring walk provided the sight of a lifetime for two Okanagan residents. Frank Serio said he and his girlfriend were out for a stroll near the dock between the S.S. *Sicamous* and S.S. *Naramata* when they came upon a large creature swimming rapidly in Okanagan Lake.
>
> 'As we were walking, we heard two large splashes and when we turned toward them, we saw a large head swimming southward,' said Serio. "The head was moving faster than anything I've ever seen swimming,' he said.
>
> Serio followed the movement, running along the shore, before being forced to stop by a fence. The mysterious creature stayed afloat for a few more minutes, then disappeared into the night. Speculation on what the creature was abounds.

More recently, this report came in on e-mail from Dale Roberts:

> August 14, 1999, Saturday 1:15 p.m. Location of sighting: Sacramento, California -Street Crossing: Riverside Boulevard and Clipper.
> I couldn't sleep too well and decided to take my Chow dog T-Rex to the Sacramento River levy. I heard what sounded like huge rocks dropping

into the river. It was a continuing noise that occurred every two minutes. I took a closer look and saw a snake-like object swimming in the river about 20 to 30 feet in length. This snake-like creature was doing something out of the water with its body, causing a loud splashing noise in the river. When I threw rocks at it, it would instantly make the sound of diving into the water. At one point when we were at the edge of the river, and my dog was lapping water, it edged closer to us so I took my dog and backed away.

As I watch beavers swimming I have to agree with Ken Chaplin that beavers swim with their heads parallel to the water, not with a raised head as the animal did in the footage he filmed. I am also intrigued by its speed and ability to change directions so quickly as it did three times before the splash. Since then I have watched film footage of beavers in action very intently. There is no doubt that the familiar tail slap mimics that of a beaver, but the way the Okanagan creature swims, with its head held at a raised angle, its agility and speed as it swims, continues to raise questions.

Even some ten years later as I write this copy, I reserve an open mind as to just what was on the video taken by Ken Chaplin. The animal I photographed swimming out of Bear Creek into Okanagan Lake that July 22, 1989, evening was in the same area that the Chaplin video was shot. If it was indeed a beaver, it was most certainly the only fifteen- to twenty-foot (4.5–6 m) beaver that I have ever seen.

The Chaplin video elicited interest world-wide with the *You* magazine, a segment of the *London Daily Mail*, being one of the most recent of the many news groups sending reporters to Kelowna for a story. The video also created a lobby group concerned about the animal's safety. One letter I received reads: "Do not ever reveal the identity of the animal's home as it would be hunted to death."

Rob Munroe, *Daily Courier* reporter, who wrote a weekly column called "In My Opinion" wrote the following on Tuesday, August 22, 1989, titled: "THE CRY FOR OGOPOGOS PROTECTION IS WARRANTED."

Ogopogo must be protected now, before it's too late. Those are the sentiments not only of the man who has apparently captured the creature on video and a woman launching a major effort to protect the creature, but also of a growing number of Okanagan residents.

Ogopogo has been talked about for years, with most people having a healthy skepticism about its existence. Reports of waves appearing in

Okanagan Lake during a dead calm are rampant. I've seen such waves myself, but never attributed them to the legendary creature.

Arlene Gaal, the local expert, has studied the animal for more than 16 years and has the rights to both the Folden and Thal films. One film showed a dark shape in a blue background, another shot showed a couple of black flipper-like shapes splashing in the water.

Ken Chaplin's video shown to the media last week, while it still does not prove Ogopogos existence, is totally different from previous footage. It is clearly focused on a shape that initially looks like a log with a bump on the front moving through the water. But that log curls toward the camera, then dives revealing a sharply pointed tail, two flippers or feet. Although shot from 75 feet away, the footage is sharp, not blurry. I thought it might be an otter, though it looks too long for that.

Paul Gasek, a *National Geographic* film producer, viewed the video and made a deal to have it sent to his company today for an expensive image enhancement. Gasek is not a marine biologist, but has worked in that field for a number of years and knows the tricks that can be played by cameras and lighting. He could obviously not identify the creature, but was impressed enough to want to study it.

Gasek's interest lends credibility to Chaplin's claim. Chaplin wants to sell the footage and his story, which makes many people suspect his motives; we are all wary of anyone who sees a profit in something like this. But Chaplin has given up his job not only to record the creature, but more importantly, to ensure its safety.

With renewed interest in Ogopogo sparked by his video, a lot more people are looking for it. From what Chaplin has said, the creature is feeding in a fairly public area and has almost been run over by motorboats. The longer he tries to keep the location secret the greater the risk that it will be discovered and hundreds of people will crowd in trying to get their view of it. More frightening is the likelihood someone will try to capture or kill it.

Chaplin seems sincere in his concern for not only the immediate, but also the long-term well-being of Ogopogo. He has an ally in Tauri Atchison, a Kelowna housewife launching a campaign to protect the creature.

Both quite independent of each other, are arguing the need for legislation to protect the creature. Tauri also wants steps taken to ensure it is not killed off by pollution in the lake. Chaplin accuses the provincial government of hiding in the weeds, in their refusal to view his video and initiate some action to ensure its protection.

At least Kelowna Mayor Jim Stuart has had the guts to stick his neck out and call on provincial authorities to protect Ogopogo. The myth of

Ogopogo has been the calling card for the Okanagan for years. So, if for no other reason, why not have a little fun and draft regulations to protect it. Then if it is found, safeguards would already be in place.

Throughout all of this remains the very legitimate question, is the Chaplin video a hoax? The fact that he was willing to turn it over to *National Geographic* gives him greater credibility.

A positive aspect of the Chaplin saga was the furore and concern expressed, when it was felt that the lair was going to be revealed and the animal endangered. Kelowna citizen Tauri Atchison voiced her opinions and stories were printed by the *Kelowna Daily Courier* and *Vancouver Province*. Tauri called me for advice and we met over coffee as she was eager to begin the circulation of a petition for the Protection Of Ogopogo. After some discussion and agreed conditions, I offered to help prepare a draft.

Petition for the Protection of Ogopogo

Due to the Chaplin video of July 19, 1989, which shows the existence of a large unidentified animal making its home in Okanagan Lake and known by most as Ogopogo, we the undersigned strongly advise the municipal, federal and provincial governments to take immediate action to protect this animal from all harm and place it immediately on the endangered species list.

The Protection should Include:
1. No projectiles, shells, missiles or anything of this nature be fired at the animal.
2. No nets, cages, or restraining holds of any kind can be placed in Okanagan Lake for the intent of capturing the unidentified creature known as Ogopogo.
3. All forms of chemicals, raw sewage or pollutants of any kind must be banned from Okanagan Lake immediately, not only to preserve the life of the Ogopogos, but also to ensure that our children and their children can swim and enjoy a pure and clean lake system and natural environment.
4. The animal cannot be hunted, chased, run over or bombarded with high frequency sound waves for the sole purpose of closer observation.
5. The Ogopogos must be allowed to swim freely around Okanagan Lake and can be observed, photographed or videotaped from a reasonable distance by boat on land or from the air.
6. No one shall remove any member of the Ogopogo family from

Okanagan Lake at any time for the purpose of biological analysis or for the purpose of observation under scientific controlled conditions.

7. No one shall disturb the lair, feeding grounds or habitat of the Ogopogo family and the areas of concern will be patrolled at all times.

***Please note: The unidentified swimming animal or animals known as Ogopogo/Ogopogos have not harmed anyone but like any animal who is provoked, it will react to protect itself. So please be forewarned.

This petition was drawn up August 20, 1989, by Arlene B. Gaal and Tauri Atchison in Kelowna, B. C.

Signatures were gathered and the petition was taken to Mayor Jim Stuart of Kelowna who agreed to find a suitable area of government to present it to. The end result was that the animal known as Ogopogo in Okanagan Lake was given protection under the Wildlife Act, which was similar to the prior protection given under the Fisheries Act in 1949 which read: "No one shall hunt, or kill fish or marine animals of any kind other than porpoises, whales, walrus, sea lions and hair seals by means of rocket, explosive materials or explosive projectiles or shells."

"This," the Attorney General commented, "would make it illegal for anyone to shoot the Ogopogo."

The Kelowna Daily Courier August 29, 1989.

Fantastic Ogo video

By J.P. SQUIRE
Courier Staff

A "fantastic" video of a 15- to 17-foot long "overgrown rattlesnake" in Okanagan Lake will likely be shipped to the National Geographic Society today.

But the location of a "feeding ground" where four sightings were video-taped will not be revealed until the provincial and federal governments secure the area, says the man who filmed what is believed to be Ogopogo.

During a news conference Monday, Salmon Arm car salesman Ken Chaplin said he expects an agreement with National Geographic would be finalized today. The society would then be sent a three-quarter-inch videotape copy of his 8 mm film.

Under the agreement, National Geographic would take the tape, produce an enhanced copy, and return the original and a copy of the enhanced version within 10 days.

The society's enhanced version would be for its own in-house use and not commercial use. His copy of the enhanced version could not be used for commercial purposes.

He expected an agreement to be signed with the society much earlier, but its legal department initially insisted the society get commercial rights for a specified period of time.

He won't reveal the location of the so-called feeding ground where the video was shot for fear irresponsible people will try to use tranquillizer darts, a spear gun, or other means to try to capture one of the creatures.

He and Kelowna Ogopogo expert Arlene Gaal now believe the creature caught on film is the offspring of a much larger parent. Members of Chaplin's family have seen two of the smaller creatures in that location.

He believes the creatures are non-aggressive, but isn't sure how they would react if cornered or wounded. The creatures go to this feeding ground for reasons which will be obvious to many people, he added, but wouldn't be more specific.

He suggested the provincial and federal government could create an ecological reserve like Robson Bight on the Coast.

He emphasized he is in no way connected with the B.C. Cryptozoology Club and is not interested in working with club members.

76

Discoveries

We have heard so often of the rediscovery of the coelacanth, believed extinct for 60 million years until, in 1938, a live specimen was netted off the coast of Africa, raising the possibility of other prehistoric finds. We are told that fifty-five new mammals were discovered in the past ninety-nine years including the white rhino and the Mesoplodon beaked whale photographed in the Pacific. Amid all of this are the innumerable fresh-water lakes throughout the world with reports of USOs (Unidentified Swimming Objects) being spotted, including Mokele-mbembe, a prehistoric-like animal in Africa.

In July of 1999 two news reports run by Canadian Press and Associated Press caught the attention of scientists world wide. On July 10 headlines read:

Scientists excited by discovery of dinosaur fossils in Antarctic

Discoveries in the Antarctic of bones from the time of dinosaurs are exciting scientists pondering the mysteries of past global warming and continental drift. A geological expedition has unearthed what project leader Jim Martin of the Museum of Geology in South Dakota called "huge deposits of dinosaur-age bones in the remote Vega Island, Seymour Islands and Antarctic Peninsular areas. The remains include bones of two giant marine reptiles: the mosasaur, a razor toothed duck-bill animal with paddles and the plesiosaur, which resembles the images of Scotland's Loch Ness Monster. Both were dinosaurs.

Martin said that the find shows at least four different types of mosasaur lived in the Antarctic. One type had previously been found in North America and Europe. He stated that mosasaurus have been found around the world from Sweden to New Zealand, but we had no idea of them in Antarctica.

77

The find is further evidence the continents were once much closer than they are now, with connecting marine corridors and also shows that the Antarctic was once much warmer than it is now. Martin said that the creatures probably came to the Antarctic around 75 million years ago at a time when the climate was probably subtropical.

"It was much warmer world-wide. That's the only way these reptiles could have swum around in the water."

Mosasaurus were fantastic animals and could be up to 10 meters long and armed with teeth up to 10 centimeters with skulls easily more than a meter in length. The lower jaw was hinged so they could eat things larger than their own heads. They were very fast in the water and tail propelled.

A team at the South Dakota Museum found striking similarities between dinosaurs found in the Antarctic and other parts of the world. It was concluded that a fairly cosmopolitan distribution of the creatures must have existed as the dinosaur age wound down.

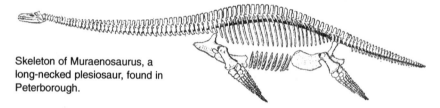

Skeleton of Muraenosaurus, a long-necked plesiosaur, found in Peterborough.

A few weeks later, headlines in a local paper read:

Secret Fossil in Northern B.C.

Hidden dig site may contain one of the world's largest marine reptiles.

Somewhere north of Fort St. John in northern British Columbia in a secret location a team of paleontologists is uncovering a fossil that may be one of the world's largest marine reptiles ever unearthed.

The team from the Royal Tyrell Museum of Paleontology in Drumheller, Alberta, is painstakingly removing the bones of the 220 million year old fossil.

The museum has an exclusive agreement with the television network Discovery Canada, which is partially funding the dig, estimated to cost $500,000. It was said that the agreement forbade the staff from discussing the project.

The Discovery Channel has maintained strict control over the site but allowed Alaska Highway News an exclusive peek. Discovery Channel spokesman Paul Lewis said the location has been kept a mystery to prevent the area from being disturbed or damaged.

"This was a way to document one of the greatest fossil finds in the country in a long time and make sure the area was preserved," said Lewis.

The fossil is classified as an Ichthyosaur (fish-lizard) and is by far the largest ever found, exceeding all other known specimens by at least 30 percent. According to paleontologist, Betty Nicolls who is leading the dig, its head is about four meters long. "Although it was air breathing, it never walked on land." A more accurate description would be a creature with a large dolphin-like head, attached to a body which resembles an over-sized fish.

Other Discoveries

An earlier *Ichthyosaur* find came from Baker City, Oregon, by a group of high school students led by a geologist who uncovered a fossil skull from the oldest vertebrate species ever found in Oregon in the Wallowa Mountains east of Baker City.

Team leader William Orr said the find bolstered a theory that much of the region was formed geologically in Asia before shifting volcanic action.

■

The skeleton of what is believed to be a 90-million-year-old marine reptile has been found 240 kilometers northeast of Saskatoon. Saskatchewan. Tim Tokaryk, assistant curator of the Museum of Natural History in Regina called it a Plesiosaur. Its a marine reptile which could be 30 to 40 feet long. Tokaryk found the skeleton while on a fossil-finding mission in the Carrot River.

■

Fossil bones found in a jungle stream bed in Thailand in 1994 have disclosed what scientist say is the oldest known tyrannosaur that roamed 50 million years before the far larger Tyrannosaurus rex some 120 million to 130 million years ago.

The newfound creature measured about 6.6 meters from its nose to the tip of its tail and had serrated teeth up to ten centimeters long. The discovery strengthens indications that tyrannosaurs evolved in Asia and spread to North America over a land bridge across the Bering Sea.

■

A few years back, this newspaper article caught my attention as this discovery could change the way we view the methods by which unidentified marine animals enter and exit our freshwater lakes, perhaps through connecting river tributaries with similar geological anomalies.

Cousteau finds lake under Saguenay River

A unique saltwater lake with frigid Arctic-like water has been discovered under Quebec's Saguenay River, French Oceanographer, Jacques Cousteau said Tuesday.

"What we found was a little Arctic Ocean under a river," he told a news conference called to give a progress report on a film he is making on the St. Lawrence River in collaboration with the National Film Board of Canada.

Cousteau's son, Jean-Michel said, "The river is deep 180 meters, but only the top 12 or 25 meters are fresh water emptying into the St. Lawrence. The salt water with its own ecology, lies under that and is kept in place by what he called a geological dam.

The river is a fiord, bounded on either side by spectacular cliffs. Jean-Michel said to get to the lake he followed one of the cliffs down under the water in a diving saucer. Going through the fresh water was like going through Coca-Cola and then through chocolate," he said. "Visibility was about a meter and the water temperature varied between 10 and 13 degrees Celsius. Suddenly the visibility increased to eight to 10 meters and the water temperature dropped to one degree Celsius. The water was nearly clear and supercharged with nutrients. We saw big shrimps and little shrimps and cod hiding under rocks."

In 1996 British and American scientists discovered a vast lake, two-and-a-half miles beneath the ice in Antarctica. Its waters, which had been isolated for 50,000 years may contain micro-organisms that may be one million years old. It was dubbed the Antarctic Dream Lake as imaginations soared and hypotheses were written.

All of the excavations and explorations, including the major find by Jacques Cousteau, allow us a picture of early animal life and perhaps gives opportunity for the hundreds of Nessie and Ogopogo-like creatures to find a niche somewhere in the hierarchy of paleontology studies.

Cousteau finds lake under Saguenay River

QUEBEC (CP) — A unique salt-water lake with frigid, Arctic-like water has been discovered under Quebec's Saguenay River, French oceanographer Jacques Cousteau said Tuesday.

"What we found was a little Arctic Ocean under a river," he told a news conference called to give a progress report on a film he is making on the St. Lawrence River in collaboration with the National Film Board of Canada.

Cousteau's son, Jean-Michel, said the river is deep — 180 metres — but only the top 12 or 15 metres are fresh water emptying into the St. Lawrence. The salt-water lake, with its own ecology, lies under that and is kept in place by what he called a geological dam.

The river is a fiord, bounded on either side by spectacular cliffs. Jean-Michel said to get to the lake he followed one of the cliffs down under the water in a diving saucer.

Going through the fresh water was like going through "Coca-Cola and then through chocolate," he saïd. Visibility was about a metre and the water temperature varied between 10 and 13 degrees Celsius.

Suddenly, visibility increased to eight to 10 metres and the water temperature dropped to one degree Celsius.

"The water was nearly clear and supercharged with nutrients. We saw big shrimps and little shrimps and cod hiding under rocks."

JACQUES COUSTEAU

Tracking the Unexplained

Decomposing carcasses can be a monster researcher's worst nightmare as decomposition makes identification almost impossible. Modern DNA techniques and tissue samples, however, moves this into the true realm of science.

One of the most controversial finds took place in 1977 when a group of Japanese fishermen netted a thirty-two-foot-long (9.75 m) animal off the coast of New Zealand. At first glance the photo of this animal dangling from a hoist, bears a striking resemblance to the classic *Plesiosaur* reptile species reportedly seen in Loch Ness and other bodies of water. Reptilian head, long neck and long appendages raised the hopes of seasoned investigators like myself who are constantly seeking an explanation for the many unusual sightings of unidentified swimming animals. It appeared to be an exciting discovery as reports hit the wire.

JAPANESE NET SEA CREATURE TOKYO July 22, 1977 (AP) A Japanese trawler off New Zealand netted a 30-foot, two-ton sea creature which a marine biologist says resembles an extinct sea reptile of 130 million years ago.

Professor Fujio Byasuda of Tokyo Fisheries University, who studied photographs of the creature on board the ship, said it looked like a prehistoric plesiosaurus. Fishing company executives told reporters it was kept on board for an hour. The crew then cast it back into the ocean because they feared the rotting creature would contaminate their commercial catch.

Upon seeing the photos, Professor Imaizumi declared it to be a reptile with plesiosaur features. Experts to non-experts offered opinions and theories for some months. Further investigations, proving it to be a very badly decomposing basking shark, quickly quelled interest.

TOKYO July 25, 1977 (AP) A marine biologist says a 30-foot two-ton sea creature netted by a Japanese trawler off New Zealand last April shows a biochemical makeup similar to that of a kind of shark.

A spokesman for Professor Fujio Yasuda of Tokyo Fisheries University said today Yasudas gas chromatography analysis of a whisker-like specimen from the creature showed it contains various amino acids seen in a species of shark Prionace Glaucus, which usually grows to a maximum length of 289 feet.

The trawler Zuiyo Maru fished up the dead creature and sent a specimen and photographs to Tokyo for analysis. The rotted carcass was thrown back because the crew feared it would contaminate their catch. The fishing company executive told of the find at a news conference here last Wednesday.

The trawler was still at sea. Japanese newspapers, focusing on a possible link to Scotlands legendary Loch Ness monster, had dubbed the new beast the South Pacific Nessie. Yasuda stressed that the report is strictly tentative and what it shows is only that the monster could have been a shark, not that it was nothing but a shark, said the spokesman.

Giant Squid

The 1997 netting of a huge squid off the coast of New Zealand measuring twenty-five feet (7.6 m) in length and weighing 250 pounds (113.4 kg) leads one to believe that the Cape Sable Monster which created quite a stir, bears similarities and is not an uncommon description of creatures belonging to the giant squid family. The giant squid attains lengths of up to seventy feet (21 m)from the tip of its head to the tip of its tentacle. It has the eyes of soccer balls, a huge parrotlike beak, eight arms and two long tentacles, each equipped with dozens of suckers armed with teeth. The giant squid is the sustenance of legend makers and a delight to writers like Jules Verne whose *Twenty Thousand Leagues Under the Sea*, became a legend.

A few years ago scientists traveled to remote Cape Nemesky in the Russian Arctic, 932 miles (1,500 km) north of Moscow to check reports of a Nessie-like monster. The muscles had been so damaged by a storm they resembled feathers and the whole animal looked like a big plucked hen. Its tail was curved into a very strange form and looked like the head of a dinosaur, while its three-foot-long (1 m) penis could be easily mistaken for a limb. The Nessie-like monster was none other than a battered sperm whale.

"What if it had turned out to be a real dinosaur? I would never have forgiven myself if I hadn't come here," biology expert Mikhail Yakovenko stated.

Perhaps the unusual photo of a creature that had washed up on shore in California in 1931 is one of the same. It warranted some attention as the head is almost identical to the sketch drawn by the Wong family after their 1977 close encounter while fishing on the south side of Okanagan Lake Bridge.

Two marine biologists revived a seventy-five-year-old debate in 1971, by stating that there is new evidence that a huge sea creature found at St. Augustine, Florida, in 1896 was part of an octopus, 200 feet (61 m) in diameter. Evidence that the creature was an octopus appears unmistakable based on microscopic testing of tissue samples preserved by the Smithsonian Institution. We can say with certainty that the tissues were not those of a whale and left open the possibility that it was either a huge octopus or the closely related squid.

Measurements of the 12,000-pound (5443 kg) carcass found at St. Augustine indicated an octopus with tentacles of between seventy-five and 100 feet (23–30.5 m), each about eighteen inches (46 cm) in diameter and was first examined in 1896 by A. E. Verill, a Yale professor and marine life expert.

David Rajter of *Unsolved Mysteries* sent me some interesting photos taken in the Quebec town of Perce, located in the Gaspe Peninsula, by Jean Dorion of Manorville, New York. It shows a large animal carcass, all of forty feet in length, that washed up on shore and attracted the attention of local residents. They walked on it, touched it and observed it with keen curiosity The creature appeared to have an unusually long tail, with a three-foot-long ridge running from the front of the tail onto the back end, appendages, a short neck and a large gaping mouth. Assuming it to be a sturgeon, I looked for the familiar fin at the base of the back, but none was to be found. The head was too small to be a shark, and the mouth showed no presence of teeth. There is still some uncertainty about the find, but Jean Dorian states that when the curiosity abated, the locals cut it up and ate it, leading me to believe that it must have been a marine species they were familiar with and that a sturgeon could not be discounted. However, the photos did not resemble a find in Lake Washington.

On November 8, 1987, this story ran in the *Vancouver Province*:

Bellevue, Washington. Fisherman around Lake Washington are swapping stories about the one that passed away. A dead 3.3 meter, (11 foot) white sturgeon weighing about 400 kilograms (900 pounds) was found last week in the lake, where tales have long persisted of a huge, duck-eating 'monster.'

State fisheries officials estimated that it was born around the turn of the century. Cathy Evans, a computer consultant for the fisheries department said that a cross section of the sturgeons pectoral fin would be cut to determine its age, using a method similar to counting the rings in a tree. The cause of death was under investigation, but it may have been just old age. Sturgeons are suction feeders that scoop up snails and small fish. They can grow to more than 450 kilograms and six meters in length, but their mouths are not structured to eat ducks.

As I compare the description of the Lake Washington white sturgeon to the marine animal that washed up on shore in the Gaspe Peninsula, they are as different as night and day. The Lake Washington white sturgeon resembles an overgrown fish with a fluked tail, quite different from the long winding tail seen in the other animal. The heads are different and the Lake Washington creature definitely does not have a neck. Both animals were in relatively good shape and there was little sign of decomposition in either. The marine animal from Lake Washington was definitely identified as a white sturgeon by Fisheries personnel, while the Gaspe Peninsula creature presents a bit of a mystery.

There are white sturgeon reported from Alaskan lakes and coastal waters and as far north as Cook Island, providing basis for the theory that the Lake Iliamna, Alaska, monster may be a sturgeon.

Can we assume that given the numerous reports of elongated fishlike creatures ranging in length from ten to thirty feet (3–9 m) that a sturgeon population may now constitute a subspecies of enormous size?

News Services TORONTO 1988—Is a giant, worm-like creature lurking in Muskrat Lake? Toronto author Michael Bradley thinks so and in August he plans to lower a big cage into the lakes deepest recess, hoping to trap something you usually only see in monster movies.

For years, the residents of Cobden, about 90 kilometers northwest of Ottawa, have reported sighting a very large water animal which would surface briefly, scaring swimmers and boaters. Descriptions give it a length of four to six meters (13 to 20 feet).

Mussie could be an example of a huge worm-like creature believed to have been extinct for millions of years, says Dr. E. L. Bousfield of Ottawa's National Museum of Natural Sciences. This kind of creature would have a long tubular body widening to a fish tail with a mouth midway along its length. The front end would look and act like an elephant's trunk, except for a razor sharp ring of teeth inside its hollow tip. Its eyes might be mounted on stalks protruding from the body.

Canadian Press TORONTO December 16, 1990—Ottawa fisherman, Dana Rogers thinks he's caught the monsters of Muskrat Lake on movie film. The 90-second clip shows two wakes moving about the lake and an object surfaces. The creatures have been described as reddish gray with sloping backs and rounded foreheads, by people who live by the lake.

In 1926, this story was printed in a Prince Rupert Newspaper:

STRANGE SEA CREATURE ATTACKS RUPERT BOATMAN Jan. 21—Attacked by a strange sea creature while fishing in the vicinity of the harbor entrance, Louis Stephens had the fight of his life to beat it off when he attempted to get into his boat. Stephens declared that he was compelled to use his utmost strength and any weapon that lay handy to force the strange creature back into the water where it finally vanished.

November 22, 1934, Prince Rupert:

The remains of a strange marine monster thirty feet in length resembling the description of sea serpents which have been previously reported in British Columbia was brought here from Henry Island by Dr. Neal Carter, director of the Prince Rupert Dominion Fisheries Experimental Station. The body was so badly decomposed it was impossible to preserve it intact. Red flesh indicated that it was a warm-blooded mammal. It had a head shaped somewhat like a horse, and a tough, rough skin. The upper part of the skin had hair and the lower part quills like spines. There were no bones of importance except the vertebrate. The identity of the monster is entirely a matter of conjecture.

In 1947 a skeleton of a snakelike creature was found by four fishermen. It was wedged between two boulders somewhere near Useless Island and Effingham Island in Barkley Sound. It was then transported through Alberni Inlet to Port Alberni, British Columbia, to be shown to the public. The skull measured one foot across (30.5 cm) and the top resembled that of a horse or camel.

Ta-Zam-a—The Mystery of Shuswap Lake

The *Native Voice*, from California reports:

On July 12, 1948, Mr. C. Dew of Salmon Arm, B.C. reported that when he and his wife were returning from a fishing trip to Tappen Bay, a huge animal surfaced close to their boat and practically upset it. Mr.

M. Mclellan reported a similar incident a few days later on July 14 while out fishing near Engineers Point.

On July 27, 1948, Mr. D. Sinclair, owner of the land, said that he saw what appeared to be one of his black steers in the water. He thought it must have drowned, but when he approached, it swiftly dived and disappeared.

At Tillicum, Leon Bernois said that the animal was well known to the Indians of the Shuswap Band and that they knew of the locations of two dens, one in Tappen and one in Ansley Arm. Tomma Sam, a Squilax Indian, had killed one of these strange animals in 1904 and had sold the skin in Enderby for $60. Tomma Sam's son Pete remembers this animal and says it is known to the Indians as 'Ta-Zam-a' which means Water Bear. He describes it as being as large as a mature grizzly with hair as fine as silk and about 4 inches in length. The head had no visible ears, but when the hide was removed, ears were found under the skin down on the sides of the neck. The feet were twelve inches in length and resembled those of a mole. The head was broad like an ordinary bear and the nose was very long. The stench was extraordinary when the hide was removed. The Indians do not like to talk about Ta-Zam-ba as they think he is a bad omen.

An Associated Press story out of Inverness tells of the carcass of a creature measuring eighteen feet (5.5 m) long and weighing one and a half tons (1,361 kg), discovered off the shore of Loch Ness, described as looking like a bear with scales and clawlike flippers. Some called it a cross between a seal and a walrus. Don Robinson, director of the Flamingo Park Zoo said, "I've always been skeptical of the Loch Ness Monster, but this is definitely a monster. From the reports I've had, no one has ever seen anything like it before, a fishy scaly body green in color, with a massive head like a bear and flat ears. I thought it looked half bear and half seal." Similarities to the Ta-Zam-ba are clear.

Frank and Mary Goller live on Shuswap Lake between Canoe and Sicamous. One day when Frank returned from fishing he had a story to tell his wife. Frank had hooked something which could have been a log, or so he thought, as he tried to reel it in. Realizing it was alive and large, he cut his motor and reached for his life jacket because of the turbulence. He heard a splash, and the bow of his boat was lifted so high that water entered the boat and he had to bail it out. His line was suddenly free. To this day, Frank wonders what was on the other end.

Although Ogopogo tales predominate when mysteries of the Okanagan Valley are talked about, it should be noted that the Indians once told of how Squally Point was home to the queer "Little People." They were described as creatures of the waves, with round heads, staring eyes and hair that floated about them. It was said that they nursed their young while rocking on top of the water.

What is interesting is that the habits of these creatures were remarkably similar to the manatee, an animal whose habitat engulfs the quiet rivers of southern Florida, South America, the West Indies and Western Africa. It has a huge, clumsy seal-shaped body and a large, swollen soft snout. An adult grows from seven to fourteen feet (2–4.25 m) in length and weighs from 200 to 1,200 pounds (91–544 kg). The tail is spade-shaped and the female stands erect on her tail in the water while holding her two calves to her breasts with her weak flippers.

Sea cow is a term sometimes applied to the dugong and manatee, which belong to a group of sea mammals called Serenian or the related Stellers sea cow, discovered in 1741 near the Community Islands in the Bering Sea. There were only one to two thousand in existence, and by 1768 it is believed that sailors annihilated the species for food and they are now considered to be extinct. The Steller's sea cow lived in shallow water near shore and fed on seaweed. It was the largest Serenian and the only one to adapt to cold water. Estimated length was about twenty-three feet and it weighed almost 9,000 pounds (4,082 kg).

In 1914 several people were camping on Okanagan Lake beach near Greata Ranch. One member of the group had gone to the edge of the lake for water and was alerted by a strong smell of rotted fish. Upon investigation, he discovered the badly decomposed body of a strange animal lying at the waters edge. His description has mystified many as the body was between five and six feet (1.5–1.8 m) in length and weighed about 400 pounds (181 kg). It had a short, broad, flat tail and a head that stuck out from between shoulders without any sign of a neck. The nose was stubby, sticking out of a rounded head, with no ears visible. The thick hide was sparsely covered with silky hair four or five inches (10–13cm) in length and of a bluish gray color, while the teeth resembled those of a dog. It had two ivorylike tusks and claws on flipperlike arms. The claws showed no signs of wear or use as those of land animals would.

For many years a shoulder blade, the tusks and great claws were shown to interested persons upon request. The find was described as something that had never been seen or heard of in or around Okanagan Lake. Although the carcass bore some similarities to a manatee, making the story of the "Little People" of Squally Point more of a reality than myth, it tends to lose credibility where the two ivory tusks and claws are concerned.

Mary Moon, author of *The Okanagan Mystery* tells of Captain Thomas Shorts, skipper of *Mary Victoria* who came across a huge bone in shallow water in the 1920s. It was taken to the Victoria Museum where it was identified as the backbone of a whale and later returned to Vernon where it was displayed until its mysterious disappearance a few years later.

What then was being described in this old London Music Hall song that was sung at the Vernon Board of Trade Banquet in 1924?

His mother was an earwig,
His father was a whale;
A little bit of head
And hardly any tail—
And Ogopogo was his name.

The catchy word Ogopogo was picked up immediately and although tongue-in-cheek, the local lake serpent was renamed for posterity, replacing the Indian reference N'ha-a-itk.

It should also be pointed out that the original song with words by Cumberland Clark and music by Mark Strong was titled "The OGO-POGO, The Funny Fox Trot." It was sung, broadcast and recorded by the Savoy Bands. I felt privileged to have a recorded version given to me a number of years ago. Dr. Karl Shuker was kind enough to send me the sheet music in 1999. The refrain reads:

I'm looking for the Ogopogo,
The funny little Ogopogo,
His mother was an earwig,
His father was a whale,
I'm going to put a little bit of salt on his tail,
I want to find the Ogopogo,
While he's playing on his old banjo,
The Lord Mayor of London
Wants to put him in the Lord Mayor's show.

THE DAILY COURIER, JULY 1990, by J. P. Squire—As a Japanese film crew wound up a documentary on Ogopogo, a Vernon resident had turned over an unusual skull to a local television station.

Ogopogo expert Arlene Gaal was in City Park with the Nippon TV crew Thursday when she was called aside by a reporter Mohini Singh of CHBC Television. Out of sight of the Japanese, Singh showed her a skull about five centimeters smaller than a regulation soccer ball, with a large rounded snout in front. It was apparently found by a Vernon, B.C., resident washed up on the shore of Okanagan Lake.

The skull had both a bottom and top jawbone with very white tiny sawtooth teeth. Crevasses on the top could indicate a nose and on the side, well back, where eyes might have been located. Gaal admitted she was not an expert on paleontology and had no opportunity to study it so couldn't confirm if it could be from a previously undiscovered creature like Ogopogo.

Following this incident, I quickly sketched what I had been shown for Gan Hanada, a Japanese Nippon TV interpreter from Los Angeles and he immediately identified it as a species of dolphin. However, the Nippon crew wanted to see for themselves and we set up an appointment with CHBC for the following morning. The complete Nippon crew walked in the station with cameras rolling and CHBC had their cameras on us. Nippon producer, Hidetsugu Honda and the Japanese crew smiled knowingly after a quick look and all agreed with Gan Hanada that it was a dolphin skull. Nippon crew members thought that it may have been a bait and trap scenario, though perhaps somewhat unprofessional.

However, the question remained: if it was indeed found on the shores of Okanagan Lake, how did it get there? Much like whales and sturgeon, the introduction of a possible dolphin in Okanagan Lake was perhaps just a trigger for the imagination.

On February 28, 1981, I received a call from Randy Nagel, a resident of Winfield. He apparently had taken an unusual picture of Okanagan Lake and was wondering if I wanted to see it and perhaps offer an explanation. He said he was driving along the road leading to Okanagan Center, when he saw a disturbance in the lake. The water appeared to be boiling and frothing and what really caught his attention was the huge spray that kept shooting up from within this forty-foot-long (12 m) mass. Randy stopped his car and began taking pictures of the event. He observed the phenomena until it disappeared and the lake settled back to normality.

Upon checking the picture, I could tell that it was a sunny day as there were reflections and shadows in the land mass across to Westside Road. The lake was not calm and had small white caps throughout, but none to compare with the size of the unusual anomaly that Randy had photographed.

If this had been the ocean, one would immediately attribute the disturbance to a whale. This was Okanagan Lake and there was nothing even remotely resembling a whale in this freshwater lake. But a spray that shot up from the forty-foot-long (12 m) mass, reaching heights of ten feet (3 m) or higher would certainly make a person think otherwise. A black shadow appeared to be beneath the water, directly behind the turbulence. I waited a week and then went back to interview Randy once again. He took me to the spot where he had taken the pictures and repeated his account. Randy appeared to be a logical individual who was not at all concerned about what anyone else thought. He just wanted to tell his story and get another opinion.

February 4, 1932, Captain Joseph Weeks was taking his steamer the Sicamous out on Okanagan Lake. It was 4:00 P.M., his chief officer called his attention to what appeared to be a column of vapor about sixty feet (18 m) in diameter and about 150 feet (46 m) high, rising out of the lake. It seemed to be driven up from the center as though it were a jet of gas escaping from the bottom of the lake. In about five minutes it disappeared and the lake was back to normal.

On June 30, 1976, at around 12:30 P.M. Lynda Peter reports seeing a large brown object creating a massive spraying action at Okanagan Center before a head and neck lifted a good ten feet (3 m) out of the water.

Rick Trembley, a Vancouver resident working at Okanagan Lake Resort in August, 1981, saw what he thought to be a whale surfacing as he looked out from the balcony at the resort. Not considering that this was Okanagan Lake and not the Pacific Ocean where he had been raised, he immediately told his whale surfacing story to fellow workers. They never doubted the fact that he had seen something, but likened it to the Ogopogo, while politely reminding him of his geography. Rick, of course, was seeing the similarities of an Ogopogo surfacing to that of a whale, something not unnatural for folks used to living on the ocean.

It was at this point that Dr. Roy Mackal's theory that Ogopogo belonged to the prehistoric whale family known as the Zeugledon began to seem reasonable. The ancestry of whales is completely unknown, but they are clearly descended from the land-living. By upper Eocene times we already encounter giant forms like the Basilosaurus, sixty feet long. By the Miocene times, two distinct lineages had developed: the toothed whales such as the porpoises and sperm whales and the baleen (whalebone) whales such as the gigantic blue whales growing to 100 feet (30.5 m) in length and weighing 150 tons (136 t).

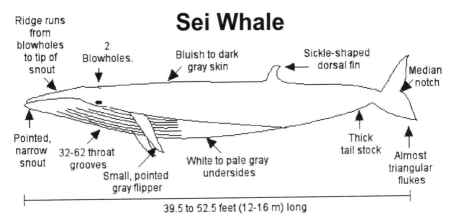

Sei Whale

Ridge runs from blowholes to tip of snout

2 Blowholes.

Bluish to dark gray skin

Sickle-shaped dorsal fin

Median notch

Pointed, narrow snout

32-62 throat grooves

Small, pointed gray flipper

White to pale gray undersides

Thick tail stock

Almost triangular flukes

39.5 to 52.5 feet (12-16 m) long

In appearance, the Zuegledon certainly bears some resemblance to the USO in Okanagan Lake but as in the sturgeon theory it lacks the obvious long neck. It's a known fact that while dinosaurs were clumping around on land, there were some frightful reptile cousins in the sea that looked just like sea serpents. These creatures were sometimes fifty feet (15.25 m) long with long necks and tails and four large paddles. Their heads were small but they had large jaws of spiked teeth. The *Elasmasaurus*, *Tylasaurus* and *Plesiosaurus* also had claims on descriptions of Ogopogo.

Paleontologists in the 1990s, found fossils in Pakistan of the earliest known water-dwelling whale. Dr. Philip Gingerich of the University of Michigan says the 46-million-year-old fossil was buried in shale in Punjab province. Whales evolved from animals that walked on land and are more closely related to other mammals than they are to fish. Until now, scientists have been unable to confirm an intermediate phase between those that lived on land and those adapted to the sea.

The team of paleontologists in Pakistan also reported that it had discovered the missing link whale, a creature that swam and also moved on land like a seal.

A 1935 midsummer Ogopogo sighting frightened little Audrey Gellatly when she saw something that resembled a log slither off the beach into Okanagan Lake, disappearing beneath the depths.

Alan Gartrell writes of a story told to him by his mother of a woman who lived on a beach in Kelowna who was washing clothes in a nearby building. When she came out, unusual footprints in the sand indicated that something had come out of the water, walked on the beach to the building she was in and gone back into the water.

"My mother also told me that she talked to an Indian while sitting on a fence at Pencticton High School. He told her that they used to put carp on the shore at the mouth of the river and go up on the clay banks and watch 'these things' come out and get the fish," stated Alan.

The Gartrells were one of the first family of settlers to homestead in Summerland in 1886. Alan's grandfather traveled the valley a great deal and told his mother of an old Indian named Charlie who was ninety-two years of age in 1925 who spoke of five creatures living in Okanagan Lake near Vernon.

"As I say in the earlier part of the letter, I think it is something like a Plesiosaur or one of the three species that have flippers and a long neck." signed Alan Gartrell.

While fishing in 1942, the Snyder family is certain the creature slithered off a ledge near Rattlesnake Island and they observed it moving at high speed through the lake toward Trepanier Bay.

Not to recognize Dr. Roy Mackal's theory that Ogopogo could perhaps be a prehistoric whale would be somewhat negligent, although it is somewhat negated by the many reports, sketches and photos showing a long neck. Perhaps less far-fetched might be to adhere to the probability that the two species bear characteristics of both *Plesiosaur* and Zuegledon.

My fascination with whale watching is well known within our family circle. I am awed by the actions of these magnificent creatures. As they swim, turn and dive, similarities to Ogopogo come to mind, which cannot be disputed while viewing film and video footage. The fact that it appears to circulate water through a structural opening on or near its head, creating sprays similar to that of a blowing whale, leads one to believe that it may be air breathing. If Ogopogo's lineage is indeed a product of the whale family then we should never discount the use of whale sounds in our attempts to lure it to the surface. Perhaps underwater cries of a similar species may help facilitate its discovery.

On September 18, 1999, the *Montreal Gazette* reported:

Norwegians record 'lake monster' sounds. Scientists have recorded mysterious noises in a Norwegian lake, bolstering local lore that it is the home of a monster. "The sound seems to have a biological source from its frequency structure," marine researcher Aud Vold Soldol said of underwater recordings made in Seljord Lake in southern Norway. She played the tape to experts from Norway, Sweden and Britain without disclosing the source. They assumed the sounds came from a large sea mammal like a whale, seal or sea lion.

The 1980 experience by Frank and Jim Rieger and Jim's six-year-old son Aurie is of importance, for not only did it take place close to where Randy Nagel took his unusual photo but also fairly close to where Rick Trembley saw his "whale," and where both the DeMara and Berry videos were taken.

Neither Frank nor Jim Rieger have any doubt that a huge dinosaur-like creature that swam beside their boat in Okanagan Lake for forty minutes and 4 miles (6 km) was Ogopogo. The father and son, both orchardists from East Kelowna, were fishing in the lake near Okanagan Center on a calm and sunny morning August 15, 1980, when they noticed what they thought was a floating log in the distance.

"Then we saw it moving toward us and it wasn't a log," stated Jim. "It was a big animal and it came right up to the back of our boat."

"When we saw what it was we were scared," said Frank Rieger. It was stirring up a lot of water because it was paddling. We could see its four legs, but it kept its head under the water."

"The neck was eight to ten feet long and it was moving from side to side. It was feeding on Kokanee, just scooping up the fish."

Frank and Jim estimated that there was about nineteen and a half to twenty-three feet (6–7 m) between the creature's front and back legs and that its total length was about thirty-three to thirty-nine feet (10–12 m). After traveling down the lake almost side by side for about forty minutes, the men gained some of their composure. "Dad said, 'let's see if we can get it to lift its head,' so we turned on our big engine. The creature just rolled slightly to one side and slid under the water. It was just like sliding off a table, a nice easy motion and it just vanished."

I interviewed the Riegers in their home a week after the experience. What really sticks out in my mind was that Jim was still in a state of shock, as he literally yelled into the tape recorder while he recounted the events. From the long tail that could have easily swiped them off the map to the front hinged appendages, to the back dinosaur thrusting legs along with Frank Rieger's statement that it was at least twenty tons (18 t), leaves very little to the imagination. The Riegers must be considered reliable witnesses. They have never deviated from the original account and have had opportunity to tell it to the rest of the world when producers sought out eye witness accounts of Ogopogo.

In the spring of 1998 Clara Shea was on a houseboat on Okanagan Lake with a group of seniors traveling north. She and her friends chose to sit at the back of the boat looking out toward the stern. The relaxed atmosphere was suddenly broken when something very much alive broke water about fifty feet away. Although most of the animal remained visible below the surface, they estimated that it must have been about twenty feet (6 m) long with a width approximately twenty inches (50 cm) or more. "We saw no fins; the object appeared to be flat and looked as smooth as an eel and was dark grey or smoky in color."

What was different about this sighting was that the portion that appeared to be the head was out of the water and it was spouting water just above the lake surface.

"I must say that it was very thrilling for the two ladies and myself," stated Clara Shea.

Clara provided a sketch to help reinforce her story.

A similar incident was reported in July of 1964. Mr. and Mrs. Durrant of White Rock, British Columbia, were vacationing in the Okanagan Valley. From Naramata Road, the couple spotted something in the lake. Mrs. Durrant stated that it had a head as large as a bucket and they both agreed that it was spouting water.

As more reports surface about Ogopogo spouting water as it moves through the lake, one can only continue to speculate.

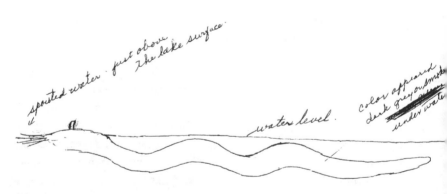

"The width from where we were sitting and looking at this object appeared to be about 20" wide. We were about 50 ft. or so from it. It did narrow some near the tail. We guessed it at about 20 ft. long. Saw no fins the object appeared to be flat—looked smooth like an eel. Must say it was very thrilling for the 2 ladies and myself made our day." —Clara Shea

Mysteries of the Lake

It is said that Okanagan Lake never gives up its dead. For whatever reason it appears to remain true. Divers located an elderly gentlemen who had been missing for almost a year near the south side of the bridge November 29, 1999. Under normal circumstances a body becomes buoyant and surfaces after a specified length of time. However, this does not hold true for Okanagan Lake.

Long ago it was believed that upon the crowing of a cock, Okanagan Lake would give up its dead.

Twenty-year-old Jack Blewitt was first reported drowned May 14, 1931, a week after he disappeared. Jackie Blewitt had started from Wilson Landing at the Paradise Ranch to cross Okanagan Lake in his canoe to his home on the other side. He did not arrive. An investigation followed and the canoe was found full of water, with a small sail still attached.

Investigation revealed that Guy Waterman had seen Jackie start out about 5:00 P.M. and watched him until he was well out on the lake. There was a good breeze to help him along. It further stated that Blewitt was a strong swimmer, and had swum from Summerland to Naramata and back many times. The assumption was that a gust of wind upset the boat, flinging him into the water, and that he died from exposure as the lake was still coming out of its winter chill.

His father, J. Blewitt, had tirelessly searched for his son's body, going out onto the lake over and over again. But it wasn't until he enlisted the help of a rooster that Jackie's body was found.

Two weeks later, he went out in a canoe and took along a rooster, following an old custom adopted years ago by people searching for victims of drowning. He passed over an area in the lake near Chute Creek and the cock crowed vigorously. Mr. Blewitt marked the place with a buoy and the next week returned again, and the bird crowed once more. He solicited the help of L. Fudge, who went out with him a third time to the same locality and the rooster crowed once more. This time the body was sighted on the shore only a short distance away.

No one will ever know what really upset Jackie Blewitt's canoe, nor understand why such a strong swimmer was not able to take control of his boat once he gained his composure.

Naramata and Summerland are across the lake from each other, yet Jackie's body was discovered on the Naramata side, some distance north. If the boat had been upset by a strong wind, the paddle and lee board should have fallen out with Blewitt. His death remains a mystery.

The year was 1932, Henry Murdoch was practicing for a marathon swim for an Okanagan regatta. His intent was to swim from the present Maud Roxby Bird Sanctuary Point to the dock at the Eldorado Hotel. His friend, John Ackland, was piloting the row boat assuming that Henry was swimming comfortably about twenty feet behind.

When they were off the south end of Boyces Field (where Cedar Avenue is today), John rested his oars, bent down to light a cigarette and when he looked up Henry had disappeared. His first thought was that Henry was playing a trick on him by swimming under the boat to hide. But soon John realized the situation was serious and for about twenty minutes he scanned the lake, which was about eight feet deep in that area. There was no sign of Henry.

John Ackland rowed frantically to shore and called the police from the nearest telephone. A search party began dragging the lake by boat while swimmers searched as best they could. This continued for two days, but a body was never found.

Everyone knew that Henry had been a life guard at the Eldorado Arms Hotel and was considered to be one of the strongest swimmers in the Okanagan. What deepened the mystery even more was the fact that the water was very clear and shallow and there was no discernable current in that part of the lake.

A similar incident happened in 1988 when Allan Skarbo of Peachland and his friends were enjoying a swim from his new houseboat. Dan Kerr's cap blew off and a member of the group jumped in to try to retrieve it. Unfortunately, he ran into trouble and very quickly disappeared. After an intensive search, which included an underwater camera, a body was never found. It was noted that the person in question was a strong swim-

Zaiser photos, 1996. Taken from Okanagan Mountain Park. A body and neck emerged from a mirror-calm lake churning up white waves around it. Six photos were taken.

Below: Zaiser photo progressive enlargement to 200 per cent. Note the neck and body of the creature are forty feet (12 m) or more in length.

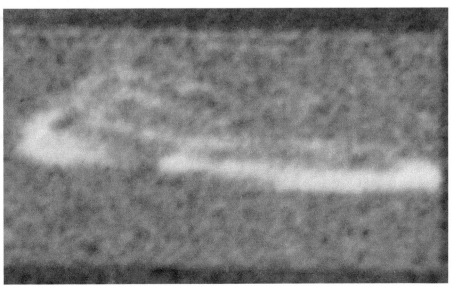

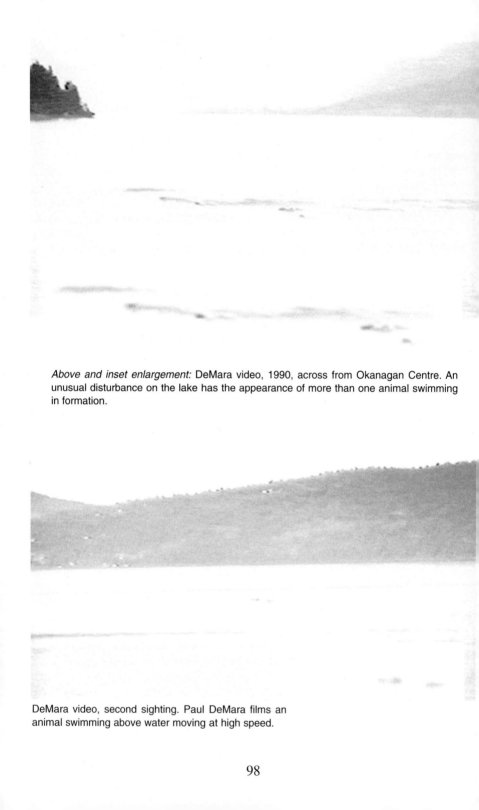

Above and inset enlargement: DeMara video, 1990, across from Okanagan Centre. An unusual disturbance on the lake has the appearance of more than one animal swimming in formation.

DeMara video, second sighting. Paul DeMara films an animal swimming above water moving at high speed.

Above and inset enlargement: Kirk video, 1987, taken from Mission Hill in Westbank.

Chaplin video, 1989, taken as an animal surfaces near Bear Creek.

Okanagan Lake—home of Ogopogo.

Right: An introduction to Ogopogo's home.

OGOPOGO'S HOME

Before the unimaginative, practical whiteman came, the fearsome lake monster, N'ha-a-itk, was well known to the primitive, superstitious Indians. His home was believed to be a cave at Squally Point, and small animals were carried in the canoes to appease the serpent.

Ogopogo still is seen each year — but now by white men!

DEPARTMENT OF
RECREATION & CONSERVATION

Local interpretation of the lengendary lake monster.

ANALYSIS OF FOLDEN FILM 1968 SINGLE FRAME

Source: **WWW**

Description: **JPEG Bitmap Compressed image 300 X 197 24-Bit Color   (original unavailable).**

Comments: Said to be frame of 8mm film. Scratching of image is consistent with film that has been projected repeatedly. However, color and contrast do not exhibit pale muted quality found on older commercially available film. This image was probably contrast and color corrected during or after the scanning process.

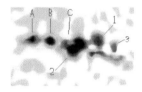

Threshold increase shows this to be a solid object as opposed to a wave or shadow effect. At least (3) distinct sections are above the water - "a" & "b" appear to be humps or coils connected just beneath the water. The greater part of section "c" is above the water and exhibits three (3) protrusions - 1 & 2 appear to extend sideways from the main body while 3 appears to be a tube or horn extending upward.

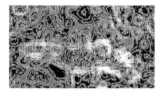

Color Contouring shows this to be a single object tapered at both ends (possible indicating submersion). Sections "a" & "b" are not visible here. This means that they are either part of the objects color or that they are humps angled or leaning toward the photographer.

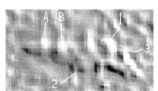

Edge Enhancement reveals a solid three-dimensional object. The "a" & "b" sections are roughly circular shaped - consistent with humps angled toward the camera. Note that the side protrusions are not level - "1" presents itself as sharp and obvious while "2" has a lesser definition. This indicates that "1" is farther out of the water while "2" is near/on the water line further supporting the object being at an angle. The tube -"3" - is pronounced, possibly indicating a reflective surface.

Light Blasting, Enlarging, and Sharpening combine to give a much more detailed view of the object. Color is green with an brownish tinge along the "spine". Object is arching out of the water and a third "hump" can be seen centered between the two side appendages. A white dot crowns the "tube" at the right end of the object - this may be reflection off the wet surface or it may be a flaw in the film. It appears to be too high out of the water to be caused by splashing. The overall shape of the object is that of a slightly flattened tube.

Analysis of Folden film performed by Kerry J. Voth.

Randy Nagel points to the area where he observed water churning and shooting up massive spray (inset photo).

Landsburg production producer Nick Webster discusses the next scene with Chief Bill Derickson. November 1977, *In Search of Ogopogo*.

Photo by Arlene Gaal (1979) near Okanagan Lake Bridge.

Above: Enlarged and enhanced version of head shot from the Thal film.

Below: Original head shot from Thal film footage (1980).

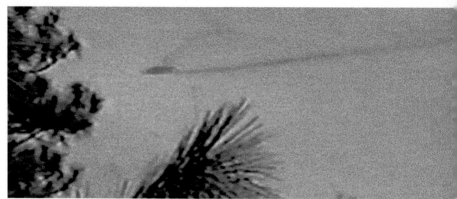

Berry video, March, 9, 2000, Okanagan Centre. An animal surfaces leaving a large section of turbulance in a calm lake, as it moves ahead in thrusts.

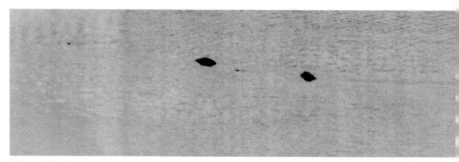

Bierowski photo, 1985, Delta Hotel balcony, Penticton.

Francey/Gaal photo, 1980, Kelowna City Park. An animal surfaces in a calm lake and moves across Lake Okanagan. Photo shows a body with a perpendicular raised neck.

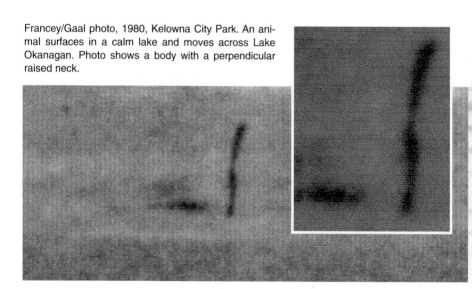

Paskal photo taken near Fintry,1990. *Inset:* Note the raised fin and spots or scales on the creature.

Svennson photo, January 28, 1984. Taken from Westside Road.

Below: Arlene Gaal photo taken near Bear Creek, July 1989. This sighting was witnessed by Ken and Clem Chaplin.

Johnson/Rolston photo, Kelowna City Park, 1992. Sudden turbulence in a mirror-calm lake is observed as an animal breaks water.

Left: Geoff Tozer and Andy Aikman are stunned as a long neck and head emerge from Lake Okanagan to grab a seagull.

Artist: Corlis Bennett

Rattle Snake Island, home of Ogopogo adjacent to Squally Point.

Photo: Arlene Gaal

Nippon TV producer Michihito Ogawa watches as ROV is loaded on to the boat for the March, 1991, search.
Photo: Arlene Gaal

Divers prepare to enter underwater cave at Squally Point to search for Ogopogo (July 1990).
Photo: Arlene Gaal

Arlene Gaal giving the interview for Nippon film crew and television Ogopogo search.
Photo: Don Defty

Photos taken by Jean Dorian, early 1980, Percé, Quebec, in the Gaspé Peninsula. No identification of the creature is given but a species of sturgeon has not been ruled out.

Potter's Prank.

Even Stranger Still!

This photo is accompanied by the story of Mr. Vincent St. Germain who swore on an affidavit before the King's Bench in Montreal on November 13, 1812, as to his finding. Legend states that Mr. St. Germain killed the creature, and took it to a far off place to sell it, as he feared the Indians would harm him for killing it. The Indians believed it to be "God the Manitou or Nahais, God of the Waters." At the time, the far off place could have been Banff, Alberta, or possibly St. Anne, Alberta, where today the creature above is encased in glass for viewing.

Another legend states that a sea creature with the head of a young negro boy with black woolly hair and large eyes would, at the change of weather, swim up and down the shores of Lake Superior crying like a baby. It swam at such speed it caused large ripples and deterred both travelers and Natives from traveling the lake when they heard the terrifying screams.

Photo Courtesy of Dorothy Bailey of Sidney, B.C.

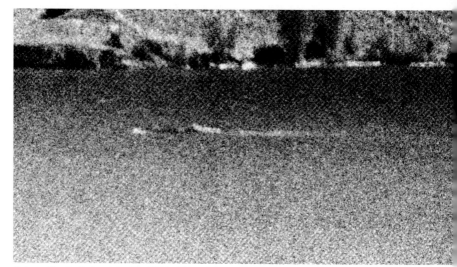

Arlene Gaal photo, July 12, 1981. This photo has pronounced similarities to the Wachlin phot (below), which was taken at the opposite end of the lake.

Wachlin photo, July 24, 1981. Seattle resident Walter Wachlin, twenty-year-old son Randy and thir teen-year-old daughter Sherri encountered Ogopogo while out fishing on Okanagan Lake. Sherr obtained this photo of the creature swimming 100 feet (30.5 m) directly in front of the boat.

110

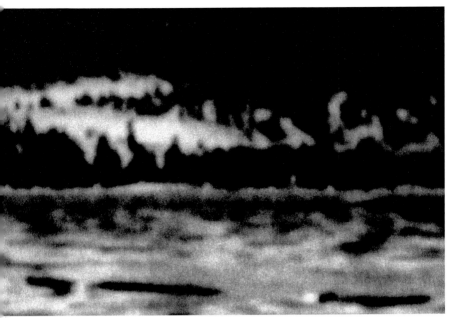

Allsup photo, 1980, near Fintry. Animal surfaces in the distance and two pictures are taken. Progressive enlargement to 200 per cent shows very long animal holding its head up with flipper-like appendage.

Fletcher photo, 1976, taken near Gellatly Bay. Ridges are seen on its back.

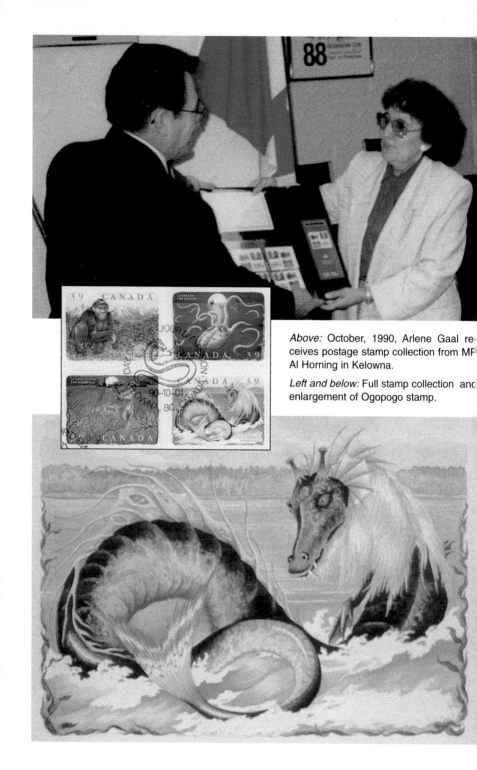

Above: October, 1990, Arlene Gaal re-
ceives postage stamp collection from MP
Al Horning in Kelowna.

Left and below: Full stamp collection and
enlargement of Ogopogo stamp.

mer. The event traumatized Alan Skarbo so much that he sold his new houseboat immediately and never ventured out on the lake again.

John Parker, a native of Australia and Kelowna resident, agreed to act the part of one of the settlers, during the *In Search of Ogopogo* production filmed by Alan Landsburg in 1977. I had come to know him through a family friend and he was an enthusiastic young man attending Okanagan College and working toward his welding certificate. However, before John could graduate, tragedy struck.

John, who participated in recreational diving, went out with his friend for a dive just off Eldorado Road in Kelowna one spring afternoon, His friend stated that when he signaled to surface, John indicated that he would stay down for awhile longer, and as he had more than enough airtime left in his tank, his friend waited for him on shore. John never came up. John's body was later discovered, but there was a mysterious bruise on his head. John either hit something or something hit him. Either way it was strong enough to render him unconscious, causing his death.

It caught my attention not because I had known John, but because he died in an area of the lake where only a few days before a dramatic encounter with Ogopogo had occurred. John was a skilled diver and knew enough to unlatch his weight-belt if he sensed any type of danger. It appeared obvious that whatever struck him was swift and strong enough to leave a noticeable bruise on his forehead. My thoughts immediately veered toward the description of the huge unidentified swimming animal with its long whiplike tail that had panicked a boater in the Eldorado Road lake site the same week.

If the animal had been feeding and John presented a threat, anything could have happened. I recalled the experience reported by Stan Baron of Calgary and Lawney Scown who were fishing near Fintry, July 2, 1976, when a creature at least fifty feet long surfaced and began swimming beside them. It appeared the animal was attempting to crowd the two fishermen out or perhaps was competing for the kokanee catch. At the first opportunity, the two men high-tailed it out, giving no thought to the fish they were leaving behind.

In 1901, H. D. Lyons was fishing near Squally Point (the area across from Peachland and bordering Rattlesnake Island often referred to as Ogopogo's lair), when something began pulling on his line. Whatever it was, Lyons was in for the ride of his life as it managed to tow him and his boat halfway round Ogopogo Island before the line broke.

It was Tuesday, July 6, 1977, Ed Fletcher, self-proclaimed Ogopogo hunter, was boating on Okanagan Lake with his daughter and her friend. Some unusual wave action was experienced and the boat received a heavy bump from below. There were no logs and the depth was near 300 feet (91 m). A massive bubble appeared in the water, moving outward from the center and a horrible smell of dead fish emanated from it, leaving a lingering stench in the nostrils of the boat's occupants.

Two days later, Erin Neely put on her water skis and went out behind the Fletcher boat. One third of the way out from shore, Erin spotted the creature's humps as it was swimming to her far right. A huge wave catapulted into a massive disturbance and as Erin stated, "I wiped out and fell flat on my face."

The sudden fall apparently stunned Erin and as she opened her eyes, part of the monster was visible and passed within arm's reach. "I must have lost consciousness, because I couldn't remember anything after that." She was brought to shore and treated for shock. I interviewed her within the hour and the terror in her voice was evident.

On August 11, 1995, two couples were motoring a speedboat across Okanagan Lake just north of Rattlesnake Island when the two women sitting in the bow noticed a strong fish smell.

"My sister-in-law said to me, 'It stinks,'" said Chris Barile, a Kelowna resident of four years. "It was gross—strong and smelly."

Moments later there was a strange churning in the water about six meters from the boat. A large object then appeared above the surface.

"This huge back of something came out of the water. It looked like the back of a snake, but it was huge," said Barile. "It had a hump coming out of the water and then went down. It didn't come up again."

Barile described the hump as greenish gray, but stopped short of identifying it as that of Ogopogo.

"I believe there's something big in there, but I don't think there's a sea monster. The thing that really made us think though, was that awful smell."

Both Ed Fletcher and the Chris Barile group experienced an offensive smell coming from the water below, while encountering what appeared to be Ogopogo The creature may have been expelling gas or perhaps emitting a natural scent due to its activity at the time. Most who encounter Ogopogo can be thankful this does not happen very often.

Inez Cooper tells of an experience in October of 1976 that provides yet another side to the Ogopogo mystery. While standing near the water's edge in City Park, close to the pier, she suddenly saw waves begin to wash up on the beach from the very calm lake. "I looked up, expecting to see a boat but nothing was in sight. Then through my binoculars I saw opposite the Kelowna Yacht Club and in the middle of Okanagan Lake, what resembled two logs swimming side by side in a slightly diagonal northwest direction, heading toward Westbank."

Could there be more than one animal out there? Logic of course tells us so, as *Capital News* owner Les Kerry and prominent medical practitioner, Dr. Underhill, saw two creatures through binoculars in 1949 and Jake Heppner confirms this in the 1980s.

Andrew Bennett writes:

Here is a recount of a sighting of Ogopogo by the Indians. This person did not wish to be identified, however this is what she told me this evening, July 24, 1993:

"In 1942, Mrs. Lawson asked her friend if she would like to go in and see Mrs. Derrickson, who was quite old and an invalid in Kelowna General, and ask her to tell the story about Ogopogo. Mrs. Derrickson stated that in those days her Indian men went from the westside to Kelowna for groceries paddling a canoe both ways. One day while going across they saw five Ogopogos swimming around the boat. The creatures were quite boisterous and fearing they would upset the boat, the Indian men had to turn back."

In 1951, Edythe March saw two creatures, at least four feet out of the water, swimming away and on September 12, 1976, Mr. and Mrs. Rowdon, while relaxing at the Peachland Lookout, see two Ogopogos swimming to meet each other. Graham Merricks observed three animals swimming out from shore in a 1990 aerial sighting and both the DeMara and Berry videos give the impression of more than one animal swimming together.

Jake Heppner, a long-time Okanagan Valley resident, tells of his many encounters with Ogopogo, and states: "I have met up with Ogopogo many times and even seen three of them swimming together in formation."

One very close encounter had him holding his breath. While out fishing, he noticed something approaching from the distance leaving a big swell behind it. It came right toward his boat, so Jake quickly shut off the motor and reeled in his line. The animal was right beside his boat. There was no snorting noise or unusual activity, but it suddenly submerged.

"Since it was less than ten feet away, it did make quite a commotion and I had to hang on to the sides of the boat to steady it."

Jake remembered some markings on its body. "There were brownish colored lines along its back about eight or nine inches apart and in the spaces connecting the lines, there was a yellowish tint or color. It had no scales or humps, just smooth skin. Since the head was submerged, and the back area exposed I surmised that the creature must be at least fifty feet long and have a girth at least as big."

Inez Cooper opens up yet another door. Following her October, 1976, experience at City Park she discovered a couple of unusual footprints in the sand, "the approximate size of one being 5 inches by 5 inches, (my two hands combined)." Her letter continues: "A man who has since died, said he had seen in the reeds, farther south on Lakeshore Road a creature that he believed to be a young Ogopogo."

John Greig was one of the few people to observe an unknown animal with reptilian features on land. It was 1948, the year of the Great Flood in British Columbia. Okanagan Lake had overflowed its banks covering Lakeshore Road and nearby fields. Greig was bicycling home from his evening shift at the CPR station. The darkness was ameliorated by a full moon, and as he rode, he heard a plodding through the fields. Assuming it to be Mr. Eaton's horses, he paid little attention until he saw a reptilian-like creature with webbed feet in the field where the horses should have been. Overwhelmed by the encounter, John watched it slowly back down and disappear. He would never forget the experience.

This letter, dated February 9, 1990, from Jo Driftmeir and her son Rick, is an important contribution to this mystery:

> After seeing the recent TV program Unsolved Mysteries, I wanted to let you know what happened to us on Lake Skaha many years ago. We were camped in our trailer near the lake and had a 12-foot aluminum boat with a 9-horse motor on it. Out oldest son, who was then about 15 wanted to take me for a ride. This was approximately 1965.
>
> We went out into the lake not too far from what I imagine is the north shore. It is the area where the town begins and also where the canal comes in from Okanagan Lake. Rick had the motor open and all of a sudden, the motor hit something which stopped it completely. We drifted on past and then he started the motor to see what he had hit. He thought it was a blob of kelp at first because of the color, but of course kelp only grows in salt water. When we looked back we saw a tremendous churning in the water just like one of the TV pictures showed. A

large part of the animal came out of the water in a loop and we could see a V-shaped cut in it with some dark liquid coming out of it. It was dark enough that it stained the water.

Not being very smart, I guess, I took the oar from the boat and lifted part of the thing out of the water. It was about 10 to 12 inches wide and maybe two inches thick through. It was a rather dark green with brown lines on it. Along the edges the brown lines were almost in scallops and there were two lines running lengthwise on the top. As I looked into the water I could see no head and no tail, although the part where the cut had been was wider than the part that I lifted out of the water.

This was a slimy, snake-like animal and had no relationship to a beaver type creature as shown in some of the TV pictures. It moved like a wide, flat, huge snake. All of a sudden the boat shot forward, and I asked Rick what he was doing, and he replied, "Getting out of here!" And I guess it may have been a good thing we did.

I don't know how long it was, but I know I saw at least 18 to 20 feet of just coils. My son claimed he would never water ski in that lake again, and he hasn't. My son's name is Rick Driftmier and I am Jo.

It was such a strange thing to have happened that it stayed in my mind almost like a nightmare. I can still see it very clearly in my mind. After seeing those pictures, I feel we were very lucky that the thing did not thrash so much that it overturned the boat.

The Driftmiers live in Washington state and addresses are on file.

The interesting thing about the Driftmiers' experience was that if it had been the 90s instead of the 60s we would immediately have thought of DNA. There is no doubt that the dark liquid oozing from the wound would have been enough for species identification.

A recent e-mail read: "SEEN IT AND MY BOAT STRUCK IT!" The writer, Adrien, identified herself as being thirty-four years of age and a resident of Penticton.

I was approaching a dock in Summerland very slowly and watching for rocks on the bottom as I had not been there before. It was a bright, sunny day and I could see the sandy lake bottom clearly with the odd scattered weed patch. Suddenly I saw this long black hump with tiny white spots that looked like barnacles. As soon as I saw the depth rising I pulled my throttle off, but it was too late.

My small outboard motor had hit the half-cylinder-shaped object and the force kicked my motor up to the land-locked position. I saw nothing move but when I looked down again I had coasted over it. The depth of the water was about 10 feet, which meant that for my boat to strike it, the size was at least 7 or 8 feet round from its belly to its back. I looked to the right but it was too long to see the end of it. No humps. No bend, just a long half cylinder shape, black and white barnacle-covered. It looked like a whale's back, but no fin or ending. Upon coming to shore, I asked the other boaters why that huge black pole that I hit was not marked. One guy replied that he had been boating for years and there's nothing there. I responded, "My motor cannot be raised other than by lifting—it's heavy and it landlocks up." A few of us went back out but whatever it was had gone.

Yes I am one of the 85% who have not reported this to anyone. I assure you I am sane and was not drinking. I know this was a large lake creature and nobody can change my mind. I also still swim and ski in the lake and I know that if it wanted to, it could have surely capsized my boat but it did not move in the few seconds when I saw it and it was not there when we went back.

While the Driftmeirs' experience in Skaha Lake was frightening, Adrien's boating encounter in Summerland created wonder and scrutiny. Both experiences left a mark and untold questions in the minds of those involved.

A few years after the Driftmeirs' sighting this news report was printed:

GIANT STURGEON SPOTTED

A 15-foot giant sturgeon has been reportedly sighted by three persons in Skaha Lake. Brent Sato of Burnaby, a summer visitor to Penticton said he ran over the fish while he was towing a water skier with a boat last week.

He said that he and two companions saw the sturgeon in the lake about a half mile south of the airport where the water is about 100 feet deep. Fish and wildlife branch officials in Penticton expressed surprise at the reported sighting.

"It's within the realm of possibility, but it's never been directly confirmed," said Cas. V. Eysinga, pubic education officer, about the idea of the giant sport fish being in the Okanagan Lake system.

Records show that the white sturgeon swims in the Fraser River and its tributaries, and Okanagan Lake is listed as a possibility.

Some sturgeon spend part of their life in the ocean, but some are landlocked. They are bottom feeders which eat crustaceans.

Dave Smith, a fish technician with the fish and wildlife branch, said that the giant fish were found in the Columbia River and there is no reason why they could not have been here at one time. However, within the history of white men in the Valley, no sightings have been authenticated. He said the fish and wildlife staffers have not gone out looking for sturgeon, but research done by the Okanagan Basin Study should have located the fish if they are in the lake system.

"The sturgeon are good active game fish," he said, and are managed in the Fraser Fishery. He said the 15-foot estimate of length in the sighting last week is reasonable because the fish run up to 25 feet in length.

"Sturgeon can be both shore and stream spawners, but possibly any sturgeon in this lake system are stream spawners," he said.

If there are any sturgeon in Okanagan Lake, it is likely they are also in Skaha Lake.

The theory held by some about the nature of the fabled Ogopogo of Okanagan Lake is that it is a sturgeon or a school of them.

News clipping of a strange animal found in California in the 1930s. The head is very similar to the Wong sketch of the head of Ogopogo on page 42.

AST
it to moder-
much change
ght to mod-
t mild.

The Daily Co

(ESTABLISHED 1858)

FIFTH YEAR   VICTORIA, BRITISH COLUMBIA, THURSDAY, OCTOBEI

SON CLOSED Awards Given
ticultural Society Contests by Mayor—Page 5

WOULD ADD TO INTERE
Women's Institutes in Conference Discuss Ways to Improve Work—

Strange Creatures Inhabit the Ocean Depths

TAKEN several years ago, when the strange specimen of a mammal shown here, was cast up on a California beach, this photograph comes to The Colonist through the courtesy of Major Hogg. Whether or not the mammal's head and general appearance resemble in any way the large creature seen in the vicinity of Victoria by a number of reputable citizens recently, it is within the range of possibility that it may belong to the same species. At any rate, it is ocular evidence that there are stranger things in the sea than are seen. Nor is the fact that such a creature should be so far north an extraordinary thing. Currents flowing along the coast vary from year to year, which have been undoubtedly responsible for turtles and other denizens of tropic waters being taken as far north as the West Coast of Vancouver Island, and may, with reason, account for the presence of a relative of the mammal monster photographed on a California beach.

Native Legends of Ogopogo

"Long ago ... when the Redman's searching gaze swept the sunbaked hills, and reflected the diamond dancing glints of Okanagan Lake, N'ha-a-itk was a name that held the awed respect of every brave. N'ha-a-itk was the lake monster or lake demon whose lair was deep in the cavernous depths of this inland sea."

You doubt that this is so?

"Seize him! Let him face the Council of Chiefs! The braves who know no fear! The mighty ones who stalk the snarling mountain cat and warriors who scorn the fury of a storm on Okanagan. Beat the tom-toms! Feed the hungry flames! Let this paleface tremble at the mention of N'ha-a-itk's name!"

Such would have been the fate of skeptics in an earlier day.

With the passing of time, N'ha-a-itk is now Ogopogo, and despite the fact that an ever-increasing host of witnesses fervently swear to having seen Ogopogo cavorting in the sun-kissed waters of Okanagan Lake, there are some who doubt the reality of the deep. But there are just as many who do not.

Ogopogo has mellowed with the passing of time. Of recent years, he frolics in the water with almost impish delight, flips a flirtatious tail and, with a sly wink, disappears in a froth—to return from whence he came.

On the surface, Okanagan Lake presents a scene of calm beauty, but this view can change in a moment. Winds rise seemingly out of nowhere whipping the lake into a fury. The Okanagan Indians have lived near the shores of the lake for centuries, long before the appearance of the white man. They hold a deep reverence for nature, believing that all creation is part of the plan of the Great Spirit and the lake invokes both fear and respect.

This lake is like a living, sacred thing. In an hour or two this lake can be a raging body of water and very dangerous. In this lake we have N'ha-a-itk, the serpent that lives in the water and it has been told to me by my great, great, grandfather and told to him by his ancestors. No Indian would attempt to cross Okanagan Lake without first offering a prayer to the great spirit or without carrying a small animal sacrifice should they come in contact with the serpent. This offering can be viewed as a spiritual act of sacrifice or as a way of appeasing a hungry monster.

—Elder Chief Bill Derrickson. (1977)

Native Elder Shares Legends

Dave Parker, known by the children as "The Story Teller," made a hobby of telling traditional Native stories—legends he learned as a child. "They reflect what it was like before the white man. In early days there was no writing or books it was all telling stories."

Native people knew about Ogopogo before the white people arrived. I heard about it as a child. People talked about it long before I began story-telling. It was supposed to have been born across Okanagan Lake from Peachland. There's a rock bluff there that goes down into the water. When you look down into the water from there, there's no bottom whatsoever. The water goes out of sight. It looks eerie.

Little waves hit the caves along the rocky shore. They make sucking sounds. The combination of what you see and hear is kind of scary. Many people who have happened along there, run away saying they saw something.

In 1923 when divers went down to the bottom of the lake to see if they could find any remains of Ogopogo bones, they did find a skeleton, but it looked much like a cow. When I tell people that they laugh. They see the story as a myth "It was a cow skeleton." What I try to portray is that there is such a thing as Ogopogo.

But here's where the story changes.

I was telling the story before 1982 in Oroville, Washington, where my aunt was living. When I told her the story she said, "I saw it!"

My aunt who's dead now, said she saw what we know as Ogopogo, not in Okanagan Lake, but above Skaha Lake, near Kaleden, south of Penticton. It was 1908. She would have been six years old. She was walking along the shore of the lake with her step-mother, picking choke-cherries. She was lagging behind when her stepmother beckoned her to hurry up.

When she caught up, her stepmother pointed down to the lake below. There, below them, lay a monster basking on the rocks. The head of the monster and part of its body were lying above the surface on the shore of the lake. The rest of the body was under water.

My aunt said the head looked like that of a horse; only it wasn't a horse. It was like a snake, only it wasn't a snake. It is true, that creature would have had to go from Okanagan Lake to the smaller lakes and back again.

In my early days I heard people talking about tracks going over the land—the kind of tracks a large serpent would make. I don't doubt for a minute what she told me. She wouldn't lie.

Many moons ago in these hills, there lived an old Indian known to all as "The Old Man of the Mountains," a friend to all animals and kind counselor to his people. He was called by them, "Old Kan-He-Kan."

There came one day to the Valley an evil man named "Kel-Oni-Won," who was possessed by the spirit of the evil one. With a club he murdered the vulnerable old man. In memory of Old Kan-He-Kan, his people named this beautiful lake in the valley, Okanagan and called upon the gods to avenge his death and to punish Kel-Oni-Won for his wicked deeds.

The Gods, unable to decide upon the punishment, left the murderer to brood on his sins until council could be held. The decision was to change Kel-Oni-Won into a lake serpent, a restless creature who would forever be at the scene of the crime where he would suffer continued remorse.

He was left in the custody of the beautiful Indian lake goddess and was known to the tribesmen as N'ha-a-itk; the remorsefulone who must live in the lake with the company of other animals. It is said that the only animal who would tolerate his company was the rattlesnake.

Monster Island of Okanagan Lake

Situated in the beautiful Okanagan Lake, about twenty to twenty-five miles distant from Penticton lies a small island. Insignificant and picturesquely barren, the islet would fail to attract the attention of an ordinary observer, but for the Aboriginals, it possesses a horrible fascination. It was thought to be the home of the monster of Okanagan Lake and while eyeing it with dread and interest, none of the Natives ever dared to approach or attempt to land there.

The Indians believe that in passing this islet they have frequently seen the blood, bones and fat of the victims strewn on the rocky shore and believed that N'ha-a-itk consumed his catch on Monster Island after having pulled them into the water to drown them. It is difficult to ascertain the exact nature of this monster, but Indians believed that it is both benevolent and malevolent.

Legend tells that Ogopogo watched over his island, and any time someone came near, he created stormlike turbulence, making any sort of landing almost impossible. Even today, this phenomenon occurs, frightening boaters enough so they leave the area.

The monster was supposed to chiefly frequent the waters between his favorite island, known also as Rattlesnake Island, and the Mission Valley, although often making excursions to both the head and foot of the lake. Some of the early white settlers believed they had seen this strange creature, and described it as resembling a large log or canoe turned upside down.

A government plaque that sits just south of Peachland looking across at Rattlesnake Island reads: "Before the unimaginative white man came, the fearsome lake monster N'ha-a-itk was well known to the superstitious Indians. His home was Squally Point. Small animals were carried in a canoe to appease the serpent. Ogopogo is still seen each year, but now by the whitemen. (Department of Conservation and Recreation)"

From *Ogopogo's Vigil*

At night around the campfire tall tales would be told, recounting an adventure with a grizzly, or the latest antics of Nha-a-itk, the lake monster. A monster that was said to have its home in a cave under Squally Point, but when a native had occasion to speak its name he did so with bated breath. The terrifying creature would race up and down the lake, and at times heaving water with its tail making a great deal of wind, preparing to devour any unprepared Indian who might be caught out in a canoe.

—Frank Buckland

Primrose Upton wrote:

All Indians rushed for shelter when the dark ridge of rising water showed that N'ha-a-itk was abroad. He churned the waters into a fury with such speed that one minute there was breathless calm and the next, the wind howling and the waves racing and clawing at one another, sinking back exhausted only to be smashed by the next wave.

After her experience with Ogopogo in 1872, Susan Allison penned a poem which tells of the awesome nature of the lake and its surroundings. She writes:

Miles to westward lies an island,
An island all men dread,
A rocky barren island,
Where a monster makes his bed.

So busy are the fishers
That they hardly spare a glance
To the black line of white crested waves,
That so rapidly advance.

From the westward -from the island,
The island all men dread,
From the rocky barren island,
Where the monster makes his bed.

Recreation of Native Indians towing horses across Lake Okanagan.

Monster or just a hoax for tourists?

KELOWNA, B.C. (UPI) — Believers say the warm waters of summer bring the demon to the surface.

Skeptics suggest the dragon responds better to the ringing of cash registers.

The faithful argue that "Ogopogo" behaves in classic reptilian fashion, it's dark, hump-backed body slithering across the lake until it dives again.

Wags counter that it behaves in a typical Chamber of Commerce manner, showing up about the same time as the summer tourists and disappearing when they leave.

Whichever is true, another tourist season has closed at Lake Okanagan and six more sightings of Canada's version of the Loch Ness monster have been logged into the record books.

'We could see six humps'

"I turned around and I saw this dark thing coming through the water," recounts Lionel Edmond, 33, who was fishing with a friend July 20 when he heard a loud rushing of water 30 yards behind him.

"It looked like a submarine surfacing, coming up toward my boat. As it came up perpendicular to the boat, we could see six humps out of the water, each hump about 10 inches out of the water and each one creating a wake.

"It was cruising between 8 and 10 miles per hour. We followed it for 10 minutes. We saw no head or tail, but it must have been some 50 or 60 feet long."

Harold Thwait, the former mayor of nearby Peachland, describes that sighting differently.

"A pile of horse ———" he starts, then stops and rephrases.

"I've never seen anything," he begins again. "A lot of it's just tourist promotion. You'll see people rigging up truck tires in the water and taking pictures of them. The next thing you know, you're reading in the newspapers about a new Ogopogo sighting."

Centuries of reports

Legend holds that a kindly old Indian once lived by the lake but was killed by an evil wanderer. As punishment, the Gods turned the killer into a giant lake serpent so he would spend eternity at the scene of his crime.

Sightings date back ———

called "Naitaka."

The first known sighting by a white settler was in 1872. Since then hundreds have claimed to have seen something huge and mysterious rise out of the water.

Dozens of scratchy films, blurry photos and sharp sketches have been submitted as proof that a monster resides in the 80-mile-long, mile-wide lake.

In 1926, British Columbia authorities considered arming lake ferries to protect them from the creature. They were never able to decide, however, what weapons would be effective.

There is no record of the demon ever attacking humans, although in the 1890s a team of horses was said to have mysteriously been pulled under water, never to be seen again.

Ogopogo's biographer, Arlene Gaal, has spent the past five years meeting people who swear they've seen the creature. She has made three sightings herself.

Her dining room table is littered with photographs, some blurry, some out of focus and some obvious fakes. She holds up a snapshot of a dark figure moving ———

drawing the glass and her camera.

"Naitaka," her movie figure surfaces times.

The lake east of Vance for touring people think her of Crescent

"Last year a $1 million Ogopogo offered $50 ———
The Northeast $1,000 for a ———
No one ———
Skeptics created by the ———
people like that it is a fish that her ———
to be seen ———

But the people like ———

"A shameful kidding," ———

Ship's Master Pens Vivid Account Of Sea Monster

The following story was written by the captain of the Ss. Santa Clara at the request of the Associated Press and radioed to New York following the ship's report to the U.S. Coast Guard that it had struck a "sea monster" in the Atlantic off the North Carolina coast.

By J. FORDAN.

ABOARD THE SS. SANTA CLARA. (AP). (By Radio)—On Dec. 30, 1947, the Grace Line steamer Santa Clara was cleaving through sunlit calm blue seas 118 miles due east of Cape Lookout, en route from New York to Cartagena.

The Santa Clara had just crossed the Gulf Stream when William Humphreys, chief mate; John Rigney, navigating officer, and John Axelson, third mate, assembled on the starboard wing of the bridge to take the noon sight at 11.55 a.m.

HEAD SEEN FIRST

Suddenly Axelson saw a snake-like head rear out of the sea about 30 feet off the starboard bow of the vessel. His exclamation of amazement directed the attention of the other two mates to the sea monster, and the three watched it unbelievingly as, in a moment's time, it came abeam of the bridge where they stood, and was then left astern.

The creature's head appeared to be about 2½ feet across, 2 feet thick and 5 feet long. The cylindrically-shaped body was about 3 feet thick, and the neck about 1½ feet in diameter.

As the monster came abeam of the bridge it was observed that the water around the monster, over an area of 30 or 40 feet square, was stained red. The visible part of the body was about 35 feet long.

BELIEVED CUT IN TWO

It was assumed that the color of the water was due to the creature's blood and that the stem of the ship had cut the monster in two, but as there was no observer on the other side of the vessel there was no way of estimating what length of body might have been left on the other side.

From the time the monster was first sighted until it disappeared in the distance astern, it was thrashing about as though in agony. The monster's skin was dark brown, slick and smooth. There were no fins, hair, or protuberances on the head, neck, or visible parts of the body.

Ogie in flight

We can't say we were surprised to hear from town busybody Bernard Stroller that Ogopogo has been spotted near the shores of Skaha Lake. To be sure, this has been a particularly trying summer for Ogie and we knew that sooner or later he would reach the point of exhaustion and head through that channel between Okanagan and Skaha Lakes for a much-needed vacation down south.

Let's face it folks, a sea monster, no matter how mature or sophisticated, can only handle so much glaring publicity. Why, we recall that during John Hindle's most recent stint as mayor, the usual sign on his office door was 'Here today, gone to Maui.' Granted, Dale Hammill was well suited for the ——— ber chicken circuit, but we ——— at Ogie is more of a Hindle than ——— was as squat as our current ——— ain inconspicuous, but how can ——— e in a lake of two-to-four-pound ——— ow trout not stand out?

——— ans coming out of the closet to ——— een him, too," to out-of-work us- ——— ying to get rich, who can blame ——— ing on down the waterway? The ——— must have been the disclosure ——— ng ground and the humiliating ——— -meaning Bruce Strachan that ——— ategory of wildlife.

——— te night parties with loud water ——— gin certainly isn't the lifestyle of ——— rumph. Wildlife indeed. Our ad- ——— Ogie hunters is summed up in

——— s fled his lair, ——— tarted to blind him. ——— ne and he'll come home, ——— behind him.

Ogopogo sightings increasing

By DON PLANT
Daily Courier Staff

Ogopogo has reared its ugly back again.

Okanagan Lake's legendary sea serpent is the prime suspect after three women spotted a strange object swimming in Okanagan Lake near Bear Creek Park about 3 p.m. Monday.

Lidia Allen, Trudy Towers and Debbie Nielsen were sitting in the picnic area of the park looking over the calm water when a black streak appeared in the water about 60 metres offshore.

"It almost looked like a wave, but it was so long and it stood there — really dark black," said Allen, 21. "Then it moved and went under. It was a thick black line and it started to go up and down. . . . It looked like a serpent."

The three women, all from Kelowna, watched the object for close to 10 minutes as it swam like a snake south along the Westside shore. They had no camera, but memorized the object's movements and color.

"We saw this black streak coming out of the water. It was really thick, like a big black snake," Allen recalled. "It went up and down, slithering.

"The part above the water was 10 to 15 feet long. It was really dark. We couldn't see a head. Its back was coming up and then going down."

The women watched the object

J.P. SQUIRE/The Daily Courier
Ogopogo got to hold Beloved Teddy Monday while five-year-old Alice Ward munched on popcorn in Kerry Park and scanned the nearby lake for the real thing.

wake from the stern of the Fintry Queen, which was docked by The Sails.

The two humps were blackish, bluey and smooth, said Brenda Massey, 23. She described it as a large water snake coming up out of the water and down.

On Aug. 11, two couples were motoring in a speedboat across Okanagan Lake just north of Rattlesnake Island when the two women sitting in the bow noticed a strong fish smell.

"My sister-in-law said to me, 'It stinks'," said Chris Barile, a Kelowna resident for four years. "It was gross — strong and smelly."

Moments later there was a strange churning in the water about six metres from the boat. A large object then appeared above the surface.

"This huge back of something came up out of the water. It looked like the back of a snake, but it was huge,'" said Barile. "It had a hump coming out of the water and then went down. It didn't come up again."

Barile described the hump as greenish-grey, but stopped short of identifying it as that of Ogopogo.

"I believe there's something big in there, but I don't think there's a sea monster . . . The thing that really made us think (though) was that awful fishy smell."

There have been five sightings of Ogopogo — or a distant relative who looks just like him — so far this summer.

disappear around a point, then reappear in the distance minutes later.

A thing that may have been Ogopogo also made an appearance last Thursday, when a Kelowna woman and her two adult grandchildren spotted two humps and a

Ogopogo joins the snowbirds

There you are!

Kelowna residents who may have wondered where our favorite denizen of the deep disappeared for the past couple of months need wonder no more.

Ogopogo has been holidaying in Hawaii.

The legendary Okanagan Lake resident has not surfaced in this newspaper since he and his family were featured in a Christmas tale.

He's back!

Ogie has been spotted on a Hawaiian beach thousands of kilometres from his chilly Okanagan home.

A likeness of the legend was built out of Maui sand by a holidaying Winfield family.

Cliff Rousel said he couldn't believe how many people recognized the sandy serpent.

"It didn't matter if they were from Canada, the States, Europe or Japan — they'd walk by and say, 'Oh, that's Ogopogo'."

Legend has it Ogopogo was a snowbird, er, snowfish, who took off to the sun for a couple of months every winter.

What was not known was that he could afford Hawaii, and Maui to boot!

Rousel was on Maui this month with his wife Vi, and two young children when the family decided to dress up the beach with a 20-foot-long rendering of Ogopogo, complete with humps, horns and snout.

It was a hot hit.

About half the people walking by recognized the likeness.

It's probably not surprising how many people know the legend of Ogopogo, since the often-sighted creature has gained a considerable measure of notoriety in the past decade, thanks to several television programs.

Ogopogo has been written about in countless magazines and newspapers — including the venerable New York Times.

And more ink and airtime are sure to surface in the media this summer.

Just in time for tourist season.

If only Ogie can tear himself away from Hawaii.

Fact or Fiction?

As involved as I have become in Ogopogo research, it is only natural that every so often someone would attempt to perpetrate a hoax. Two of the more colorful attempts, Potter's prank and the Bierowski photos, came at the peak of a well-publicized tourist promotion.

In 1984, the Okanagan Similkameen Tourist Association took out a Lloyds of London policy for one million dollars to be paid out to anyone who could capture Ogopogo. The rules, although quite ridiculous, were somewhat straightforward. You were to go out on the lake with rod and reel, latch onto this monstrous whalelike animal and pull him or her into shore. The next step was to build a pen or fence around the creature, which would, of course, calmly wait as you ran for your tools. Once secured, it was then necessary to make a telephone call to a biologist at UBC who would catch a plane to Kelowna, identify the animal and if it looked like Ogopogo, you would then waltz to the bank with a million-dollar check, to the delight of all your family and friends. Spotting scopes were set up on specific areas of the lake bordered by a colorful set of rules along with a written history of the Ogopogo. It was a very attractive display.

The project was duly launched during a reception held at the Royal Anne Hotel. The mayor, members of council, chamber of commerce and media made it even more eventful. As the resident expert, I was also invited. It was all somewhat tongue-in-cheek. As the months passed, unsurprisingly, no one came forward to claim the reward.

One day I received a call from Dave Henshaw, managing editor of the *Kelowna Daily Courier*, to come down to the office as he had some pictures for me to see. I looked at them, shook my head and Dave com-

126

mented, "I think he thought we would publish them, like they did in Penticton." He then proceeded to show me the photo reproduced by the *Penticton Herald*, showing a massive science fictionlike animal swimming in Okanagan Lake below Munson Mountain near Penticton. "You can do what you like with them, the guy's phone number is on the letter."

The letter was headed "Ogopogo Sightings by John Potter." He gave his address as Skaha Lake Road, Penticton.

He describes taking some visitors from England up to see the view from Munson Mountain in the early fall of 1983 and tells of seeing a big wake around the shoreline of the Delta Hotel where an animal with a long neck and two very distinguishable humps appear. He takes some pictures as he claims it moved from the lakefront of the Delta Hotel at a tremendous speed.

The letter continues:

Earlier this year I took my youngest daughter for a drive out to Kelowna and to my surprise OGY came swimming under the bridge just as I was about to snap a photo of my daughter. The City Park Beach was deserted and again I managed several shots of OGY as he glided adjacent to the beach on his way northwards.

I am in the tourist business, owning a motel in Penticton and I think my photographs will give the tourist business and towns of the Okanagan, a great shot in the arm. I am in the process of preparing the photographs for our Okanagan towns in the form of plaques, decoupage, wall hangings, postcards etc. so our tourists can take home proof that OGY does exist.

The photos Dave gave me were taken from City Park in Kelowna and showed an animal swimming underneath Okanagan Lake Bridge and then a second shot as it swam in the lake beside the park. Making it all the more authentic was having his daughter in one of the pictures. The animal was so out of proportion that even the most gullible would be able to see it as an obvious hoax.

I telephoned Penticton and spoke to the photographer, and he began to tell me this story of Ogopogo making an appearance at a time when he had his camera handy. He did not back down and stood firmly by his story. So I did the next best thing, although it cost me money. I had the photos enlarged and the reality of the hoax was even more obvious. Then I wrote out an air-tight affidavit and a week later I called again and proceeded to tell him that I would believe his story only if he would agree to sign the affidavit I had prepared. After reading it to him over the phone, there was an uncanny silence at the other end. Then a meek voice replied, "I faked it."

"Why on earth would you do something like that?" I blurted back. "I just wanted to see how far it would go," was his reply. He explained that he had drawn and cut out a replica of Ogopogo, positioned it on a small piece of glass with the lake and bridge in the background and shot the photo. Ogopogo sightings were down, the weather was poor and it had affected tourism. As a motel owner, his reasons are obvious.

A few years later, the news was screaming about someone taking some great photos of Ogopogo from an open balcony at Penticton's Delta Hotel. The sighting was convincing and the photos apparently so good that the tourist/photographer, who was being identified as Wallis Bierowski, ran out as soon as the one-hour photo lab was opened and had the film processed. One of the local DJs, Jim Hart, who worked for a Penticton radio station and who is now a member of Parliament for the Reform Party, took control of the story immediately. His beat was local tourism. Jim had conducted a telephone interview with Bierowski soon after the early morning sighting and picture-taking and continued to lead the airwaves with the story. Bierowski then proceeded to hand out photos like candy to everyone he saw. This in itself appeared odd. Pictures of Ogopogo were few and far between in 1985, and if you ever snapped that great a photo it could mean more than a few dollars in a photographer's pocket.

Wallis Bierowski, a visitor from Toronto staying at the Delta Hotel in Penticton, stated that he awoke at 6:00 A.M., June 28, 1985, and upon looking out of his sixth floor window overlooking the lake, he spotted a "very, very large creature" in the water and he grabbed his camera. After taking several pictures from above, he then took the elevator down to the main floor, ran out to the patio and continued shooting until the creature swam away toward Kelowna.

According to Margaret Hayes of the *South Okanagan Review*, the pictures showed a serpentine shape that Bierowski said circled around the shallow water. He told Hayes that it was a green and yellow striped creature. "It was snakeylike, thirty feet long with humps. At times two and upwards to six showed above the water."

The radio station was notified as was the local paper, and interviews and photos (showing Bierowski with his back to the camera) were obtained. I could see that he was about five foot eight (1.75 m), with broad shoulders and somewhat on the heavy side. It looked as if he might be wearing a wig.

Not having seen the photos and hearing all the hype, I grew increasingly interested. I called the Delta who directed my attention to Jim Hart at the radio station. Jim agreed to send me a copy of the taped interview along with any pictures he had in his possession. I was not given any directives to just where Bierowski could be found as I naturally wanted to talk to him in person. In a matter of hours, Bierowski disappeared and gave out a Toronto address on Yonge Street (Eaton's store) where he could be reached. I really did not become suspect until I listened to the interview Jim Hart had conducted. Bierowski had a thick Russian type accent, but every now and then a normal and very clear English word would creep out between the accent. I listened to the tape a few times over to make sure that I had not been mistaken. In all appearances, Bierowski was not the man he claimed to be and supposedly left Penticton following his hasty interviews. So once again, it was necessary to don my investigator's cloak in an attempt to sort out what had actually taken place.

Dave Duncan, reporter from the *Penticton Herald*, and I had a chat and he began telling me how tongue-in-cheek the staff at the Delta were and that the snickerers concerning the sighting far outnumbered the serious believers. I then told him that my attempts to locate Bierowski were futile and that the address he had given was for the Eaton's store complex in Toronto. A few days later Dave telephoned me saying that he had learned that the Delta had a bill for $600 payable to local divers, just after the Bierowski photos were shot. A diver friend of his then agreed to check the area out, and reported that it appeared that something resembling a hose or pipe had been dragged along the bottom where the photos were alleged to have been taken.

Before closing the file, I prepared a series of questions that I posed to a member of the Delta management. There was little response, even when I implied knowledge of an alleged invoice for divers and that Bierowski may have been related to Delta Inn staff. There was also the refusal by Delta officials to allow Dave Duncan access to take pictures of the area where Bieroswski took his photos.

Paul Leblond, UBC biologist, stated that the photos were the best yet. I, in turn, was glad that I had reserved comment. After looking at the back profile of Bierowski showing head and shoulders in that infamous photo, I have my own opinion as to just who Bierowski really is, wig and all.

Incidents like this that involve the tourist industry never make a researcher's life any easier and only enriches the imagination of the Eric Beckjords and Adrian Shines who choose to explain away even the most authentic of sightings.

Interest in Ogopogo never goes away. On July 1, 1992, a large twenty-three-foot (7 m) fiberglass replica of the "beastie" created by K-5 Manufacturing in Summerland was launched with real dignity by a champagne breakfast at Peachland Marina to help celebrate Canada Day. The fiberglass monster was towed by boat to Kelowna and viewed by hundreds as it passed by City Park like royalty with Rhonda Kent holding the Canadian flag and Theresa Guzzi riding the monster to Paul's Tomb. Following a public picnic, it was submerged thirty feet (9 m) deep, to become an underwater attraction. The replica near Paul's Tomb is just north of the bridge and close to where broadcast journalist Yvonne Svennson took her photos in 1994. The replica was the brain child of CKIQ news director, Mike Guzzi, who kept a watchful eye on the necessary details. The area around Paul's Tomb has become popular with local divers and television producers.

In 1989 *Unsolved Mysteries* brought along their own fifty-foot (15 m) lake monster, created by Dan Schillberg, for the *Ogopogo Kelowna* production. Danny even promised the replica would be mine, when *Unsolved Mysteries* no longer needed it. I envisioned placing it on my front lawn to the delight of my neighbors. Although I did not receive the replica, he did send me a beautiful framed photo of it with Okanagan Lake in the background engraved: "A Legend Come To Life. To Arlene Gaal, thanks for all your help. Daniel R. Schilberg Unsolved Mysteries 1989."

Canada Post even got into the act in October, 1990 when it launched its stamp series of Canada's monsters which of course included Ogopogo. In the presence of Member of Parliament Al Horning, Canada Post staff presented me with a beautiful folder which housed the entire series. The stamp depicted Ogopogo as a fierce, red-eyed monster complete with mane and horns, fanglike teeth and tail. It was an artist's perception of the animal and thankfully not the real thing.

Ogopogo has been a theme float at the Rose Bowl Parade, a hot air balloon, a telephone card, on the menu as a noodle dish at a local restaurant and even the center piece in a watch. I was consulted while each of these items was still on the drawing board. In 1999, due to the popularity of the hydroplane races, Ogopogo took on the persona of The Monster Hydroplane and was being prepared to represent Kelowna in upcoming events.

At the beginning of the 1999 hockey season there was yet another surprise. The Kelowna Rockets had commissioned Nike to design a logo for their new sweatshirts. Much to my dismay, the Kelowna Rockets new jersey was sporting a menacing Ogopogo complete with devil-like horns, brandishing a hockey stick. The logo may have represented the violence expected in hockey for the 1990s, but sadly did nothing for the image of the creature living in Okanagan Lake.

I cannot conclude this section without mention of the statue that sits in Kerry Park at the base of Bernard Avenue overlooking the lake. This Disney-like reproduction has been sat on by children, provided a photographic background for enthusiastic tourists and has even had some teeth repaired by local dentists to help maintain the respectability of its toothy grin.

Ogopogo memorabilia is in abundance and strongly in demand during the summer months. An Ogopogo fishing license sits in my files, an Ogopogo ivory tooth adorns my lapel, and Ogopogos of every size and shape peek out from my bookshelf. Kelowna City Council even declared the Order of the Ogopogo to be presented to a city resident who has attained a meritorious honor. Henry Hobson, a Kelowna poet, was the last to be so honored in 1980 by Mayor Hilbert Roth.

Telephone card with the image of Ogopogo.

131

In the News

Montreal Gazette, December 26, 1926:

MYSTERY MONSTER DIED BATTLING ICE
Half-breed Describes Watching 'Ogopogos' Thrashing for Freedom
(by Canadian Press).

Heaving, cracking ice thrown up into the mounds near the shore on Okanagan Lake, a few miles north of Kelowna, B.C. says a dispatch from there published today by the Morning Star formed the basis of reports that Ogopogo mystery monster, died during the recent cold weather.

Peter Simon, a half-breed Indian, according to the dispatch, said that while hunting along the shore he saw the ice torn asunder by some monsters struggles and fragments thrown far up on shore. Timidly venturing nearer, Peter said he could see the giant form, sinuous and powerful, outlined beneath the ice, the tail feebly thrashing for freedom and the huge head, bearing a ghastly resemblance to a sheep, raised twice in the agony of its struggle.

From his vantage point behind a tree, Peter watched the final battle for life, saw the great form become more and more feeble, then subside gently into the ice. Creeping to the lakeshore, he made certain the monster was dead, then rushed frantically back to Kelowna.

Calgary, December 28, 1926:
SOLUTION FROM CALGARY
Calgary newspapermen, aided by encyclopedia, old prints and authentic legend, believe they have solved the Okanagan Sea Serpent Mystery from a vantage point on dry land. They only await examination of the "Ogopogo's" dead body, if it is dead, for confirmation of the theory that the mystery animal is an oarfish which has given rise to sea serpent stories on the north Atlantic for centuries.

How the Ogopogo migrated from the sea to the Okanagan Lake is a matter for investigation by scientists. The oarfish or ribbon fish, a deep sea monster has very occasionally been cast up on the North Atlantic shores and has been photographed. It has been found to reach a length of 15 to 20 feet, 10 to 20 inches deep with a continuous dorsal fin. It has a pronounced sheep-like head with a small mouth and imperfectly developed teeth. The tail fin is either rudimentary or directed upward like a fan.

Written descriptions and photographs of the oarfish coincide exactly with stories which occasional, but frequent glimpses of the Okanagan Ogopogo, with its sheeps head and other sea serpent attributes have furnished.

Kelowna, B.C. December 28, 1926:

LITTLE ICE AT KELOWNA
Although reports that 'Ogopogo' has died, caught in the ice north of here, are believed unfounded because there is very little ice in that district. Investigations into the rumors are being conducted...

What one is able to determine from these early news reports is first of all, Ogopogo did not meet an early demise in December of 1926 trapped underneath a sheet of ice, because the lake did not and rarely does freeze over. However what is interesting is Peter Simon's 1926 description of the animal which is close to what is being reported today. Either he had a sighting or his account was second-hand, stemming from either news reports or stories from people who saw the animal.

The newspaper story from Calgary identifying the lake creature as an oarfish, although convincing enough, refers to the sheep's head and ribbon structure down its back to reinforce the theory. Two determinents however do not a monster make. Other physical attributes including length are missing.

Rod and Gun and Canadian Silver Fox News, (R. Leckie Ewing) February, 1928:

OGOPOGO
Some of your readers, I dare say, have seen the above name as it has gained considerable publicity throughout B.C. and its fame went further afield last summer.

Like many others I used to be very skeptical of its existence, but the actual accounts from those who have seen it have come from men whose word is above suspicion and that I and other doubters are now perfectly convinced of the existence of Ogopogo or more than one in Okanagan Lake.

Perhaps I had better carry my readers back with me to the time when I first heard anything about such an animal living in the waters of this lake. It is some twenty odd years since the Indians used to make a living by catching quantities of the splendid steelhead trout which were so plentiful in Okanagan Lake. I, and the few other white men who were some of the first lakeshore settlers, used to meet the Indians, whilst out trolling. There was always a stretch of water at the north end of the lake which we found was one of the best spots for the big fellows, but we never saw the Indians on it and I used to wonder why. One day I remember asking an old Indian why they never trolled there; his language was limited but he said something about being afraid of Big Lake Devils.

To this remark, which long since had escaped my memory, I paid no attention at this time, nor subsequently, and none of us old timers ever saw or got any definite word of any such sea serpent. However in light of what has been seen during the last three summers, it is probable that such monsters must have been in the lake. At any rate, the fact is worth recording.

I will cite one very definite and absolute reliable description (vouched for, checked and re-checked and re-checked independently) by myself when the animal was seen by five men at the same time and place.

"It was a dead calm summers day; the serpent was seen some fifty yards from shore going at tremendous speed and throwing up behind, a wash exactly similar to that made by a fast launch. Neither head nor tail was visible, only a big broad dark back shaped like a balloon tire of a car, and the color of an eel. It traveled some 200 yards and then submerged. The length of the body was between 14 and 20 feet.

Another man who was out trolling and whose description I can again absolutely vouch for said he was going slowly when to his right about 200 yards, he saw what looked to be a smallish tree trunk with its roots sticking up. He was not paying attention to it, to his amazement it began to move toward shore quite slowly. He admits that he was afraid of the creature and rowed away as fast as he could lest it might capsize his small boat.

The subject is a most fascinating one and I only hope that this coming summer some definite steps will be taken to capture the animal. Personally I am pretty sure there are more than one. To anyone who is fortunate to do so, it would be one of the most important captures of modern times. It has been suggested that it may be a sea lion. Personally I dont think it is, in fact I might positively say no.

Okanagan Lake is certainly connected to the sea via the Columbia and some small rivers and lakes, a distance of some 700 miles. For a sea lion family to a make its way through such turbulent waters is practically beyond belief.

Other Known Unidentified Swimming Animals

Stories of unusual marine animals go back to the earliest of times. Biblical text speaks of the leviathan in Job 41 where God discusses the powerful creations of the behemoth in the River Jordan and asks Job, "Can you pull in the leviathan with a fishhook or tie down his tongue with a rope?" and states: "If you lay a hand on him, you will remember the struggle and never do it again! Any hope of subduing him is false; the mere sight of him is overpowering." As one continues to read the biblical description of this animal, it is impossible not to compare this text to the descriptions of the aquatic animal reportedly seen in Okanagan Lake and other lakes throughout the world.

"His back has rows of shields tightly sealed together. Strength resides in his neck. When he rises up the mighty are terrified, they retreat before his thrashing. He makes the depths churn like a boiling caldron and stirs up the sea like a pot of ointment. Behind him he leaves a glistening wake, one would think the deep had white hair."

Psalm 74:14 speaks of God's salvation saying: "It was you who split open the sea by your power; you broke the head of the monster in the waters. It was you who crushed the head of Leviathan and gave him as food to the creatures of the desert." Again, Isaiah 27 states: "The Lord will punish with his sword Leviathan the gliding serpent, Leviathan the coiling serpent, he will slay the monster of the sea."

If I were a lawyer presenting evidence regarding the existence of such creatures, I would complete my summation to the jury with the above text, for what greater power can we turn to for sorting out truth!

As we consider the reports of the many unidentified swimming animals throughout the world, the data reveal that the more popular water monsters inhabit water systems near the fiftieth parallel, with Canada making claim to some sixty or more. This immediately elicits the question of why. Do we take into consideration the ice age and the possibility of a species surviving this great phenomena or are we just observing creatures that have eluded mankind by their ability to remain beneath the depths for countless hours surfacing only when they find it necessary? Perhaps this is a species that has inhabited water systems that go back as far as the leviathan. It's a known fact that mankind has considered the exploration of outer space far more important than the many amazing discoveries still awaiting underwater exploration on planet Earth, thus allowing this species and no doubt many others the opportunity to remain unidentified.

One interesting fact to consider about water monsters in lakes and rivers of the northern hemisphere, which encircles the Arctic polar belt where such creatures abound, is that the majority of them fall within the vegetational zone referred to as the boreal forests, which extends southward into Montana and Idaho due to the high altitude.

Although stories of sea monsters have been reported from the southern hemisphere, the monsters of the south are often mistaken for giant squid or octopus and even known reptile species such as the monitor lizard. The more contemporary sea or lake serpent phenomena appear to be dramatically confined to the rather narrow belt of northern latitude and could rightly be labeled "The Water Monsters of the Fiftieth Parallel."

For the purpose of examination, the following ocean and lake monsters have maintained an almost constant environmental presence near or above the fiftieth parallel, with most registering an above-average percentage appearance ratio over the years.

The Loch Ness Monster— 57° Latitude, Loch Ness, Scotland

Well documented and sought after is the Loch Ness Monster, affectionately dubbed Nessie by our Scottish friends. Records of an unusual animal breaking water goes back as early as 585 A.D. when Saint Columba reported seeing an aquatic animal rise from the loch with a great roar and open mouth, about to devour Lugne Mocumin. Saint Columba invoked the power of God, commanding the ferocious monster to go back with all speed. The beast of Loch Ness was seen twice between 1600 and 1700. A book written in 1769 tells of two leviathan creatures sighted more than once by road builders along the loch. In 1934 the British government passed a law that officially protected Nessie from being harmed by enthusiastic hunters.

People such as Dr. Robert Rines, Tim Dinsdale and even Adrian Shine no doubt helped lay the foundation for future investigators and expeditions by uncovering evidence that could not be disputed by the most hardcore skeptics. Robert Rines' 1972 underwater photographs of a flipperlike appendage and Tim Dinsdale's film footage both left impressions of a living creature. Adrian Shine, while trying to disprove the existence of Nessie-like animals, did admit that there was something there after making forty or more unusual contacts through the Furano sonar between May and September, 1982. Even as I write, teams continue to flock to Loch Ness hoping for that conclusive proof. However, in 1999 Adrian Shine announced that he was raising a sturgeon in the loch, and Nessie believers are attempting to second-guess his motive. He stated: "I am not saying that the Loch Ness Monster was a sturgeon, and I am not trying to debunk the legend, just the opposite in fact. I want to prove that the local traditions were correct all along. My experiment is not anti-Nessie."

If ever there was an individual who sought evidence with passion and sheer love of the investigations for Nessie, it must be said to be Nora Jones, an American and fellow cryptozoologist. Her desire would be to live on the banks of Loch Ness and watch Nessie for the rest of her natural life. The initiation of the web-cam scanning Loch Ness was the second-best choice, and Nora set up an almost constant watch. Her success is registered in the number of photos she and her mother managed to capture, bolstering Nora's belief to the point of elation. Web-cams could very well become the way of the future for lake monster watchers.

Morag—56° Latitude, Loch Morar, Scotland

Unlike his close cousin in Loch Ness, Morag seems to live a rather peaceful existence in Loch Morar, which at 1,017 feet (310 m), is considered to be the deepest lake in Britain. Reports of Nessie-like animals spotted in Loch Morar have been investigated by the Loch Morar survey group. Prior to his Loch Ness investigations, Adrian Shine accepted a similar challenge in Loch Morar, determined to find out just what species was creating all the furore. The possibility that Nessie and Morag are one and the same and that a subterranean channel allows them to commute back and forth elicits a strong denial. The locals at Loch Morar prefer to believe that Morag is their very own monster.

The Storsjon Lake Monster— 50° Latitude, Storsjon Lake, Sweden

There have been many attempts to capture lake monsters over the years, but none more zealous as those by fishermen living in the town of Ostersund, Sweden. An unexplained frequency of sightings in Lake Storsjon between 1820 and 1898 of a large reptilian creature that was ruining the local fishing trade prompted the fishermen to built a massive trap, similar to a bear trap. They also constructed large barbed spears for protection to use against the monster of the lake. These spears, now displayed in the local museum, failed to put an end to the animal's appearances. Similar in description to Ogopogo, the Storsjon Lake Monster continues to be seen from time to time.

The Krakens—50° Latitude, Norway, Denmark, and Sweden

Sailors of the North Sea, the Baltic Sea, the Norwegian Sea and the Northern Atlantic Ocean reported encounters with herds of monsters who inhabited the regions. These monsters, called Krakens (from Scandinavian folklore) were hunted and killed to extinction in the1800s. One theory is that the Krakens were actually a northern herd of manatee or sea cow that grew much larger than their southern cousins. The carcasses of such creatures were reported to have washed up on the shores of the bordering countries and as far west as Newfoundland.

NORWAY

Search resumed for alleged lake monster

■ **More than 100 sightings have been recorded since 1750**

By FLORA BOTSFORD
The Guardian

SELJORD, Norway — International efforts are under way to prove the existence of Norway's version of the Loch Ness

something unnatural in the lake. More than 100 sightings have been recorded since 1750, when the first sighting of a mysterious aquatic beast was made. In that year, Gunleik Andersson-Verpe from nearby Bo was "attacked by a sea horse" while rowing on the lake. In 1880, Bjoern Bjorge and his mother, Gunhild, reportedly killed a "strange-looking" lizard on one of the lakeside beaches.

As a young boy, retired farmer Torge

The Monsters of Lake Baikal—50° Latitude, Lake Baikal, Russia

Lake Baikal is situated in the far eastern region of Russia. According to the Soviet government, the Baikal monsters have a rich heritage and folklore that dates back to Peter the Great. Lake Baikal is one of the largest freshwater lakes in the world and is home to the indigenous species of freshwater seal, the only species of its kind in the world. This could well explain the monster folklore that originates from the lake. Films and unclear photos help, but reliable proof is limited to eyewitness accounts. Russian officials are quick to point out unusual dragonlike monsters in other lakes such as Lake Kol Kol and Lake Uri where a forty-five-foot (14 m) marine animal with a three-foot (1 m) wide head has been reported.

Issie and Kushi—43° Latitude, Lake Ikeda, Southern Island of Japan

The people of Japan have always had more than an average fascination for the concept of monsters from ancient caverns on land or from the depths of oceans, seas or lakes. Their history and folklore abound with tales of ferocious dragons and prehistoric Godzilla-like monsters that wreak havoc on our world.

Lake Ikeda, situated on the southern island of Kyushu, continues to elicit sightings of a water serpent named Issie, first reported by an English physician who resided near the lake prior to the second world war. He was enjoying a picnic with his family when the creature suddenly appeared. He wrote of his experience to friends in England.

On January 4, 1991, Issie was at last videotaped. Mr. Hideaki Tomiyasu and his family noticed a big black object in the center of the lake while driving. It disappeared and reappeared 656 feet(200 m) from them when they reached the lakeside. The object moved sideways, surfacing and submerging when a motorboat went by. Soon after, two similar black objects surfaced close to each other and then disappeared. Upon seeing a broadcast of the video, a Mr. Kazuo Kwano came forward with a videotape of another experience that occurred October 21, 1990. He too, saw a long black creature from sixteen to thirty-two feet (5–10 m) long.

A photo taken by Mr. Matsubara at Lake Ikeda in 1978 bears a striking resemblance to pictures taken by Wally Wachlin and myself in July of

1981 from opposite ends of Okanagan Lake. Each show solid protrusions and huge waves.

In 1978 this news report came out of Kagoshima, Japan: "Nessie-Like Creature—A Loch Ness Nessie-like monster has been witnessed by more than 20 people at Lake Ikeda on the Satsuma Peninsula on the southern tip of Kyushu Island. One of them, Mr. Yukata Kawaji, said he saw a huge monster with two humps on the back swimming swiftly from south to north. In two minutes the monster sank and vanished into the water."

It is rumored that a photo similar to the Mansi photo was taken of a lake monster in Lake Biwi near Kyoto. Another creature, referred to as Kushi has also been seen in the lake waters of Japan, fueling the evidence for freshwater lakes, world-wide, being home to unidentified swimming animals.

Ogopogo—49°–50° Latitude, Okanagan Lake, Canada

"I turned around and I saw this dark thing coming through the water," recounts Lionel Edmonds, who was fishing with a friend July 20, 1986, when he heard a loud rushing of water 30 yards (27.5 m) behind him.

"It looked like a submarine surfacing coming up toward my boat. As it came up perpendicular to the boat we could see six humps out of the water. Each hump about 10 inches out of the water with each one creating a wake. It was cruising between 8 and 10 miles per hour. We followed it for 10 minutes. We saw no head or tail, but it must have been some 50 to 60 feet long. I know what a sturgeon looks like. This thing was no sturgeon. It wasn't like anything I've ever seen before. I believe we just saw Ogopogo!"

Keeping pace with Nessie and sometimes referred to as Canada's Loch Ness Monster, Ogopogo is alive and well in the seventy-nine-mile (127 km) long Okanagan Lake. An average of three to seven sightings are reported annually, mainly during the spring and summer months. Described as being from twenty to seventy feet in length, dark in color with a reptilian head, bulbous body, long tail and appendages. Photos, film footage and videotaped images abound along with hundreds of witnesses who report seeing an unusual creature break water or move swiftly through the waters of Okanagan Lake from as early as 1872 to year

2001. Ogopogo has been given world-wide billing in the many documentaries that have drawn film producers to the Okanagan Valley since 1977. Skaha Lake south of Penticton, Woods Lake and Lake Kalamalka, south of Vernon, have reports of similar creatures. There are thirty tributaries leading into the lake systems. Other surrounding lakes in British Columbia also reporting similar water monsters include Osoyoos Lake, Shuswap Lakes, Williams Lake, Lake Tagai and Kootenay Lake.

At least twenty years ago while we were waiting for the ferry to cross Kootenay Lake I was searching for unusual rocks with my children. To my surprise I picked up a piece of soapstone about an inch long and three quarters of an inch wide (2.5 x 2 cm), that had tiny images carved into it. One in particular caught my attention, it showed an obvious lake monster with a long body, head and small appendage. Every so often I take this out to remind myself of the history of these unknown animals.

Cadborosaurus—47° Latitude, Pacific Ocean, Vancouver Island

"A huge head reared out from the rocks on the north side of Cadboro Bay. The head was shaggy, with a large underslung jaw like a camel. Behind the head appeared the monstrous undulations of the body judged to be between 75 and 80 feet long, and as thick as 20 feet at the widest point," reported the *Victoria Colonist Daily* newspaper.

This description was given by a Victoria lawyer in 1933 and his story soon led to many more similar reports of Caddy sightings that total well over 600 personal testaments. There are tales of Caddy being shot at, rammed by cantankerous fishermen and in the midst of World War II, was said to have been torpedoed by a Japanese submarine scouting the waters near Vancouver Island when they mistook Caddy for a new Canadian secret weapon and opened fire. Recorded sightings persist, books and studies have been written and speculations as to what it may or may not be are in abundance. Ed Bousefield and Paul Lablond must be credited for their investigations into this Pacific Coast phenomenon.

The Shunkalas—49° Latitude, Harrison Lake, Canada

Although relatively unknown in the marine monster set, the Shunkalas are found in the heart of the homeland of the mysterious creature known as Bigfoot or Sasquatch. According to Native elders, this lake serpent can change, or shape-shift, to look like anything it wants to. Sometimes it resembles a horse and other times a large snake. It dwells in Harrison Lake in southern British Columbia. Veteran skipper Jack Stirling confessed to hearing tales of such a monster in this bottomless lake. Although the creature is rarely reported, it is a definite part of Native folklore and there are strong claims that Shuny continues to exist.

The Serpent of Saddle Lake—55° Latitude, Saddle Lake Indian Reserve, Canada

On Halloween night,1984, an Alberta government helicopter flew out to Saddle Lake to hunt for a mysterious lake monster, according to a report in the *Globe and Mail*. A series of sightings prompted the band manager to request that the government investigate. University of Alberta social science professor, James Butler, stated before the search, "We don't know if there is anything in the lake, but we aren't sure that there is nothing either, so we see this as a real phenomena. The effect is very real and the people who live beside this lake are very afraid."

Those who have seen it agree to a similar description and it is very unlikely that they all could have contrived similar details with equal accuracy.

Turtle Lake, near North Battleford in the neighboring province of Saskatchewan, is home to the Turtle Lake Monster, a freshwater animal very similar to the creature spotted in Saddle Lake. A young lad noticed what appeared to be a log near the shore. He called it to the attention of his friend, who took chase in a motorboat. He was unable to overtake the animal as it disappeared beneath the depths.

Is there a monster living in Turtle Lake?

LIVELONG (CP) — Would you believe in a beast called the Turtle Lake Monster?

It lacks the romance of the thing from Loch Ness and B.C.'s Ogopogo — but despite its prosaic name, it provides ammunition for lively conversation in the cozy beer parlor at the Livelong Hotel south of the turtle-shaped lake about 50 miles east of Lloydminster.

According to the believers, the monster is big and black.

In winter, they say, the beast lets fishermen know its around by tearing huge holes in their nets. In the summer, well, it breaks the surface to frighten onlookers with its enormous size.

The stories about the monster, with three humps on its back, a long neck and head like a horse, pig or dog depending on which version you believe, have been kicked about for 55 years.

Indian legends — as usual in these reports — tell of "the big fish" inhabiting the picturesque resort lake.

"Some people say it's 14 feet long and there might be more under water," says Ben Blatz, a school teacher and co-owner of the lake's Northlander Inn.

Girls scared

"Two girls saw it last year while water-skiing and were so scared they couldn't go back in."

Blatz, who calls himself a half-believer, says he saw a creature in the lake one day. It looked like it had three humps on its back.

Disbeliever Gordon Kenderdine, who has also seen the "creature," thinks it is a large sturgeon about two or three metres in length similar to a 500-pounder caught near Saskatoon.

"You have to be realistic," says Kenderdine, a sawmill owner. "I think it's a sturgeon but I don't know what you'd catch it with. Many times you get your net torn by it."

He agrees that what he saw had two or three humps, but figures them to be the creature's dorsal fins.

There are those who say they saw the creature surface and poke a dog- or horse-like head into the air.

One of them is Iana Sandwick, 17, of Calgary, who used to live near the lake.

"It didn't look like a fish's head — it sort of looked like a dog. I saw it when it jumped out of the water."

Miss Sandwick describes the creature she saw two years ago as being greyish in color and "big and ugly."

Al Pruden likes to talk about the monster over an ale or two.

"I was out fishing one day and it was absolutely calm. All of a sudden there were these waves that came from nowhere. I never saw what made them but I've often had huge holes in fishing nets."

What do government and RCMP officials have to say?

Saskatchewan sturgeon don't grow to three metres long, a government fisheries biologist says.

"I don't know if there's anything to it," says RCMP Constable Al Morgan of the nearby Glaslyn detachment.

Blatz hopes to catch the creature to end all speculation.

"A lot of people see it but they don't say anything because they think people will say they are crazy."

Igopogo—45° Latitude, Lake Simcoe, Canada

The Lake Simcoe monster, referred to as Igopogo or Iggy, is described as being a dog-faced animal with a neck the size of a stove pipe. The creature has been part of local Indian legend for centuries with a heritage of sightings that closely match those of Loch Ness.

A Presbyterian minister, a funeral director and their families all claim to have seen Igopogo. The Reverend L. B. Williams of Mount Albert, Neil Lathangue and their families were out boating when something suddenly came toward them. Mr. Lathangue said it was charcoal in color, about thirty to forty feet (9–12 m) long with dorsal fins. People on surrounding lakes such as Muskrat Lake, Lake Erie (Bessie) and Lake Ontario have all submitted reports of mysterious creatures.

Lake Champlain Monster—44° Latitude, Lake Champlain, U.S.A.

Lake Champlain is situated on the border between New York, Vermont and the province of Quebec in Canada. Several sightings of Champ have been reported over the years with a rash of sightings in 1987, along with video footage and photographic proof. One important photo taken by Sandra Mansi has put Champ on the map, and is considered the best evidence to date, as studies by experts have never disputed its authenticity. Joseph Zarzynski, a local teacher and research writer, must be credited for his efforts to keep the legend alive. His investigations include diving expeditions, witness interviews and the writing of his first book, *Champ Beyond the Legend*.

Scientists in Debate: Does Monster Dwell In Lake Champlain?

Special to The New York Times

SHELBURNE, Vt., Aug. 30 — Scientists and others interested in speculating about monsters convened here yesterday to discuss the possibility that a large creature lurks in Lake Champlain. None of the scientists would say that such a creature existed, but they did call for renewed study.

The event, sponsored by the Lake Champlain Committee, was billed as a scientific seminar on the subject, "Does Champ Exist?" Champ is the name given to the purported Lake Champlain monster photographed in July 1977 by Sandra Mansi of Winchester, N.H.

Current speculation holds that the creature, if it is real, may be a primitive whale or reptile, and that others like it may inhabit other bodies of fresh water created by retreating glaciers in the last Ice Age. Loch Ness in Scotland, one such lake, is the possible home of a

Ponik—44° Latitude, Pohenegamook, Canada

The resident serpent of Lac Pohenagamook, Quebec, was described in an issue of the *Hamilton Spectator* as "a thing from another time, black and dragon-like, as long as three canoes, fast as a power boat, yet quiet as a midnight breeze." Around the same time, fifty local residents claimed to have seen Ponik while fifty-four-year-old Louis Fournier claimed to have sighted Ponik eight times in one year. "Sixteen years I'm here and I never

143

saw it," he said. "Then on July 8, 1976 at 11:45 a.m. I'm leaving the corn-field to get a beer and I'm sitting on the balcony. All of a sudden I yell to my wife, "Ah, la bete du lac' (lake creature). It was very black and as long as three canoes." The lake creature has been photographed and sketched and was the subject of a ten-day search.

Much like the Shinkalas of Harrison Lake, British Columbia, sight-ings have been relatively few, but this did not prevent the locals from adopting it as the official mascot for the town's centennial celebration in 1974. Reports of a serpentlike animal have also come in from surround-ing lakes such as Mocking Lake and Lac Duchene, Quebec.

Manipogo—51° Latitude, Lake Manitoba, Canada

Canada's Lake Manitoba holds claim to a monster legend that dates back to 1908. Manipogo, often referred to as Manny, was the subject of a search in 1960 by Dr. McLeod, a University of Manitoba professor and head zoologist. Dr. McLeod failed to spot the eight-foot (2.5 m) aquatic animal or its remains. His belief, however, was bolstered by the discov-ery of an unusual bone on the north shore of Lake Winnipegosis, twenty miles (32 km) from Burrows Landing.

In the summer of 1999, Russ and Tricia McGlen led a one-week adventure safari to Manipogo Park to search for Manipogo and interview witnesses. A year 2000 search was to follow. Vincent Konefell's photo-graph has convinced some observers, including Dr. McLeod.

The Lake Utopia Monster—44° Latitude, Lake Utopia, Canada

"It is still fresh in my mind, and I was never so frightened in my life," said Mrs. Fred McKillop when a reporter asked her to recall her brush with the serpent of Lake Utopia in New Brunswick.

> Suddenly, I watched water begin to boil and churn up waves that came in and broke on the shore. Then a huge creature of some sort emerged from the water; it showed a part of its head and body. It looked like a huge black rock, but it moved and churned all the time. I was alone with the children at the cabin, and I was so terrified that I took the children inside and locked the door. After a short time had passed, I realized that whatever it was belonged in the lake and we were in no danger. I watched it from inside. I had never heard of the Lake Utopia Monster

before and therefore had no idea what it was. It was a very frightening experience.

Reports of this monster go back as far as the 1800s and sightings generally occur just after the winter ice breaks up on the lake.

The Cape Sable Monster—44° Latitude, Cape Sable Island, Canada

In 1976, a Cape Sable Island, Nova Scotia, fisherman came home with the ultimate story about the one that got away. "At first I thought it was a whale," Eisner Penny told reporters, "but it kept coming out of the water. By the time it got near my boat it was a good 14 to 15 feet out of the water."

Two days after Mr. Penny's experience, Keith Ross and his son were fishing in the same area when they were confronted by what the elder Ross described as a sea monster. He said, "I've never seen anything like it in my life! Its neck was covered with things that looked like giant barnacles. Its eyes weren't in their sockets. They seemed to look out from the side of its head. It had two tusklike appendages which protruded from the top of its head, maybe two to three feet long and four inches or so round. It was a terrifying thing to see."

Another fisherman, named Edgar Nickerson, said that he found the sea monster reports funny. Then one day he was fishing with his son when the creature appeared. "My first thought was a whale and I kidded my boy that the monster was coming after us. I turned on my sounder which usually scares whales away, but not this thing. It kept coming and coming. It was a horrible thing to behold, I tell you that if there is a devil, that was one."

The Flathead Lake Monster—48° Latitude, Flathead Lake, U.S.A.

The state of Montana has been the sight of many prehistoric fossil excavations and is considered to be the site of a Jurassic sea that once filled the Montana plains. It is believed that *Plesiosaur* was one of the species living in the Jurassic sea.

In 1963, Ronald Nixon and friends were fishing in Flathead Lake when they saw a creature described as reptilian in appearance and similar to descriptions of Canada's Ogopogo. No one would believe him, so Mr.

Nixon posted a $1,000 reward for its capture. Sightings, although few in number, are still reported.

The Creature of the Grand Bank—
46° Latitude, Grand Bank, Canada

The Atlantic Ocean is home to many mysterious creatures, some identified as giant squid and eels. Others, like those spotted off the coast of Newfoundland, cannot be easily explained. On August 30, 1913, two officers of the steamer *Corinthian* saw something near Grand Bank according to a report by second officer G. Bachelor.

> First appeared a great head, long fin-like appendages on the sides of the head, and large eyes. The eyes were mild and liquid with no indication of ferocity. Following said eyes came the neck. It was a regular neck all right, all of 20 feet in length and resembling that of a giraffe. The monster took its time in emerging, but it kept on and on to a point that I wondered what the end would be. The neck seemed to be set on a ball bearing, so supple was it and easily rhythmically did it sway, while the large liquid blue eyes seemed to take on the ship with a surprised, injured, fearful stare. Three horn-like fins surmounted its bony head which could probably be for defense and attack or for ripping things up. For a minute the creature inspected the Corinthian with its roving gaze. It seemed to be trying to comprehend a curiosity which might be a new danger. I almost felt a tenderness for it as it emitted a piercing wail, like that of a baby.

This creature has continued to make appearance at different intervals throughout the years, and is still a strong part of Grand Bank, Newfoundland folklore.

The Lagar-Ormssmarin—65° Latitude,
Lagar Fijot, Iceland

This denizen of the deep lives in a lake called Lagar Fijot in Iceland. The lake itself is very similar in general size and shape to that of Okanagan Lake and Loch Ness of Scotland, and is considered to be bottomless. Stories of this creature date back to the first settlers of the area. A lengthy and detailed examination of this particular phenomenon was conducted by a British journalist. Sightings of Lagar-Ormssmarin often mirror those of Ogopogo in description and size.

"We Saw Ogopogo"

Evidence surrounding the existence of Ogopogo in British Columbia's Okanagan Lake can no longer be disputed as film footage, photographs, sketches and videotaped evidence provide the needed proof that an unidentified animal continues to make its presence known. Each year Ogopogo Archives are added to and reality takes precedence over myth.

Eyewitness accounts number in the hundreds. Sightings range from individual experiences to families on boating excursions or large gatherings such as summer tourists vacationing at Blue Bird Bay resort at the time Larry Thal took his film footage in 1980. A Greyhound bus driver saw something that convinced him to stop the bus and allow his passengers opportunity to observe the serpentine like animal frolic in the lake near Peachland for at least five minutes June 29, 1950. The animal has even been spotted by passengers in both private and commercial air flights. Witnesses are rarely disreputable, and some are surprised and shaken, as to them, Ogopogo was unknown.

Many individuals who call to report a sighting are reluctant to speak about it, although they are somewhat relieved to know that there is someone to whom they can talk—someone who will listen with interest and not accuse them of imbibing or having illusions.

■

Pat and Irene Dineen called me to report the first sighting for 1999. It was April 25 and the couple were out for their daily walk along Beach Avenue in Peachland. They provided this written account as well as a sketch.

Lillian M. Vogelgesang sketch.

147

It was 80 feet long, six serpentine humps, water like glass and very clear. Close to 100 feet from us and we were about 12 feet from the beach. It passed by us for another 100 feet and we expected it to disappear as it approached. It continued to go through the swim markers without disturbing them which were some 60 feet from shore. Two humps went by the third marker, three in front of the second marker and the sixth between the first and second marker. The objects continued on toward shore and disappeared 20 to 30 feet from shore. The first group vanished before the last one entered the area for swimmers. The waves also quit with just a ripple reaching the beach.

To us it proves our famous beast is really six beasts or the children of the master beast. Our instant thoughts were that we were looking at dolphins or porpoises having seen something similar in salt water. As they passed we noted that the bodies were about 16 inches thick, black with an unusual floppy fin that was on the shoulder behind the head.

Pat commented: "I was lucky to have Irene see it at the same time, or she would accuse me of a liquid visit to the Legion."

■

On April 3, 1997, I received a telephone call from a gentleman who wished only to be known as Bill. He had been relaxing on a bench overlooking the lake near the concession stand in Kelowna City Park when something in the lake caught his attention. The lake was mirror calm as he observed a fifty-foot (15 m) creature swimming around for almost an hour.

It appeared to be feeding and the skin was similar to that of a halibut. Bill did not have a camera, and was somewhat embarrassed to talk about the incident.

■

"Helen Galigan has believed in the Ogopogo for years. Now she's doubly sure that the legendary lake creature exists after spotting it from Okanagan Lake Bridge July 3, 1997," reported *Daily Courier* reporter Rob Munro.

Galigan grew up in Kelowna. In the 1940s her late husband and father were working on a house in Okanagan Landing. "They saw a log out on the lake then looked away for a few seconds. When they looked back, it was gone. There's no way it could disappear that fast," she said.

For years, every time she drove across Okanagan Lake Bridge with her husband, she would look through the openings in the railings at both ends. "I would say to him, 'No Ogopogo today.'"

But at 1:30 p.m. on July 3, 1997 while crossing the bridge, she saw something out of the corner of her eye. "I thought it was a boat flipping over, but when I looked I couldn't see any color or anything." What she did see about 600 yards away on the south side of the bridge looked like a log with evenly spaced bumps sticking out of the water. It was about the length of a telephone pole. She thought about pulling over at the west end of the bridge but the traffic was too heavy.

"I wasn't going to let anyone know. I told a few friends and neighbors but I didn't think anyone would believe me."

She was so convinced that she rushed to pick up the *Daily Courier* expecting to see a front page story about the sighting. There was nothing. Her daughters convinced her to draw a sketch of the creature and to finally phone Ogopogo expert Arlene Gaal.

■

In 1997 I received and saved two interesting voice mail messages. Both came in about a week apart. First message: "Arlene, I was wondering who to report it to. Last year I took a picture when we were driving by Kal Lake or the next lake. My kids said 'Look at that, Dad.' I looked over and I got a photo of something in the water, I don't know what it is." The mature male voice left a telephone number, which I naturally called. Other family members appeared somewhat embarrassed and I have yet to see the photo.

■

Lake Kalamalka sightings are not uncommon, but certainly not reported as often as those from Okanagan Lake. During a 1980 radio talk show in Vernon, a caller spoke of an elderly man who made his home at the base of Lake Kalamalka. Whenever he had opportunity, he told stories of an Ogopogo-like creature churning up the waters near his home. Lake Kalamalka and Woods Lake are joined by a small canal and were first known as Long Lake with feeder tributaries leading to and from Okanagan Lake.

■

In 1985 I received a letter from David Kerkonen of High River, Alberta. He was a young man on the trek of lake monsters.

I saw something in Kal Lake in August of 1982. At the time and for a long time later I was certain it must have been a dead tree, it looked too good and almost identical to a photo of Nessie, I still don't have an opinion on what I saw, but now that I've read the 1978 newspaper account there was something there. Trouble is I stood and watched it for at least 15 minutes, just in case. It didn't move at all. I didn't report it as I thought it was just a fantastic coincidence.

149

Davids sketch shows a creature with a reptilian head, long neck and part of the body up out of the water. Too bad he left his camera at home.

■

Linda and Walter Bauer who had just moved to Kelowna from Edmonton reported seeing something break water in Lake Kalamalka in the early morning of June 27, 1998. The lake was clear as glass and the object created a V-wake as it swam toward Vernon.

■

CKOV Newsroom in Kelowna faxed me this account of a June 23, 1997, sighting in Vernon: "The mythical lake monster was seen late yesterday afternoon around 5:30 p.m. making 30 to 40 foot hump-like ripples in the north arm of Okanagan Lake, by Doug Alexander who watched for about 10 to 15 minutes from his Kin Beach residence. He didn't have a camera ready."

■

For reasons not as yet determined, there are fewer actual sightings reported in and around the vicinity of the city of Vernon itself. However, a person has only to travel a few miles south to find markers where some of the better sightings have taken place.

A second voice mail in 1997 was also interesting. "Hi Arlene, I believe you're the Ogopogo lady. My name's Dan Pearson in Westbank here. I saw a twenty-foot long eel-like thing in the lake today, I don't know what it was. I saw an eel head; it was the weirdest thing I ever seen and I'm the biggest skeptic of the Ogopogo there is in this country. But it's an eel and it's twenty foot long and it was black. You can call me if you like." Dan Pearson was much more receptive than the previous caller and repeated his story without much hesitation.

■

Springlike November weather had evidently created some confusion for Ogopogo, who by all accounts should have taken to his winter retreat. On November 22, 1997, Gary Sorenson and Terry Horton reported seeing something unusual on Okanagan Lake. The two men were returning from the Bear Creek area and upon hitting Westside Road they spotted an unusual object swimming at a good clip toward Okanagan Lake Bridge, in what was a very calm lake. No boats were in sight and the animal appeared to be at least forty feet (12 m) long. Sorenson and Horton pulled over to the side of the road to observe the phenomenon and were soon joined by another car. Neither group made contact, as all were intent on watching without comment for fear of missing something.

What made this sighting somewhat out of the ordinary was that Sorenson's wife decided to call the RCMP to see if anyone else had spotted anything. Gary Sorenson stated that the RCMP evidently had another report of something on the lake and sent a boat out to investigate that same afternoon.

■

In the spring of 1996 Mike Zaiser had just purchased a new camera. He invited his brother and sister-in-law for a relaxing afternoon drive around Okanagan Lake, which led them to Okanagan Lake Mountain Park. Mike was anxious to try out his camera. The lake was calm, and the weather ideal. Out in the distance, the group saw something unusual that did not appear to be a boat. Mike took a few photos, but knowing that it was quite far away gave no real thought to the results. A few weeks later he called to talk to me about it and brought me both the negatives and prints of his experience. There was doubtless something above water that was almost lost in the dark shadows of the surrounding mountain. The long wake on the surface of the calm lake showed an animal swimming, oblivious to everything but the serenity of the afternoon sun.

As I concentrated on the photos for the book, each effort provided clearer results as I manipulated the brightness and contrast switches. A very long brownish colored animal could be seen on the surface with what had to be a elongated neck and head, according to its direction of travel. This was an exciting find. Mike would, of course, be pleased.

This brought to mind a set of pictures that were taken a few years before at my prompting. There are similarities, as both sets of photos seem to have a body and neck out of the water.

■

It had been a hot sunny day. The temperature neared 28°C. The time was 8:05 P.M., June 28, 1995. Brian and Janet Hutchinson of Peachland were having their evening meal on the upper deck of their home overlooking Seclusion Bay on Okanagan Lake.

I noticed what appeared to be a disturbed patch of water in what was a relatively calm lake, some 500 yards from the shoreline. I looked around for a boat or anything else which could have created this or any other connection such as a reflection from the clouds, sky or any land object, but couldn't find an answer. I fetched my binoculars, (7 x 50 mm) and observed the water surface which appeared to be in a flurried

151

condition with two patches of blue-gray over the area, which I put down to sky refraction. I then passed the binoculars to Janet as she wanted to take a look. Suddenly and quite excitedly she said, "There's something coming out of the water! I can see three humps." I said, "Let me see."

By the time I had focused on the area, the humps had gone and an animal's head and neck were visible about five to six feet above the water. The head looked distinctly egg-shaped, about 10 to 12 inches in length and probably 7 to 8 inches in diameter at the widest point. The neck was narrow at the head, doubling in size at the water level (perhaps 6 inches, expanding to 12 inches). It was not possible to see any features or skin texture due to the failing light. The head remained motionless for several seconds, then sank slowly to half its height, then again rose slowly to its original position, keeping well erect all this time. Then it once again went slowly and vertically down until it submerged. The whole episode took approximately 20 to 25 seconds and no further sighting took place.

Janet later said that she felt the protrusions she saw may have actually been the top of the head as it was surfacing. The Hutchinsons provided an interesting sketch.

■

While enjoying a boat ride with his grandchildren on Okanagan Lake Sepember 26, 1995, Anthony Hyde was paid a surprise visit by what he thinks was Ogopogo. Hyde said he and three companions spotted the lake monster while boating off Carrs Landing. "Whether it was an eel, sturgeon or Ogopogo I don't know, but there was definitely movement in the water," said Hyde who claims perfect vision for everything but reading.

He said he, his grandson, daughter-in-law and her father rented a motorboat near Fintry, Thursday and headed south toward Kelowna. "The lake that day was smooth," said Hyde. "All of a sudden waves began rising from under the water around the boat. Next thing, we see these waves about 10 feet long and 16 inches high. There was something moving in the water at a good pace." Through the side of the wave Hyde is sure he saw the snout and face of a reptilelike creature about seventy-five feet (23 m) away.

■

May 12, 1994, newspaper headlines read:

OGOPOGO APPEARS IN PEACHLAND
Ronda Caplan and her friend Michelle Horne saw the legendary lake monster in Okanagan Lake three times this week. They were visiting

one of Horne's friends who lives in the first row of houses off Princeton Avenue, above Peachland's town center.

"We were sitting outside on the lawn drinking tea while watching the waves come in," said Caplan. The house is about 200 meters from the waterfront. I saw something that caught my eye for two or three seconds. I thought: 'is that a black boat?' I looked up again and all of a sudden a big black thing was there, a foot out of the water with white caps on top of it. The protrusion was about 13 meters from shore, grey-black in color with a shiny surface like an eel," she said.

"There was another break in the water behind it and a smaller break behind that. It disappeared but came halfway out of the water again. Something clicked and I said, 'I'm looking at Ogopogo.' It was kind of neat. The object was definitely not a log," insists Caplan. "It was moving. I know I saw Ogopogo. I should have brought my camera."

Caplan said she has always believed Ogopogo exists and hoped she would see it one day.

■

July 26, 1994: J. P. Squire of the *Kelowna Daily Courier* writes:

OGOPOGO SIGHTING ONE OF THE BEST
Darlene Viala, two other adults and five children believe they spotted Ogopogo in Okanagan Lake about two kilometers west of Hotel Eldorado in Okanagan Mission at 6:15 p.m. July 13.

"It surfaced about 20 feet from them which makes it one of the more dramatic sightings," said Gaal, the local Ogopogo expert who is busy working on her third book.

Viala, a 29-year-old interior house painter, was riding across Okanagan Lake with her friend Tammy Duncan who was operating the small boat. Duncan brought the boat to an abrupt stop, shutting off the motor when she thought she saw the creature. She pointed it out to Viala who was just as startled. The three adults and five children, all from Kelowna, saw the body of a creature 13 to 18 meters (50 to 60 feet) in length swimming slowly through the water.

"We were about 20 feet away. It was snakelike with eight to ten fins on it. The water came through the fins. The tail was as clear as day and like the end of a snake. The skin was blackish green and soft like the skin of a dolphin," said Viala.

She estimated the body at about one meter (three feet) in diameter at the thickest part, but they never did see its head in the one-minute sighting.

"This was no beaver. This was no fish. This was no sturgeon. We saw different humps coming out of the water. It was something I've never seen before. I can't explain it. I've been known to get a little crazy, but I'm no lunatic. All I know is that this was very real," she said. "We all panicked. The kids were just as hysterical scared. Tammy was bawling her head off. We were just shaking. All of us are still in shock. It was moving really slowly and I wanted to get closer, but the second we started the motor, all of a sudden it started ripping. It dove real fast."

Unfortunately, none of them had a camera. Viala's six-year-old son, Billy George, had asked her about Ogopogo, so when it appeared she held him up saying: "Now you can get to see the real thing." Other witnesses were Duncan's mother, Marilyn McLean and Duncan's children, Jamie 8, Scott 9 and Laura 10.

■

Startled staff and customers at Mary's Kitchen in Peachland watched in disbelief as a long slender, slimy thing bobbed up and down on Okanagan Lake in September of 1994. Doug Mallo doesn't know if it was Ogopogo, but it certainly was something out of the ordinary. "It was about 30 feet long, with a black body," he said. "I was kind of numbed by what I was seeing."

Mallo, the new owner of Mary's Kitchen Café, called over some people after noticing the creature a couple of hundred yards offshore just before 1:00 p.m. Friday.

"I wanted there to be some other witnesses," said Mallo, a new arrival from Regina, Saskatchewan who knows there are some people who doubt Ogopogo exists. In all, about a half dozen people gathered on a veranda at the lakeside café to watch the object rise and submerge four times as it moved slowly northward. It sank from view after a couple of minutes.

"This is the second time I've seen Ogopogo," said café's former owner, Mary Mckee. "I've got a picture of him up on the wall that I took in 1991. "It came right up out of the huge wave and kind of leaped a bit, then disappeared." Mckee said. "It was kind of gray-green-black. We all could see it." McKee said the Friday sighting was more dramatic than her early morning encounter in 1991.

■

Guy Banks and his friend Larry Burton saw something unusual while driving across Okanagan Lake Bridge at 6:50 A.M. June 20, 1993. Banks, who has lived by the water all his life said he has never seen anything like what he saw that morning.

"It was absolutely astounding. It was really strange." He saw a wave break when there was nothing around and move at a walking speed with a ripple breaking out from a point. He said the wave was seven to ten meters across.

■

Three women spotted a strange object swimming in Okanagan Lake near Bear Creek Park about 3:00 P.M., August 3, 1993. Lidia Allen, Trudy Towers and Debbie Nielsen were sitting in the picnic area of the park looking over the calm water when a streak appeared in the water about 197 feet (60 m) off shore.

"It was almost like a wave, but it was so long and it stood there really dark black," said Allen. "Then it moved and went under. It was a thick black line and it started to go up and down. It looked like a serpent. The part above the water was ten to fifteen feet long It was really dark. We couldn't see a head, its back was coming up and then going down." The women watched the object disappear around a point and then re-appear in the distance minutes later.

■

Ogopogo put in a rare appearance August 26, 1993, for a Kelowna grandmother and her two adult granddaughters visiting from Hamilton, Ontario.

"We were sitting at the back of the *Fintry Queen* about 1:45 P.M. when we saw two humps about fifty feet (15 m) from the rear of the boat for a minute or so," said Ada Massey.

The three women were the only ones sitting at the rear of the paddlewheeler's top deck as it headed back to downtown Kelowna. At the time, the *Fintry Queen* was in the middle of the lake opposite the log booms on the west side of Okanagan Lake, south of Bear Creek Provincial Park.

"The two humps were blackish-bluey and looked fairly smooth," said Brenda Massey.

"You could tell they were moving because they came up and down out of the water, like a water snake except it was much bigger. There was no head or tail, but you could see the wake. I was quite surprised. At first I didn't know what to think, but it was too big to be anything else." Brenda had her camera with her but by the time she got over her surprise and fumbled with the camera case, the humps had disappeared.

■

Robert Noakes, artist and resident of Westbank sent an interesting watercolor of his encounter with Ogopogo in July, 1992. It clearly illustrates what he observed as told to his friend Phyllis Winter.

155

I shall try and describe what Robert told us this last summer in July at the Summer School of the Arts in Penticton, regarding his sighting of our Ogopogo. Robert came from Kelowna and rode his motorbike down each day. He seemed quite shy and was a good artist. One morning while parking my car near his bike he said, "I saw something funny going back to Kelowna yesterday afternoon." I asked him to tell me about it. He said it was raining so hard around Peachland that he had to stop and wait awhile. He was down by the lake when something surfaced. This huge monster rose up and then plunged back down into the water. He was so astounded, I guess he had never heard about our Ogopogo before.

I was really so excited and when we got to class I announced that Robert had something to tell us, but he was shy, so we encouraged him and everyone was so thrilled to hear it. When I got home I phoned the radio station and told them the story. A few minutes later here came my story on the radio. Such excitement!　　　　　　　　—Phyllis Winter

■

For Burt Johnson it was out of sight, but not out of earshot. Burt had been totally blind for years and was head of the Kelowna Branch for the CNIB. "At first I could hardly make out the sound of waves lapping against the beach. All of a sudden I could hear waves getting bigger and bigger. By the sound of the pounding, the waves must have been a foot high." Johnson alerted his wife Brenda and brother-in-law Byron Rolston who turned to look.

Brenda Johnson provided this account of their encounter near Kelowna City Park, October 13, 1992.

It was a beautiful sunny day so my brother Byron Rolston of Abbotsford, B.C., my husband Burt and myself decided to go for a walk in city park and take some pictures. I spotted what looked like a wave-like churning about 20 feet long, in an otherwise calm lake between the Fintry Queen paddle-wheeler and the entrance to city park. It was about 50 feet out from shore. I said to my brother, "What the heck is that? Take some pictures." It looked like something had suddenly emerged straight up out of the water with a rolling, churning action. The water seemed to be going up over its body with a tremendous force which caused quite a wake toward shore. At that time I made no movement either forward or backward. I was struck by the force of the water running over its body and its ability to create such a large wake. Its color was bluish-black, no tail or head. It stayed in this position for about two minutes then went straight down without bending its body at all.

Inside Edition joins lineup in hunt for Ogopogo

A blind man is among the Ogopogo eyewitnesses likely to be interviewed next week by an American television crew.

Burt Johnson, head of the Kelowna branch of the CNIB, will recount his brush with the legendary sea serpent for the producers of Inside Edition.

"I'm a firm believer in Ogopogo," Johnson said Thursday. "I used to be skeptical, but now I know it exists."

Johnson's conversion came at exactly 12:10 p.m. last Oct. 13, as he walked in City Park with his wife and brother.

It was a calm day, and Johnson could barely make out the sound of waves lapping against the beach as the trio strolled along the foreshore path.

"All of a sudden I could hear the waves getting bigger and bigger. By the sound of the pounding, the waves must have been a foot high," he recalled.

Johnson told his wife and brother-in-law to look out on Okanagan Lake. What they saw startled them.

"There was bluish-black thing, about 20-feet long rising straight up out of the water," Brenda Johnson said. "It didn't move forward or backward, and it didn't have a head or a tail. It just looked like the body of something."

Her brother, Byron Rolston of Abbotsford, was carrying a camera and snapped a few pics before the creature submerged in less than two minutes. The photographs, which Johnson enlarged 65 times on a special CNIB reading-assistance machine, seem to show a large object rising out of the water about 75 feet offshore.

"I've never, ever in my life seen anything like it," Brenda Johnson says. "We were all pretty shook up afterwards."

In retrospect, though, Burt Johnson figures Ogopogo must be harmless.

"While it was up making all these waves, I could hear a bunch of ducks just quacking away nearby," he says.

ROBERT NOAKES/For The Daily Courier
Kelowna resident Robert Noakes painted these watercolors of his encounter with Ogopogo. They illustrate what he saw for a few

"Ogopogo must be a friendly fish, otherwise those ducks would have got all excited."

Along with a few other Ogopogo spotters, the Johnson's will re-enact their experience next Thursday for a film crew from Inside Edition, a so-called tabloid TV program that's based in New York.

Arlene Gaal, Kelowna's resident expert on Ogopogo, says the producers of the program called her after the New York Times wrote a feature article on Okanagan Lake's most celebrated inhabitant.

Ogopogo has already been the subject of several television programs, and Gaal figures interest will never subside in the reclusive reptile.

"Whenever you have something unusual like this happening, you're always going to attract the attention of outsiders," she says. "It's a big story. It's never going to go away."

EVIN DUNN/The Daily Courier
Ogopogo witnesses Doug Mallo, front, Delores Leuning, Mary McKee and Vic Bozowski scan the waterfront from Mary's Kitchen Cafe in Peachland where the group spotted the legendary lake beast.

Lake encounter eerie

September, 1994

By RON SEYMOUR
The Daily Courier

Startled staff and customers at a Peachland cafe watched in disbelief as a long, slender, slimy thing bobbed up and down on Okanagan Lake.

Doug Mallo doesn't know if it was Ogopogo — but it certainly was something out of the ordinary.

"It was about 30 feet long, with a black body," he said Saturday. "I was kind of numbed by what I was seeing."

Mallo, the new owner of Mary's Kitchen Cafe, called over some other people after noticing the creature a couple hundred yards offshore just before 1 p.m. Friday.

"I wanted there to be some other witnesses," said Mallo, a new arrival from Regina, Sask., who knows there are some people who doubt Ogopogo exists. In all, about a half-dozen people gathered on a veranda at the lakeside cafe to watch the object rise

utes.

"This is the second time I've seen Ogopogo," said the cafe's former owner, Mary McKee. "I've got a picture of him that I took of him in 1991 up on the wall."

McKee said the Friday's sighting was more dramatic than her first encounter.

"It came right up out of a huge wave and kind of leaped a little bit, then disappeared," McKee said. "It was kind of gray-green-black . . . We all could see it."

Local Ogopogo expert Arlene Gaal described it as a credible sighting, especially since there were a number of witnesses.

"Peachland is becoming a real hot spot for sightings," Gaal said, noting that several area residents have said they've seen something strange in the water recently, and a few have captured unusual objects on videotape.

This was the fourth reported sighting of Ogopogo

He saw Ogopogo

...le enjoying a boat ride with his grandchildren on ...nagan Lake, Anthony Hyde was paid a surprise visit ...hat he thinks was Ogopogo. Hyde said he and three ...panions spotted the sea monster while boating off ... Landing. "Whether it was an eel, sturgeon or Ogo-... I don't know, but there was definitely movement in ...ter," said Hyde, 51, who claims perfect eyesight for ...thing but reading. Hyde said he, his grandson, ...er-in-law and her father rented a motorboat near ...Thursday and headed south towards Kelowna. The lake that day was smooth, said Hyde. All of a sudden waves began rising from under water around the boat. "Next thing we see these waves about 10-feet long and 16-inches high. There was something moving in the water at a good pace." Through the side of the wave Hyde is sure he saw the snout and face of a reptile-like creature about 75 feet away from the boat.

...mson News Service

My brother was able to snap two pictures, one when it was submerging. It was interesting to note that the second picture showed fins or humps just above the water line. When it submerged, the lake returned to its calm.

Byron, who had rushed closer to get a better shot, agreed that it was indeed about 20 feet long. "It made quite a loud splashing sound and the waves coming on shore were about one and a half feet high and very audible."

"I believe what I heard and my wife believes what she saw," stated CNIB manager Burt Johnson. "In this case, I think it was Ogopogo."

The pictures were later magnified on a reading assistance machine and appeared to show a large shadowy body rising from a calm lake, substantiating the experience.

The Johnson/Rolston sighting alerted me to an interesting experience I had October 28, 1980, at 1:30 P.M. in exactly the same area of the park. While driving along I observed a break in the water which appeared to be about seventy feet (21 m) long, creating a wake with solid sections above water. I stopped my car in a no parking zone, and noticed a woman sitting on the park bench holding a camera. I urged her to take a few shots. The activity lasted for several minutes and the lake regained its composure as the animal traveled across the lake and out of sight. Photos show a long, dark object above the surface and the second shows a classic pose with a long neck straight up out of the water.

■

July 26, 1991, *The Daily Courier* featured this front page story:

OGOPOGO REPORTED NEAR PEACHLAND

A mysterious wake, a furtive figure and a quick exit all witnessed by a single observer. Sound familiar? It should. It's the story of Ogopogo, another chapter of which was written Thursday.

A Calgary tourist says he spotted the slippery sea serpent in calm waters off Peachland. What he can't understand is why no one else did. "I had fully anticipated I would not be the only one sighting (the creature)," Ron Elies said. The self-employed vending machine operator says he was one of scores of motorists heading down Highway 97 about 10:30 a.m. Wednesday when a wake suddenly appeared about 300 yards off shore. Water was spurting into the air and a large black form was visible just beneath the surface of the water, Elies said.

"It looked like a small island slightly submerged," he said. "It was about 30 to 40 feet long and the main body was about six feet wide."

Due to traffic, he couldn't pull over and hop out for a better view, and Elies who was visiting friends in Peachland, said it never occurred to him to head to the lakeshore for closer inspection. Elies, who has visited the Okanagan almost every summer for the last 15 years says he thinks Ogo is a friendly fish. Elies knows some might scoff at his story, but he takes comfort in knowing he's one of many people to report seeing Ogopogo.

"I've always thought that there can't be thousands of liars out there!"

■

August 8, 1991, *The Spokesman-Review*, Spokane, Washington edition ran this story:

REPORTS OF OKANAGAN LAKE MONSTER SURFACE AGAIN
Vernon, British Columbia. Ogopogo, the legendary monster of Okanagan Lake has surfaced again. Or was it a family of sturgeon?

"We couldnt believe what we were seeing," waitress Sue Court said Wednesday. "We could see this black thing sticking out of the water. It was only there for a minute and then it was gone." Court was among 30 staff and guests at the Lakeside Marina Hotels outdoor patio lounge who said they saw a huge rippling offshore disturbance Monday night. They said it moved rapidly through the water, then briefly rose to the surface. Several said a six-foot-tall hump-like protrusion jutted briefly out of the water.

Carmen Zieman, who operates a jet-ski rental operation was among the first to notice.

"I looked out and saw these huge white wakes moving up the lake," he said. "They were moving against the rest of the waves and in the opposite direction the wind was going."

Ziemen said the area of churning was about 600 yards offshore. The frothy water moved along the lake at a speed of about 10 miles an hour, kicking up waves more than 3 feet high, witnesses say.

"Part of it came right out of the water," Ziemen said. "It was black and it came up like an arch, and then went right back down again."

"A bunch of guys jumped into boats and drove to the spot, but by that time they couldn't see anything," said Bartender Grant Nikolaychuk.

Some witnesses were reluctant to suggest it was Okanagan Lake's mythical resident monster.

"There's no way there could be anything like an Ogopogo," said photographer Murray Martz. He suggested what people saw was a school of sturgeon, similar to the kind he regularly saw on freshwater lakes in his native Saskatchewan.

That's an idea that has already occurred to Arlene Gaal, a 20 year veteran Ogopogo hunter who has written two books on the subject. But she said the provincial Fisheries Ministry has never recorded a confirmed sighting of a sturgeon in the lake.

■

Two painters at work at a home in Naramata claim they saw something in Okanagan Lake, September 21, 1991 that may have been the legendary lake serpent, Ogopogo. Andrew Mayes and his partner Brad Virtue were on the roof of the home when Mayes noted some movement in the water. "There was this dark spot," Mayes said, "and then this V shape started on the water, like a wake."

Mayes said the object moved slowly for about ninety-eight feet (30 m) before disappearing. Virtue said he thought he saw a head. Mayes estimated the shadow was about thirty-three feet (10 m) long.

■

Gloria Fanslau made the following report:

On August 21, 1991, while camping near Bear Creek, my husband noticed whitecaps on the lake moving parallel to the shore. My husband, son and I ran to the beach to get a better view of what was happening. The waves were a few yards beyond the markers that divide the swimming area from the boating area. The whitecaps were moving from south toward the north end of Bear Creek Park where the logs are tied up in the bay. After reaching the logs, the waves moved toward shore, then a large shadow appeared underwater moving back in the direction the waves came from.

The moving shadow was about 20 to 25 feet long with a much smaller shadow along each side. The smaller shadows were about 6 to 8 feet long. A part of the largest object surfaced. The part that was visible was log-like, shiny, blackish and about 10 feet long and 20 to 24 inches in diameter. It was huge. This part was visible for about 10 seconds and moving parallel to the shore. Then it submerged. The shadows were still visible but became less and less as they moved along. Finally they vanished from sight as they moved into deeper water. The creature was moving at about 5 mph and the total sighting took about 8 minutes. The lake was very smooth and calm, the sky was clear and there was no wind. There were no tugs or boats in the area.

Another family who was in the beach area told us they saw something too, but did not pay close attention. However before we talked to them about the sighting, their son, around 7 years old was singing, "I saw Ogopogo, I saw Ogopogo." Sincerely yours, Gloria Fanslau

■

Susan and Michael Filiatrault of Kelowna believe they had an Ogopogo sighting at 1:35 P.M. on Sunday, February 4, 1990 at Bear Creek Park.

We had started at viewpoint #6 and worked our way down to viewpoint #1. We sat for a rest and naturally looked out to the water, looking for you-know-who. When you look down the mountain to the lake, you look between two large trees. We figured the distance between the trees was 30 to 40 feet. We looked down and saw a long dark brown line from tree to tree. Not a log, it was underwater. Waves just kind of rolled over it, no wake or anything. As we watched, it just moved out of sight toward the middle of the lake, or possibly more accurately toward Okanagan Lake Bridge.

■

The first day of spring, March 21, 1990, is a day that Graham Merrick of Lethbridge Alberta, will never forget. He was flying out of Penticton on an Air B.C. flight at around 9:30 A.M. when looking out the right side of the plane he saw three animals shoot out quickly close to a large sandbar at the south end of the lake. The creatures varied in size from 30 to 70 feet (9–21 m). Their color was a sandy light brown, very similar to the sandbar and very noticeable in the crystal clear blue water.

The Air B.C. plane had to return to the airport due to mechanical problems, and as they neared Penticton, Graham's eyes were glued to the lake. He saw the smaller animal on the surface of the lake. It appeared to have a narrow, beveled body, much like a birch bark canoe and as it moved sideways, he noticed a shimmering light or a very bright reflection off its body. It submerged very quickly, perhaps scared by the plane's motor. Graham was very excited and did not hold back as he told his fellow passengers what he had just experienced. It appears he was alone as no one else seemed to be watching the lake. Graham provided a useful sketch along with a written account.

■

On June 12, 1990, a group of twelve people observed an object swimming offshore in the vicinity of Bear Creek Park. One of the group was Natalie Butler, a teacher at Rutland Senior Secondary School in Kelowna.

A few weeks later on June 17 Lily Granfield and her husband see something large rise three or four feet out of the lake while driving in their car near Peachland.

■

John Keery, *Daily Courier* staff reports:

THEY SAW OGOPOGO BUT CAN'T BELIEVE IT

Ann Kline thinks she saw Ogopogo from a window in her Kelowna home July 17, 1990 but is having a difficult time believing it. Kline and her husband Richard were sitting in the kitchen overlooking Okanagan Lake at about 10 a.m. when they saw a snake-like creature with three humps, a head and a tail swim by their beach home.

"I took the binoculars and I couldn't believe it. It wasn't a wave, I have seen lots of waves," said Kline. Richard Kline, a former seaman who works part-time as a ship's pilot on the B. C. Coast said the creature was about 20 feet long and seemed to be swimming at about 10 knots, 800 feet from shore.

"It had a determined direction, it was just going across. It was weird."

Kline said he has never seen anything like it in 45 years at sea. "I said to my wife: 'Dear, if you want to see Ogopogo, there he is.'"After her husband pointed out the creature, Ann Kline picked up her binoculars and had a better look. She said the humps looked like half truck tires and the head was like an overgrown snake. It swam across in front of their home on the south side of Kelowna, heading northward toward Okanagan Lake Bridge. They lost sight of it after it passed their house because the view was blocked by a row of ornamental cedar trees.

Ann Kline said she had never believed in Ogopogo. "I feel stupid about this. But if there is an Ogopogo, I saw it today."

■

The time was 7:30 P.M., Friday, July 27, 1990. The place, 600 yards (549 m) offshore from the S.S. *Sicamous* in Penticton, B.C. Ken Evans sent this account.

My girlfriend and I were parked with our 18-foot-boat in flat calm water. We noticed a wave appear about 50 feet away from underneath the water. The wave was 40 feet long, one foot high and within seconds the wave grew to 60 feet long and four feet high. At this point we got scared and started the boat up to get out of the area. The 60-foot long wave then started to move slowly north in a long 'S' pattern. The waves it created rocked the boat and we really had to hang on.

Then, at about 100 feet away, the front part turned and headed east. That's when we saw the neck and head dipping in and out of the water. This went on for 50 feet and then it submerged. There is no doubt in our minds what we saw was very large in body, the neck and head approximately twelve to fifteen feet long and about 2 feet around. We could not see eye or mouth or where the head began on the neck.

It was signed Ken Evans and E. Sutherland.

■

Later that year in early August, 1990, I received a call from a couple vacationing in Kelowna from Fort McMurray, Alberta. They were excited about some photos they had taken the day before while out boating on the lake. I quickly got into my car and headed for the motel. It was there that I met Mike and Tina Paskal and their five-month-old son Jamie. I was anxious to see and hear about their experience.

Tina and Mike did not hold back. It was a hot day and they rented a boat and headed out to the Fintry area with little Jamie tucked safely in. The lake was flat calm, the temperature bordering 90°F (32°C), just a grand day to be out on the lake. As they neared Fintry, Jamie started fussing so they decided to stop and try to find a quiet place where Tina could feed him. Tina recalled that she had just finished feeding the baby and happened to glance over her shoulder and saw a couple of waves heading toward the boat.

"Then this thing surfaced right out of the water and I screamed to Mike, 'Thats it!'" meaning Ogopogo. Mike said that while he watched the creature, about ten meters of its back came about a meter high out of the water. Tina yelled at Mike to grab the camera and in a state of shock she screamed and dropped Jamie. Mike took two shots and then moved quickly to start the boat as he was uncertain about the animal's reaction. Wanting to protect his family, he turned and headed back to Kelowna at high speed.

In the safety of their motel room, Tina remembered, "It looked like a humongous snake with a body all smooth and shiny. It came up like a submarine and you could tell that it was big by the swooshing noise."

The two pictures that Mike was able to take are exceptional. A solid section of its body is definitely visible in both photos. It's hard to determine whether it is the front or back end of the animal or a shoulder structure, but in any case, there appears to be a protruding fin up out of the water parallel to it. Two white spots are clearly visible on the side in both photos. There is a beveled look to the section out of the water, similar to what Graham Merrick described in his aerial experience.

Tina and Mike were boating where the lake is 350 to 500 feet (107–152 m) deep, and the sighting cannot be explained away as either a log or rock as was later suggested. The photos definitely show something very much alive.

Both Mike Paskal and Graham Merrick call me at least once or twice a year from Alberta to check on the status of Ogopogo sightings. I have them placed in the category of "lifetime believers," individuals who truly know what they saw, and no amount of ridicule from friends or relatives could ever change their minds.

Photos or video footage are always appreciated as backup for any sighting, but few people are camera-ready and, thus, miss out on great photo opportunities. The next best thing is a sketch and in most cases, the results generally confirm the story.

■

A group of eight people from Victoria had the experience of a lifetime. Majorie McCraig, one of the group, sent this letter:

As with all observed happenings, each of us registers impressions and we all ran true to course on this. The women had more difficulty with estimating distances than the men and as you will see in the space of a very few seconds our observations differed. I will set out the generalities of our day and then give you the names and observations of the members of our group. Barbara and Shel Rowell have written and Barbara has illustrated, what they saw. As you will learn from the account by the Rowells, there was an early morning second sighting by them on July 27th, 1988.

Okanagan Lake Provincial Park, July 26, 1988 12:40 p.m.

Our houseboat was on the beach at the park and eight of us were attracted by the very excited calls of two girls lying on the beach a few yards from our boat. As soon as they alerted us they called and pointed to the water. We all ran to the stern of the boat. After the sighting, Arch McCraig spoke to the girls, learned they were from Quebec and that they had never heard of Ogopogo. They told us that they had seen the object for some time before they called and that it had been much higher out of the water at first. Unfortunately he did not obtain their names.

WITNESSES

Jim and Margaret Black: Length: 15 feet, Distance from shore: 150 to 200 feet. Description: Flat, ribbony loops that disappeared suddenly leaving no trace on the water surface. One head. Margaret Black saw something white (perhaps water).

Donald and Francis Beresford: Length; 10 feet, Description: The Beresfords did not see a head but did see something white. There were two ripples, looked like an eel. It disappeared very suddenly and although it was traveling fast and was large, there was no wake.

Arch and Marjory McCraig: Length 20 to 30 feet; speed 5 to 6 knots; distance from shore, 200 feet.

Marjory McCraig: The object moved very fast in a writhing manner, a sleek pointed head appeared (like a seal or sea lion). There was something white in front of the head that could have been made by a fast moving object breaking through the water. This head was only visible for two or three seconds and immediately a second head appeared, less visible, not as high in the water and looked smaller, but again white appeared. The object disappeared suddenly without a trace of water or ripples, bubbles etc. Arch McCraig agrees with this description but did not see a head.

Barbara Rowell and Marjory McCraig were the only ones who saw two heads, Barb and Marjory were standing side by side. This sighting was radioed in to Shelter Bay Headquarters later in the afternoon and shortly after, a transmission was overheard from another Shelter Bay Houseboat that they had seen an object in the water too.

We hope you find our baffling experience helpful in unraveling this mystery and wish there was some way to prove to all those unbelievers out there that Ogopogo does live in the lake. Yours sincerely, Marjorie McCraig.

Sheldon Rowell, a retired Naval Officer who was very familiar with judging water distances and water phenomena, provided his account entitled: "As I Saw It." His wife Barbara included a very detailed sketch.

LOCATION—Provincial Park near Peachland. We were beached on the northern end of the beach about 50 feet north of a pile of large rocks that rather divided the beach at that point. Two girls were sunbathing near the rocks and a few family groups were located south of the rocks.

THE SIGHTING—Our attention was caught by the two girls on the beach frantically pointing out to the lake. We ran to the stern of the boat to see what had attracted their attention. The sighting at first appeared to me to be some kind of wake. However, the wake did not act as a wake. It was 20 to 30 feet long and there was only one leg to the wake or should I say one half of the normal "V." Also it did not trail out behind as one would find from a swimming animal or boat on such calm water. The movement was sinuous, like a snake movement and the water flowed smoothly over and around "the sighting."

I cannot remember clearly identifying a head but did see white near the forward part. The sighting was moving parallel to the beach at about 6 knots and was visible for about 20 seconds. It was about 50 to 100 yards off the beach. (130 to 300 feet)

POST SIGHTING—The two girls said that they had the "sighting" in view for a longer period than us and it had initially been higher out of the water. No boats, no swimmers, no wind, no haze, flat calm, clear sunny skies, no meteorological phenomena existed, no noise, no sightings' obstruction. Looking from landward to sea, no currents in the water.

SECOND SIGHTING—Eastern side of the lake opposite Peachland at the Okanagan Mountain Provincial Park. Houseboat beached and secured. At 6:38 a.m., while leaning against a rock I saw this large head protrude about 1 feet from the water vertically. No movement but remained at 1 feet for about 5 to 10 seconds then slowly disappeared. Absolutely no wake or bubbles to mark the area. It was about 50 yards out. (150 feet). The head was pointed. A few seconds later and at a point slightly 10 yards northwest of where it first showed we once more saw the head about one foot out of the water and about 10 yards from the first spot. It remained only for about 5 seconds and disappeared as before. A couple of minutes later much further to the northwest something once more broke the surface for a couple of seconds.

POST OTHER SIGHTINGS—Difficult to describe, dark color, slightly muddy colored on underside. Perhaps it could be likened to a log. However there had to be movement as the three sightings occurred at three different points. By my calculations it was moving at about 1 to 2 mph. There was no tidal wave action, no currents so therefore it could not have been a log. Also as there was no swell, there was no vertical current to project a water-logged tree.

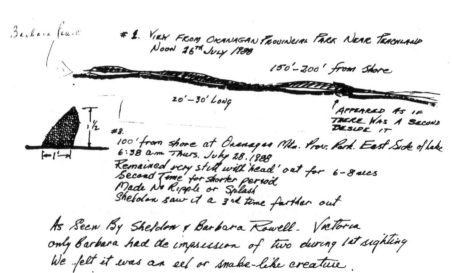

166

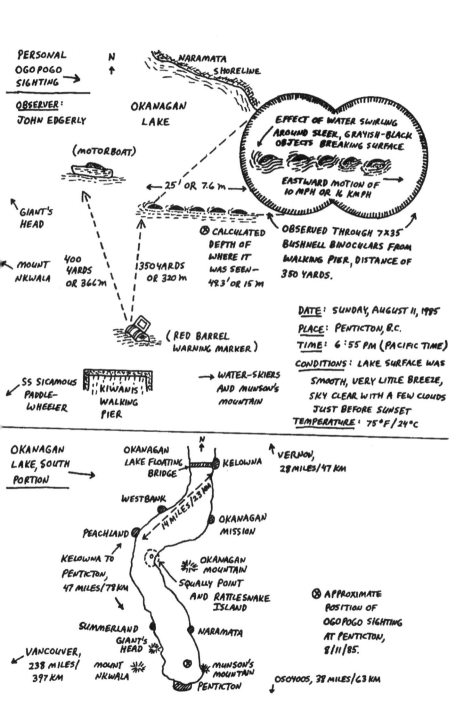

■

On August 11, 1985, John Edgerly arrived in Penticton from Montana and, after a few days rest, decided to explore the town.

I strolled out to the Kiwanis walking pier adjacent to the Delta Lakeside Inn. A fellow nearby was playing bagpipes which initially drew me to the pier. The lake's surface was very calm, just like a sheet of glass. I trained my 7 x 35 Bushnell binoculars on several fishing boats and made a sweep from Mt. Nkwala and the west shore road up to Kelowna across the lake eastward to Narmata. I noticed a black wave just before a fishing boat, around 400 yards out. It started to move eastward and I took a closer look. The object was greyish black, sleek and water appeared to swirl around it as it was moving with some speed to the east shore. All the time I was telling myself, not to jump to conclusions and think that anything spotted was Ogopogo. But what really caught my attention was observing that instead of the water being stirred up by a boat, it was being disturbed by some object beneath it.

I decided to concentrate on it. I saw five objects in a consecutive line break the surface, greyish-black and smooth as they proceeded to the Naramata shoreline. The water kept swirling around them by the force of the motion. No fins of any kind visible, only a sleek surface. Estimated that it extended along for 25 feet or 7 meters. I watched it for about a minute or so before it moved out of my line of vision. For a long while after, I sort of had empathy with Clyde Tomlaugh, recalling his elation when he discovered Pluto in 1930 at the Flagstaff Observatory. I sat down and made notes and continued with them back at the hotel.

John Edgerly provided a very detailed account and sketch of the incident a few days later at my home in Kelowna.

■

In 1989, Stella Friedel was crossing Okanagan Lake Bridge when her attention was drawn to something in the water.

On September 5, 1989 at 3:30 p.m. I saw the head, eye and neck of the real lake creature in Okanagan Lake. The water was still and the afternoon sunlight was brilliant. As our car moved westward, two thirds of the way across the Kelowna bridge, a small rise appeared in the water about forty feet off the bridge embankment. When the water surface broke, a long cylindrical black-looking neck with a smallish head rose up some twenty-feet or so. The creature held an upright position for over thirty seconds or more.

The creature's head was smooth-shaped; smallish in relation to the height and neck above the water. The neck was the width of the steer-

168

ing wheel of the car. It had a smoother top-lip and a wide closed mouth. I was observing him from the side. The creature's eye was the rich brown, living color and shape of a horse's with no sign of an iris aperture. I was looking at a one-color eye-ball surrounded by a wide band of white. An oval-shaped eye encircled by a somewhat rectangular band of white. I could not see any ears or open nostrils. I was totally amazed by what I saw and recorded these details on my return home and sketched what I saw as best I could.

This was no iron pipe or radio-crews prank. The glare from the sun prevented any vision of what may have been submerged beneath the water. I thought that the even black surface of the neck was short fur. If it was not fur, then no lines mark the surface. I stand by the truth of what I saw.   —Stella Friedel, B.Ed. M. Ed.

Her sketch was much different than that provided by the Wong family in 1979, but it fit the description of the long necked, small headed creatures that have also been reported. Stella was in a moving car while the Wongs were on the lake in a fishing boat.

■

This chapter would not be complete without recounting the 1976 dramatic sighting by Betty and Harry Staines and the experiences of Ed Fletcher who photographed the animal in 1977.

Betty and Harry were out fishing in their fifteen-foot (4.5 m) boat near Rattlesnake Island, when a huge creature surfaced and swam alongside their boat for about thirty seconds. Betty had an opportunity to observe it with her binoculars and was able to determine that it had fins on its back. Shaken by the experience they too joined the ranks of the lifetime believers.

■

On August 3, 1976 Ed Fletcher and his daughter Diane were idling along in his high-speed runabout in Gellatly Bay in Westbank when an unusual animal swam across the bow of the boat within fifteen to thirty feet (4.5–9 m) of them. "If I hadn't shut off the engine, I could have run over him or even jumped on its back," Fletcher said.

They were so intrigued by the event that they rushed back to shore for a camera and headed back out accompanied by a friend, Gary Slaughter of Kelowna. Just as suddenly, a strange wave appeared on the surface and Ogopogo came up again.

"I saw his whole length this time, about seventy to seventy-five feet.

I shut off the engine when we got near him and coasted to within fifty feet of him and I shot the first picture."

The animal submerged and when he re-appeared, Ed accelerated the boat toward him, cut the engine and took another picture. They continued this process for a good hour.

"It would submerge, swim for at least two city blocks, then surface, and all the while we chased after him and took pictures."

In total, Ogopogo surfaced twelve to fifteen times and Ed managed to take six pictures. They estimated the creature to be at least forty feet (12 m) long in its coiled up position and between seventy to seventy-five feet (21–23 m) stretched out. The skin was smooth and brownish and blended in with the clear blue water. Ed's daughter said that there were no scales and it resembled a whale's skin with small ridges on its back. She estimated the visible section to be at least four feet (1.25 m) in diameter and felt that it swam in a flattened spiral cork-screw motion.

Both Diane and Gary saw the head from the back and it looked like a long flattened snake's head at least two and one half feet long (.75 m) and had two projectiles sticking out, resembling the ears of a Doberman.

Ed became a firm believer and almost obsessed with the creature. He had a plan that would involve passing a form of electric current through the water in his quest, but this was quickly frowned on by the Department of Fisheries. So certain were they of the animal's existence, the Fletchers returned in 1977 to experience even more encounters, further enhancing the drama.

■

I would be somewhat remiss if I failed to delight you with one of the more unusual experiences of the century, and one that in my books warrants the Groucho Marx Award for Ogopogo sightings. It is really more about human nature, our thought process and one individual's reaction to a face-to-face encounter with Ogopogo.

Kelowna's Dick Lucas was reserved in nature and as serious as any postmaster could ever be. When he spoke, people listened. He had gained the respect and public trust of his community so when Dick Lucas stepped forward to tell his family and friends that he had seen Ogopogo, no one would dare question his integrity.

Dick called me one day and invited me over. His wife Dollie said that he had an experience to share. It was in the late sixties or early seventies when he was out fishing just off Cedar Creek Bridge. He rowed his boat out 300 feet (91 m) from shore and settled in for a leisurely afternoon of fishing with his faithful dog at his side. The area was jumping with fish and Dick was expecting a fair catch.

"Quite suddenly the fish made a hasty retreat, the dog jumped up barking loudly and its hair stood on end." As Dick turned to calm the dog, there was a sudden rush of water nearby, creating a current of leaping waves in what was once a calm lake. Unable to believe his eyes, he observed a large portion of what appeared to be a snakelike creature surface at least twenty-five feet (7.5 m) in length. The section on the water's surface was approximately twelve inches wide and light green in color.

"Dick's reaction was most out of character and for those who knew him could be described as somewhat erratic. Realizing that it could be Ogopogo, he immediately thought of the $5,000 reward and threw safety to the wind. He looked around the boat for a rope, made a lasso and began rowing frantically toward the lake monster. When he was within arms length, he quickly recovered his sense of reality and brought the boat to an abrupt stop.

"You damn fool," he thought, "it probably eats people!"

Not wanting to have his boat overturned, he maintained his position, sitting in quiet fascination observing every detail of this amazing and unbelievable animal. There was no head or tail and it appeared to be feeding off something beneath the surface. Just as suddenly as it surfaced, it submerged much like a submarine, leaving a wake and ripples on the lake's surface. Dick, numbed by the experience, and realizing what he had been about to do, cut his fishing trip short and returned home to tell his story to his wife and friends.

Ogopogo Summary

As we enter the new millennium, fewer sightings of Okanagan Lake's unidentified swimming object are being reported. We can attribute this partially to the inconsistent attitude toward the use of polluting substances in our lake system that not only contribute to continued disease in our own species but to the annihilation of aquatic subspecies that no longer have a clean environment.

From 1997 to the present time thousands of kokanee were reportedly found floating atop Okanagan Lake, a major disaster to say the least. The Department of Fisheries biologists' investigations were unable to provide a reason for their demise and ruled out a virus or bacteria as cause of the fish kill. They believed similar die-offs were caused by sharp temperature increases in the water, low oxygen levels or a high concentrations of ammonia. Plain and simple, they just didn't know!

Peter Dill, a biology instructor at Okanagan University College, said the kokanee population has been virtually wiped out. He pointed to poor water management, like bad flood control practices, and diking as the main culprits. A grant of some $350,000 was given in an attempt to come up with some rationale for a very troublesome situation.

Then came the report that *Mysis* shrimp were the cause of the disappearing kokanee, and the Department of Fisheries gave approval to Bob Bowker and his west coast shrimp boat *The Trident Isle* to harvest the shrimp from the lake bottom for a ten-day period in the late summer of 1998. Scientists from the Ministry of Environment hoped that the 100-foot net would scoop up hundreds of tons of *Mysis* shrimp, the pesky creature that has been blamed for decimating the kokanee fish stocks.

When the ministry introduced the *Mysis relicta* or opossum shrimp to lakes such as Okanagan as feed for kokanee, it turned out to be a major competitor for feed with juvenile kokanee and today it's being blamed for having a major impact on kokanee populations according to Environment Ministry fisheries biologist Steve Mathews.

"This is the first time an experiment like this has been tried in a lake that has a problem with *Mysis* shrimp," fisheries biologist Dave Smith said. "We have no idea how well it will work."

"Though the trawler's net will be spread far behind the boat ," stated Smith, "there's little chance of catching species other than *Mysis* shrimp. The net should be just a few meters off the lake bottom."

In early 1999 there was an interesting article about trawling for *Mysis* shrimp in one of the newspapers that implied this method of harvesting *Mysis* shrimp actually increases pollution in a water basin and is basically unfriendly to the environment. Considering the fact that they have plans to continue trawling for *Mysis* shrimp into the millennium, without doing a proper study of its effect on the lake system, it is necessary to document the data for future reference.

As an Ogopogo researcher and advocate, my concerns were kindled when I learned that they had chosen an area around Okanagan Center, a part of the lake often frequented by Ogopogo, according to documented sightings. This did not sit too well with me as I awaited news reports hoping that shrimp were all they were going to net.

Frank Rieger, who had one of the more dramatic sightings of Ogopogo in 1980, speculates that the whalelike creature they saw feeding on kokanee must eat about ninety-nine pounds (45 kg) of fish a day, and he fears the sharply dropping fish population in Okanagan Lake will soon give Ogopogo hunger pangs.

"I wonder if it will eat its way into public view as it has to come closer to shore to feed," he said. "There used to be millions of kokanee in that lake and now there's almost none. The trout limit used to be 25 a day and now it's only six and you have a tough time getting six. I've almost quit fishing, its not worth the time."

Of course no mention was ever made of the disbursement of molybdenum into the lake from the former Brenda Mines site as a contributing factor to an already existing condition. Nor has mention been made of human feces and raw sewage that were found seeping into the lake system because of crossed connections and that allowed seepage into the drinking water, creating a cryptosporidium outbreak in 1996.

Fred Alcock took a dip in Okanagan Lake almost a quarter of a century ago and he has never gone in since. As Chief Public Health Inspector from 1948 to 1978, Alcock disagreed with the government's decision to use the herbicide Killex to battle milfoil in the lake.

"I didn't agree with dosing the lake with cholorinated hydrocarbons," recalls Alcock. It was enough to keep him from swimming in the pristine lake he loved. Alcock, along with David Clarke, the medical health officer for the southern Okanagan, fought city council tooth and nail to keep sewage and chemicals out of the lake, with little success.

Twenty-five years ago the *Daily Courier* quoted Clarke's plea to municipal officials: "I have spent the better part of my professional life trying to save that great lake out there and I am not going to sit idle and see it ruined forever."

One would assume that harmful substances would not be introduced due to the thousands of people who use Okanagan Lake as the major source of drinking water, and therefore would present no threat to the human population, the marine species nor plant life. But once again, no one really knows the long term ramifications of experimental decisions such as the molybdenum run-off, decisions designed to appease the general public in order to obtain approvals. Personally, I prefer to err on the side of caution.

The hydroplane races that have become an annual summer event in Okanagan Lake only add to the problems. Not only was the intense sound creating an environmental havoc to all aquatic life, it could prove disastrous for species of the Ogopogo community. There is no doubt that this event has driven the animals to greater depths and away from the downtown area of the city of Kelowna. All one has to do is check the decrease in the number of sightings during the peak Ogopogo months of July and August. No mention of possible oil spills and other fuel-related problems that could arise has even been mentioned, as large water craft raced up and down the lake adjacent to the popular beach areas in Kelowna.

Ironically, a new hydroplane, dubbed *Lake Monster*, complete with snarling teeth, ferocious red eyes and sharp claws, is being built. If all goes according to plan, this powerful, noisy mechanical monster will soon be making its racing debut.

Most interesting was the Endangered Species Exhibit held at Okanagan University College in May of 1999/2000. Species were listed and discussed, but there was no mention whatsoever of the Ogopogo family, which is truly endangered and should be one of the most protected animals of our time. Protection under the Fisheries Act or Wildlife Act does not afford assurance that those who continue to create a hostile environment in Okanagan Lake will stop the practices or even consider long-term effects.

On March 28, 2000 I wrote the following letter:

> When I wrote my first book on Ogopogo in 1976 and even with the publication of the second book in 1986, I would not have had the courage nor the visual proof to suggest putting this unidentifiable species on the Endangered List. However as I complete the third volume and work with recent photographs including one that clearly shows a large unknown animal with body, neck and head out of the water there is the realization that somewhere "we have perhaps missed an opportunity." Recent videotape reveals that these animals swim together in small groups of two or more. Whether we wish to admit it or not there is a species in Okanagan Lake that is being considered a myth or legend when in reality they are a group of large unknown aquatic animals, very real and very much alive.
>
> I would hate to challenge this myth or legend during a scuffle as I would clearly lose. Pollution, both sound and chemical, is harmful to all aquatic life in our lake system including these unidentified animals we all know as "OGOPOGO."
>
> It is this recent evidence that has convinced me of the need to place this creature or creatures on the Endangered Species List. We are privy to having this species as a resident of Okanagan Lake, not for the purpose of promoting tourism, but for the appreciation of its very existence. —Arlene Gaal

I remember a telephone conversation with a gentleman in Seattle, Washington a few years ago. This person, who shall remain nameless, claimed to have tossed dynamite into Okanagan Lake near Peachland in an attempt to frighten Ogopogo into surfacing. He had plans to return, and I wasted no time in questioning his rationale and pointed out the probable consequences should he ever get caught.

Ogopogo friend and advocate Andrew Bennett has created a link to his SunnyOkanagan.com website under Endangered Species, leading to a B.C. Conservation field observation form, which also allows an individual to document Ogopogo sightings. In time, if enough sightings are registered, it could eventually pressure government into proclaiming Ogopogo an Endangered Species.

We still have opportunity to protect one of the most scenic and picturesque lakes in Canada, but time is certainly not on our side. That will be up to the overseers of this fine valley, and only if they have the ability to take a stand on issues that matter most.

I ponder the words of my three-year-old grandson, Joshua. He looked at me intently one day as he watched me working on this latest addition to my Ogopogo scripts and stated: "Dinosaurs are extinct," and then added, "They are not around any more."

This could very well be the anguish of a young child in the year 2010 or 2050 when discussions or stories of Ogopogo are being told. If we fail to take control of our lake system and present practices continue, the existence of this fine animal could go the way of its predecessors.

As I complete the final chapter of this book, I do so with some relief and knowledge that N'ha-a-itk/Ogopogo is alive and well in Okanagan Lake as we enter the year 2000.

This reassurance can be attributed to the last documented sighting for the twentieth century which crossed my desk within hours of the experience and the first videotaped sighting for the year 2000.

It is late afternoon, December 8, 1999. A call has just come in from a Westbank couple who had a most dramatic sighting while shopping in Peachland at noon. Stan and Nellie Bayrack, both retired, stopped to talk to an Electrolux salesman before going into the bakery. Stan's eyes moved out into the lake as he saw something large and dark on the surface. At first he thought it was a moose, and as Nellie glanced over she commented that it could perhaps be a boat. The salesman said, "It might be Ogopogo."

Another portion surfaces, and the object begins to move. They keep watching while in conversation and very suddenly, "Something shot straight up, its head looked both ways and then it dove down. It was the most exciting experience of my life, if I never have another, this has to be complete," said Nellie. Stan agreed. The salesman has not as yet been found for comment.

The lake was flat, it was snowing slightly and the temperature was bordering forty-two degrees Fahrenheit (6°C). The lake of course, was much colder. Nellie prepared a sketch of their experience.

A December sighting is rare, but the Bayracks are in good company for in 1969 *Kelowna Daily Courier* publisher, R. P. Maclean after twelve years of speculating about the animal's existence, observed several protrusions surface only a few yards away as he was feeding the geese from his lakeshore home on Abbot Street. The ducks flew off in fright and Roy

Patterson Maclean watched in amazement as the animal made a right angle turn and moved off into deeper water. He later noted: "To casually brush off the evidence is to charge a large and responsible section of the population of the Okanagan Valley with a conspiracy to bamboozle the world. R.P.M."

The time was 7:00 A.M., the date March 9, 2000. Kevin Berry glanced out the bedroom window of his home at Okanagan Centre. He alerted the rest of the family by yelling, "Ogopogo." His children, Jackson and Layana and his brother Roy headed for the deck to see for themselves as Kevin searched for his videocamera. They observed a large animal with a long contrail moving swiftly in a southerly direction. Kevin rushed out, video-camera in hand and taped the last few seconds before the animal made three distinct forward thrusts, displacing a good fifty feet (15 m) of water around it and then submerged. The head and neck could be clearly seen with each thrust. When looking at the video there is another angled contrail about thirty feet (9 m) long moving toward the main animal from the right. The question of perhaps two animals is raised when the tape is advanced frame by frame and two clear dark objects appear to be swimming parallel to each other with a definite ten to fifteen feet (3–4.5 m) of water in between. It is just after this sequence that there is the unusual commotion or thrusting movement, making the front end of the animal visible.

Kevin Berry shot his first videotape of two animals swimming together in the same area of the lake March 15, 1994. Almost six years to the day, on March 9, 2000, Kevin was privileged to videotape the animal once more. In both instances the lake is perfectly calm and the animals are clearly visible.

The year 2000 known as the year of the dragon was followed in 2001 by the year of the snake according to Chinese culture. Here in the Okanagan Valley, however, the new millennium was a capitulation to Ogopogo. The hype and interest generated by this animal, considered myth by some and a firm reality by others, rivals no other period in the years of my investigations.

Kevin Berry's March 9, 2000 sighting near Okanagan Centre, ignited the enthusiasm of film crews from Los Angeles with the *Extra* team being the first to arrive in Kelowna. They were soon followed by Next Entertainment filming a series for Fox's *Million Dollar Mystery* and Indigo Films shooting a segment for History Channel called *History's Mysteries*. The pace was set for a very busy season and requests for information and interviews were nonstop and included CTV's morning show with Wei Chan, *Toronto Sun*'s "View from the West" by Daniel Girard as well as Suzanne Wilton's article for the *Calgary Herald* "The Search for B.C. Lake Monster," to name only a few.

The 2 million dollar reward, announced by Penticton's Rotary Club and the Penticton and Wine Country Chamber of Commerce, to be paid to any person finding alive and definitely verifying Ogopogo's existence, was no doubt the calling card. However, Bill Steciuk and his *Search for Ogopogo* team also managed to stir up the waters.

Plans for the year 2000 search for Ogopogo began to materialize in early January through talks with Primal Productions in Winnipeg. However, as time moved closer to the July 15 designated start date, Bill Steciuk found it necessary to seek new producers to take over the search, reducing the lake time to three weeks. Can Pro Production's Kelowna underwater specialist, Len Melnyk, joined forces with Steciuk and Tripod Productions. It looked like a winning team would be out on the lake from August 10 to September 1.

The plan was to conduct a daily search of Lake Okanagan based on predetermined quadrants from the chronology of Ogopogo sightings over the past fifty years. Two types of sonar imaging equipment included a forward dual-axis scanning sonar produced by Interphase Technology of Soquel, California, chosen for its user friendly characteristics and ability to scan forward, downward or a combination of both, and a side scan sonar. Can Pro's remote operations vehicle (ROV) was capable of reaching depths of 984 feet (300 m), more than adequate to cover the greatest depths of the lake. A back-up boat and divers were ready to move on a moment's notice should anything come into view. With all the bases covered, all they could do was wait and pray.

As the search wound down, the team, tired but optimistic, decided to recheck the area near the mouth of Bellevue Creek. It was late August, and only a few days remained, so there was nothing to lose. They drove the boat at a slow cruise determined not to miss anything. Upon entering an area registering a depth of 20 feet (6 m), the sonar picked up a large animate object. As luck would have it, they were able to save the image on the computer's hard drive. Bill Steciuk was elated by the hit. The search had not been completely in vain. In fact, he and Len Melnyk were already making plans for a 2001 search. "All the hours I logged on the water has taught me something. I really think I know how to find Ogopogo," stated Steciuk.

Just as Can Pro Productions moved out, Tokyo's Nippon Television moved right in for what would be their third visit to Kelowna in ten years. We had been communicating for almost a month discussing plans to search for Ogopogo for their *Special Project 200X Unidentified Mystery Animals* program to be aired in Japan October 8 and 15. The team would conduct an intense underwater and ondeck search of Lake Okanagan in hope of finding something.

Tokyo project director, Wataru Ito was in charge. Upon his arrival to Kelowna, he and Yoshi Nishimoto from Office Kei in New York came to my home for a meeting. I had agreed to act as a consultant, and they needed information. Many questions and ideas were bounced around an a plan of attack formulated.

Masaji Yoshida, Yoshiro Yasuoka and Isao Zaitsu were also part of the Tokyo team. Pauline Heaton and Chris Hanson of Watervisons drove in from Vancouver to join Patrick McGuillon who had arrived earlier. Mike Blackshaw was in charge of the ROV, Mike Muirhead the side sonar operation and the Diving Dynamics team of Vern Johnson and Teresa were prepared to follow through with their expertise.

Dr. Roy Mackal, biochemist and zoologist for the University of Chicago, would supervise the search. A recognized cryptozoologist, Dr. Mackal carried a set of impressive credentials having authored books and papers on cryptozoology as well as a treatise on his efforts to find Mokele-mbembe, an African dinosaur-like aquatic animal. We both had worked together as consultants for an *Unsolved Mysteries* episode on Ogopogo in 1989.

It was decided to place five buoys strung with bait at strategic points along the search path as a lure for Ogopogo. An underwater camera attached to a smaller boat was positioned and the main side-scan sonar and ROV was positioned on the lead vessel. They had a well-coordinated plan and everything appeared capable of moving like clockwork. The first two days were disrupted by poor weather conditions and equipment failures. However, on the third day sunshine returned summer to the Okanagan and the search team headed toward Rattlesnake Island, the legendary home of Ogopogo, with great expectations. Much like the previous search, the Japanese reported two interesting sonar readings, one near Bear Creek and close to one of the baited buoys. One object was at least forty feet (12 m) long and Nippon talked about entering it as evidence of Ogopogo's existence in the 2 Million Dollar Reward Competition.

A still photo taken in September across from Monteo Beach Resort in

Kelowna by a local minister shows an unusual object surfacing about two thirds out on Lake Okanagan while in October, the shrimp boaters were quite shaken when an animal over forty feet (12 m) long broke through their nets leaving a gaping hole. The year 2000 could not have ended on a more dramatic note.

On January 16, 2001, my attention was drawn to the CHBC evening news as weatherman Mike Roberts reported that their cameras had picked up an unusual animate object swimming swiftly through the lake just north of Okanagan Lake Bridge near the west side.

Cameraman, Colin Macdonald says he was scanning the lake for a weather shot when he spotted a one-foot-long aquatic animal above water, moving quickly and leaving a long wake. Macdonald captured one minute and forty-five seconds of footage and reported that it was visible for a few minutes. It submerged before it traveled under the Okanagan Lake Bridge. Macdonald was unable to determine the nature of the beast. "It seems odd for a beaver to be swimming so far out in the lake," stated Mike Roberts.

A few days later, a call from Erik Loney, newsman for KREM Television in Seattle, requested an interview for a program they would produce on legends, myths and monsters to be aired in the Pacific northwest. The team would arrive in mid-February. I braced myself for another busy season for Ogopogo and its solicitors.

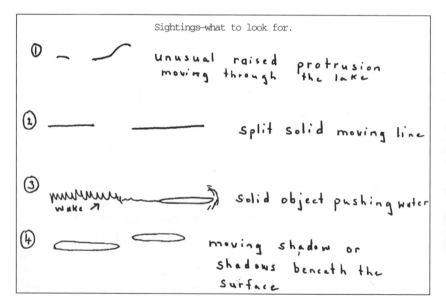

Sightings—what to look for.

① Unusual raised protrusion moving through the lake

② Split solid moving line

③ wake → Solid object pushing water

④ moving shadow or shadows beneath the surface

merged. The whole episode took approx. 20 to 25 seconds and no further sighting took place.

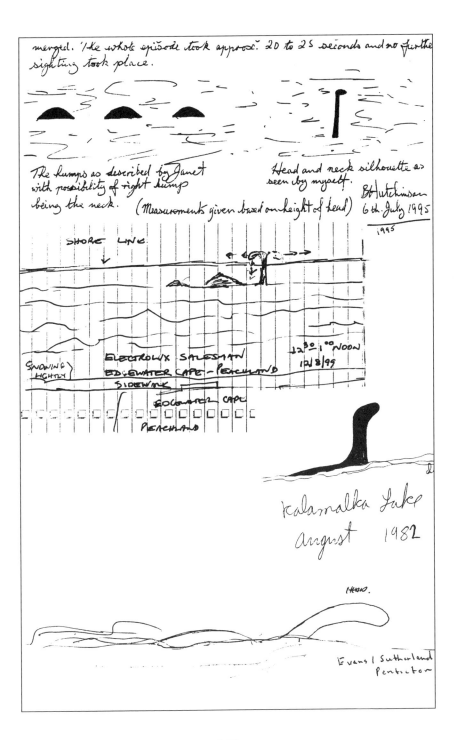

The humps as described by Janet with possibility of right hump being the neck.

Head and neck silhouette as seen by myself.

B. Hutchinson
6th. July 1995

(Measurements given based on height of head)

1995

SHORE LINE.

ELECTROLUX SALESMAN
EDGEWATER CAPE - PEACHLAND
SIDEWALK
EDGEWATER CAPE
PEACHLAND

SNOWING LIGHTLY

12:30 - 1:00 NOON
12/8/99

Kalamalka Lake
August 1982

HEAD.

Evans / Sutherland
Penticton

181

Find Ogopogo, win $2 million

Penticton agencies organize contest that begins Labour Day, with prize money underwritten by Lloyd's of London

By STEVE MacNAULL
The Okanagan Saturday

Wanted: Ogopogo.
Reward: $2 million.
The Penticton Chamber of

which a $2-million prize will be paid to anyone safely capturing the mythical Okanagan Lake monster or providing scientific proof he exists.

"There has to be something out there. There's too many people who have seen something," said Penticton Chamber of Commerce manager John Singleton.

"This initiative is meant to be a Valley-wide one to create some fun for families and tourists alike."

An insurance policy from Lloyd's of London is underwriting the $2-million prize. It cost about $2,500 to buy.

Lloyd's of London is known for insuring some unusual requests, such

Corporate sponsors have already come up with the money to cover the cost of the Ogopogo policy, and the prize money could grow if more money is raised to buy a bigger policy.

While the search promotion was announced Thursday at an Okanagan Chamber of Commerce Week reception in Summerland, doesn't actually kick off until Labour Day.

The contest from then runs one year to Labour Day 2001.

OUC will evaluate and verify any contest winners.

The search stemmed from millennium project discussions and spread to a Valley-

mayors from throughout the Okanagan expressed interest in it.
Making Ogopogo the centre of it just made sense.
He's already captured the imagine

Many details of the latest search have to be worked out, but plans call for printing up thousands of free souvenir search permits.

Mean machine

KUHA's snarling Lake Monster a speedy cousin for Ogopogo

By RON SEYMOUR
- The Daily Courier

Ogopogo sightings are always a bit suspect, but there's absolutely no doubt the Lake Monster will be seen this April.

And there'll be no mistaking this powerful, noisy creature with a giant eel or salamander.

The first hydroplane to be made in Canada since 1961 will roar across Okanagan Lake in racing trials set for early spring.

"It's taken a lot of time and a lot of work, but we're almost ready to go from concept to combat," said Jay Logie, president of the Kelowna Unlimited Hydroplane Association.

Graphic artists last week applied a distinctive green-and-black design to a prototype of the hydroplane. The Lake Monster with a heavily clawed, snarling and scaly beast, sure to turn a few heads on the hydroplane circuit this summer.

"Obviously, we're trying to draw on the Ogopogo connection," Logie said. "But we want to develop our own legend, too."

The prototype will be taken to Ontario next weekend for a tour of boat shows. Though it's the same size as a hydroplane, it lacks an engine "so it only goes as fast as the truck it's in," Logie jokes.

The boat that will actually be used in racing must still be assembled by KUHA's team of more than 100 engineers, journeymen and other craftsmen. The hydroplane association, created in 1996, has the support of about 50 Kelowna companies, including such heavyweights as Western Star Trucks, Kelowna Flightcraft and Campion Marine.

"We've got experts in every field working on the project," Logie said, adding that the association has also consulted with hydroplane builders in the U.S.

GARY NYLANDER/The Daily Courier

Jerry Ashley, foreground, and Mike Brodie of Sign Craft use airbrushes to create the Lake Monster paint scheme on the Kelowna Unlimited Hydroplane Association's prototype boat.

Even before its sleek hull touches the water, the Lake Monster should have already acquired a reputation for originality. Logie says it's the first high-speed boat to combine aircraft and hydroplane technology, and should have no trouble reaching speeds of up to 200 miles per hour.

Logie, who has more than 10 years

experience as a jet mechanic and troubleshooter, estimates the value of donated material and labour in the Lake Monster at about $500,000.

"You just don't go out and throw a boat like this together overnight," he said. "We all wanted to be in the water right after we started, but it's taken time to do it right."

Ogopogo may come home after all

Filmmaker says he'll consider shooting some scenes in the Valley

By DON PLANT
The Daily Courier

Ogopogo may ham it up in Okanagan Lake for a feature film after all.

The English producer who wrote the script for a $25-million movie about the lake creature says he's keen on exploring Okanagan locations and would consider shooting a few scenes here.

Barry Authors is committed to filming the bulk of his independent family drama in Manitoba. But he was surprised to learn Thursday about the uninhabited shoreline along Okanagan Mountain Park, which suits the isolated terrain he's looking for.

"I'm sorry I hadn't heard about it," Authors said from his home just outside London. "We'd have no objection to shoot in the Okanagan. The director and I would be quite prepared to come for a look. Maybe we could shoot a portion of it there. It's certainly open for discussion."

Authors flew to Vancouver last year to inquire about B.C. locations for his project. Local film commissioner Mark Flett sent him photos of the area, but Authors concluded it was unsuitable because the Okanagan appeared too developed and commercial.

"We've got to have a place you believe this creature has been hiding in for centuries," he said. "It has to be a remote lake where a helicopter crashes and loses its equipment."

The movie is about a New York oil company troubleshooter who is brought to a remote lake in B.C. to look for the lost machinery. Cancelling a trip to Disney World with his son, he decides to bring the boy and they meet up with bad guys and Ogopogo.

Authors settled on Lake Winnipeg and the Whiteshell region of eastern Manitoba for the film's main locations because industry representatives in Winnipeg "bent over backwards" to accommodate him. They're offering tax credits of up to 40 per cent on labour costs, professional crews are available and executive producer Kim Todd is willing to do much of the fund-raising.

Thursday, Flett said he the City of

Trawler netting harvest of mysis shrimp

By J.P. SQUIRE
The Daily Courier

The Trident Isle is pulling pounds of mysis shrimp from the bottom of Okanagan Lake.

The 42-foot boat from the Coast had several trial runs north of Kelowna on Sunday and continued harvesting Monday.

"We're in the middle of letting out the net on a hot spot right now," said fisheries biologist Dave Smith in a cellular phone call about 10 a.m. Monday.

"We're catching shrimp the way we expected – about two pounds in 15 minutes."

The Environment Ministry is paying Bob Bowker, owner of the Trident Isle, $25,000 to trawl for shrimp in the lake

GARY NYLANDER/The Daily Courier

Fisherman Bob Bowker checks over a special net he's using to catch mysis shrimp in Okanagan Lake. It's hoped harvesting will reduce the shrimp population.

for 10 days.
Scientists are testing a new 100-foot net which Bowker can tow behind his boat at depths of 200 metres.
Mysis shrimp stay close to the bottom during daylight hours while at night, they can be found at various depths. Bowker will trawl primarily around Okanagan Centre, where the highest concentrations of the mysis shrimp

have been found.
The shrimp, which grow as large as a centimetre long, were introduced to the lake in the early 1970s to provide food for the kokanee.
The plan backfired when the shrimp started competing with the kokanee for plankton.
The ministry has issued six shrimp permits on an experimental basis but only one fisherman from Lumby has actively caught shrimp during the last two years.
Lee Granberg sold his catch to fish food buyers but he's reduced the mysis stocks by less than one per cent per year.
Scientists hope the larger shrimp boat and new net can reduce the stocks by five to 10 per cent annually.

182

Last Word

To date, there is no one who can truthfully say just what animal species live in the waters of Okanagan Lake and similar lake systems throughout the world. There are those who attribute the sightings to the lake rolling over, a volcanic gas eruption, and even a creature from a parallel universe. More serious scientists like Dr. Roy Mackal attest that it may be a *Zuegledon*, a prehistoric whale that was in its prime about 20 million years ago, and believes remnants of the species may inhabit underground rivers and lakes connected to the seas. Others adhere to the reptilian *Plesiosaur* theory believing the animals became landlocked during the Ice Age. The sturgeon theory will not go away, and even though Fisheries Departments state that no sturgeon has ever been reported or caught in Okanagan Lake or the surrounding lakes, they do not entirely close the door. The perpetuation of a mystery is perhaps not in the not knowing, but it is the knowing that provides vindication to all who dare come forward.

As the final chapter is written, there is little doubt of my affirmation. Some cryptozoologists believe "we, as investigators, should not state that there is a large unknown animal living in a lake. Witnesses do." However, for those of us who have personally witnessed a large object that is neither whale, submarine nor man-made creation, break water in Okanagan Lake, there is no rational explanation other than Ogopogo, a stand must be taken. To do otherwise would be wavering in the sight of truth and sending an uncertain signal to future witnesses who, at the best of times, report in the face of ridicule.

To my cryptozoologist friends who chose to make me an Honorary Member of the B.C. Cryptozoology Club, may this book be a strength in the continued search for unknown animals.

For those of us who know that Okanagan Lake can indeed sustain large Ogopogo/N'ha-a-itk animals, a silent prayer goes out to the Creator that our children will continue to have an opportunity to enjoy the mystery that pervades this beautiful Okanagan Valley and its surrounding lakes.

In the sunny Okanagan, where the sun forever smiles
Lies a lake of sky-blue waters stretching for a hundred miles
Long before the first white settlers made this lovely land their home
Indians knew of a strange creature which these lovely waters roam;
Known to them as "Ogopogo", or the one with many humps
Frisking in the summer evenings, making great waves as he jumps.
But the white man laughed about it—put it down to Indian lore,
How could a great sea-serpent live so far from Ocean's shore?
But after they themselves had seen it, swimming there—
　　they laughed no more.

So today the summer tourist strolling on the sandy beach
Keeps his camera at the ready, always there within his reach.
Some there are who claim they've seen it basking in some quiet bay;
They will swear they're not mistaken swear it to their dying day.

Now an evil thing has happened! Curse that awful milfoil weed.
Choking all the lovely beaches. Like the fabled mustard seed!
It will multiply by millions spreading with amazing speed.
How to fight this green invader? I hope not with 2-4-D!
The risk of losing Ogopogo is too great, you will agree;

If we poison Ogopogo can we face our children's scorn?
Knowing he is lost forever to generations yet unborn
Shall we cynically keep saying, "Ogopogo is a fake,"
Till we see his bloated body belly upwards in the lake!

　　　　　—Dudley Fuller (*Shoppers Guide*, May 24, 1977)

Chronology

1700s According to Mrs. Louise Gilbert, the Okanakane Indians made a huge dugout canoe with a carving of N'ha-a-itk, the water god, on its bow.

1860 White settlers saw the monster and patrolled the waters edge at Mission Creek with rifles to protect their families should Ogopogo attack. • John MacDougal swims his team of horses across Okanagan Lake behind his canoe. They are pulled under by a mysterious force and are never seen again.

1872 Mrs. Susan Allison, from her Westbank ranch, sights a creature swimming against the waves.

1873 While riding the trail from her husband's ranch, Mrs. Susan Allison met a group of Indians who tell of seeing N'ha-a-itk on the lake near Squally Point.

1886 Richard Wellington tells of an elderly Scot visiting Ewings Landing who was greatly disturbed by what he saw on the lake, and spoke about a moving log going faster than he could row.

1888 Alfred Postill sees N'ha-a-itk swimming on the surface of the lake while building a raft to transport lumber from the family sawmill to Penticton.

1890 Indians towing venison behind a canoe, see two greenish black animals four feet high with snakelike heads surface one behind the other. • Captain Thomas Short while sailing the steamer *Jubilee* close to Squally Point observes a fifteen-foot (4.6 m) creature with a head like a ram and visible fins moving through the lake.

1900 At age ten, Mrs. Ruth Richardson remembers seeing Ogopogo a good three feet (1 m) out of the water, "looking at me as though I was as much of a curiosity to him as he was to me." She observes scales and three points on the back of the neck. • While fishing near Squally Point, H. D. B. Lyons finds himself being dragged part way around Rattlesnake Island by an unknown force. • Mrs. Maude Chrichton is frightened by Ogopogo as she sits brushing her hair on the beach near Okanagan Mission.

1914 A party of Westbank and Nicola Valley Indians find the decomposed body of an unusual animal across from Rattlesnake Island. The creature weighed in at 400 pounds (181 kg).

1919 David Lloyd Jones sees an animal cavorting in the lake near the Bear Creek log booms while on board his Kelowna Sawmill tugboat.

1923 Manuel Louie, his son and five friends, while swimming in Okanagan Lake, observe a large creature surface, swim in their direction and submerge just before reaching them. Terrified, everyone quickly leaves the water. • Captain Matt Reid of SS *Okanagan* spots Ogopogo near Rattlesnake Island across from Peachland. • **July 21:** Mrs. Lydia Hodgson of Ewings Landing observes an unusual creature among the weeds in Okanagan Lake.

1924 Captain Joseph Weeks of the Okanagan Steam boats and Angus McKinnon agree to blow their boat whistles to alert the locals should they see N'ha-a-itk. Whistle sounds are often heard. • Mr. Angus Gray, manager of Captain Dew Waters Farm sits with a group of men on the wharf at Fintry having just finished stacking boxes of apples aboard the lake steamer, SS *Sicamous*. An animal traveling at an estimated speed of 30 mph (48 km/h) close to shore and heading north is seen. • When Mr. Boyd returned home from his early morning fishing trip, his face was blanched. He talks of seeing a head and snakelike body emerge a half mile from shore, look around and quietly submerge.

1925 **August 16:** Ogopogo is sighted by James Mitchell while boating between Penticton and Summerland. He refutes the sturgeon theory proposed by J. P. Babcock, deputy commissioner of fisheries. • **August 17:** At 7:00 A.M. J. Mitchell Boyd of Ewings Landing is out fishing when he spots an unusual object moving at high speed. • **September 1:** Six Pacific coast centers hold discussions on the formation of hunting parties to capture Ogopogo.

1926 **July:** Ogopogo appears to at least nine witnesses four or five times during the month. A low trout catch is noted. • **July 19:** John L. Logie finds himself racing Ogopogo in his car early morning near Peachland. His wife and two grandchildren are astounded by the creature's appearance as is P.J. Dodwell of Summerland who was driving the Logie car. • **August:** Two unnamed Ashcroft men are reported to be waiting on the west side of Okanagan Lake armed with rifles and with intentions to kill Ogopogo. • **August:** Joe Spurrier, a sporting goods owner, fires a shot at N'ha-a-itk with a high velocity rifle. He misses as the animal submerges but hits a nearby cottage. • **August 23:** Ogopogo, is now the official name of the famous Okanagan sea serpent. Vernon Rotarian dubs creature in a song while at a Vancouver Board of Trade delegation touring the Okanagan. • **August 28:** First report of more than one Ogopogo in Okanagan Lake as Joe Spurrier attempts to shoot the family of three from his boat a mile (1.6 km) south of the Aquatic Club in Kelowna. • **August 29:** On the second day of the regatta R. E. Taylor, F. A. Taylor, and Messrs. St. George, Baldwin and Foster were shocked to see what they first thought to be a fake Ogopogo submerge. • **August 31:** An announcement is made by the B.C. Government: "Okanagan Ferry To Be Armed Against Ogopogo Tribe." • **September:** While J. S. Stockwell observes the creature chasing its tail near south Kelowna,

Manley Barnes sees it almost sixty yards (55 m) out in the lake. • **September 16:** Thirty carloads of people are stunned by the creature cavorting off a beach in Okanagan Mission. • **October:** Summerland residents spot Ogopogo fifty yards (46 m) from shore and note a sheeplike head. • **October 17:** Faster than the "speediest motorboat" is how George Henry describes his sighting of the lake monster. • **November 23:** Headlines read: "Ogopogo is Uninvited Guest at Baptismal Service" and is seen by over fifty people including L. L. Wilkins, his father-in-law Mr. Guerney, and simultaneously by Mrs. H. Clifton of Penticton and Mrs. Fenton of Westbank.

1927 **January:** A shiny black log suddenly submerges into the lake near Okanagan Mission as Primrose Upton (Walker) is mystified.

1928 **August 16:** As Captain James Roe backs the SS *Pentowna* out of Naramata, passengers Mr. and Mrs. H. Neil see Ogopogo blocking the way.

1930 **July:** Melvin Currie and friend Aaron Lewis are swimming in the lake near the Mission. They wade out chest deep about ten feet (3 m) apart when Melvin spots a thirty-foot-long (9 m) object which tapered to the far end, slowly swimming in front. Both return quickly to shore, and Melvin Currie never again ventured out in the lake.

1931 **August:** An object fifteen feet (4.6 m) long surfaces and submerges several times near Mrs. Mary Gartrell and Mrs. Lizzie Gartrell at around 9:00 A.M. near Trout Creek Point in Summerland. • **October:** A huge eel-like fish swims rapidly through Okanagan Lake about fifty feet (15 m) from shore as Mr. and Mrs. O. Jennens eat breakfast at their Vimy Avenue home. The object is twenty feet (6 m) long with an animal-like head and large fin. • Pat Ireland and friend see Ogopogo's head, neck and body up out of the water just north of Okanagan Lake Bridge. Pat recreates the event with a sketch.

1932 Captain Joseph Weeks of the SS *Sicamous* is mystified by a column of vapor sixty feet (18 m) wide and 150 feet (46 m) high, rising out of Okanagan Lake near Gellatly Bay.

1933 **July:** Mrs. Agar of Wilson Landing comes within twenty feet (6 m) of a huge log which suddenly disappears as she returns home in her motorboat.

1935 **Midsummer:** Audrey Gellatly, a frightened little girl, sees a log slither off the beach into the lake. • Four Vernon residents encounter Ogopogo by moonlight as it comes to within fifteen feet (4.6 m) of their rowboat and circles before heading toward the center of the lake. • **October 6:** While fishing at the north end, Edward and Charles Graham and Jim Ripley of England see Ogopogo.

1936 Geoffrey Tozer and Andy Aiken are terrified when a large creature lunges twelve to twenty-five feet (3.6–7.6 m) out of the water and pulls a seagull under while they are fishing near the mouth of Mission Creek. • Percy Hancock of Naramata is fishing opposite Paradise Island when he is startled by a splashing 200 yards (183 m) out. A sheeplike head is followed by a snakelike body as the creature swims about and then moves off toward Rattlesnake Island.

1940: Mrs. Stella Fenton, while walking with her children along a Westbank beach, is alerted by a large animal coming out of the water chasing a terrified bird. Instinctively they throw rocks at the creature who disappears below the surface as it releases the bird. • The lake creature is seen by Naramata orchardist, Mr. Smith and his two sons. It surfaces, submerges, then rises up as though at play and swims off in an undulating pattern. • Mrs. Root Lyon, wife of the Penticton Mayor, and companion Dote wade out into the lake along Lakeshore Drive. What first looks like a speedboat coming at them soon becomes a large animal humming and splashing. They see a sheeplike head with spiky hairs sticking out from its mouth swim by. Realizing it was Ogopogo, they head for shore and observe three humps swimming away.

1942 While looking over the lake from Knox Mountain, Frank W. Smith sees a creature moving in large circles as it surfaces and submerges. • The Snyder family is certain the lake creature slithered off a ledge near Rattlesnake Island as they were fishing. It then took off toward Trepanier Bay.

1946 Mrs. Kay Bissett, her children and other witnesses from Summerland see Ogopogo at play for half an hour before it hits the water sharply with its tail and heads out.

1948 **February 26:** Don Nourse observes Ogopups in Okanagan Lake and collects a number of witnesses to see them swimming fifty feet (115 m) from shore. • As John Greig returns home, he sees a reptilian-like creature with webbed feet in the field that had flooded off Lakeshore Road. It slowly backed down and disappeared.

1949 **June:** A crowd of people off Penticton Beach encounter a black, fifty-foot (115 m) object shortly before 8:00 A.M. • **July 2:** Mr. and Mrs. L. Kerry and visitors Mr. and Mrs. W. Watson Jr. and families excitedly call Dr. Underhill and his wife after observing the creature for a time. Dr. Underhill sees more than one animal through his binoculars. • **July 10:** An unidentified animal follows Rita Bridges and Louis Guide as they row their boat off Siwash Point. • **July 16:** One-time skeptic, Captain Jack McLeod of the CPR *Tugboat*, becomes a firm believer when Ogopogo surfaces. • **July 20:** A request is made for the protection of Ogopogo by R. P. McLean, publisher of the *Kelowna Daily Courier*. The attorney general responds, protecting the animal under section 26 of the Fisheries Act. This protection remains in force today. • **August 11:** While working on the roof of the Kelowna Growers Exchange, Cedric Boyer, Jack Riorda and Albert Cicho see a fifty-foot (115 m) long creature in the lake. It was also later seen by cubmaster Marjorie Thompson and eight cub scouts on the west side near Bear Creek.

1950 Mrs. Campbell reports seeing two heads surface in the lake four or five feet (1.2–1.5 m) out of the water. • **June 1:** A. W. Gray, writer and historian, along with his wife and three children and Rosemary Hobbs, observe Ogopogo move as fast as a motorboat near Squally Point. • **June 23:** Ogopogo swims by Gyro Park as Basil Sellick and other property owners conduct an open-door meeting. • **June 25:** As Jack Schell and his wife are heading off to work at 9:45 A.M. the creature is seventy-five feet (23 m) from shore. • **June 29:** Greyhound bus driv-

188

er Gordon Radcliffe pulls the bus to the side of the road just north of Summerland as he and fifteen passengers observe a serpentine-headed creature frolic in Okanagan Lake for over five minutes. • **August 12:** Ogopogo resembles a large garden hose thrashing in the water, according to Reverend W. S. Beams, rector of St. Saviors Anglican Church in Naramata, who spots the animal at 4:30 P.M. • **August 14:** A creature between sixty and seventy feet (18–21 m) in length is observed for over thirty minutes by R. A. Roylance and his crew of orchardists. • **August 18:** Milton Haner, George Flondra, A. Dewiles and M. Cryderman watch an unusual object speeding in the lake near Okanagan Landing.

1951 January: David Gellatly, his wife and daughter along with a houseful of guests see an unusual wave with no boat in sight. One of the guests takes chase in a car when the wave makes a sudden right-angled turn and swims across the lake. • **May 18:** Cedric McNair Stringer and Vic Cowley, both local businessmen, report an encounter with Ogopogo while fishing off Bear Creek at about 8:00 A.M. • **June 1:** Budge Barlee finds himself forty feet (12 m) away from the creature near Okanagan Mission and is able to distinguish fins. • **June:** While steering a tugboat at around 10:00 A.M. near Boucherie Mountain, Edward Schindel is startled by a log that suddenly comes to life. • **July:** Mrs. Harvey Spence and her mother Mrs. H. Dutton observe the animal traveling at high speed between Peachland and Poplar Point. • **July 8:** Insurance agent Monty DeMara and teacher Bill Fisher chase Ogopogo after it comes within thirty-five feet (10.5 m) of their motorboat near Squally Point. • **July 28:** A sixty-foot (18 m) animal is seen by resort owner Albert Moore and Marvin and Ernie Sherman of Bashaw, Alberta, while fishing in Trepanier Bay. They attempt to follow it. • **July 31:** As Mrs. James Gawne returns from Penticton to Naramata at about 4:00 P.M. Ogopogo makes an appearance near Trout Creek. Fearing ridicule, she remained silent until a radio broadcast confirmed the sighting by others. • From her home in Peachland, two creatures are observed by Edythe March at least three to four feet (1–1.25 m) out of the water heading toward the center of the lake. • **August 3:** First she sees a head, then a large black animal surfaces, undulating as it moves. Mrs. Charles Smith of Pascoe, Washington, thought it odd to see a whale swimming in Okanagan Lake, as she was not aware of Ogopogo. • **September 25:** Mrs. J. Fraser and Mrs. D. Johnson get a glimpse of Ogopogo near Okanagan Landing. • **September 29:** Ogopogos frighten the mudhens as nonbeliever Mrs. Alice de Pfyffer watches from her window at 9:30 A.M. She becomes a convert. • The same day, seven Red Cross workers see the majestic creature a few miles north of Penticton. Mrs. June McArthur stops the car as Mrs. Thorkelson and others see it moving to the north in an undulating manner.

1952 July: Ogopogo makes his debut at a public beach as twenty-five people including, Yvonne Roberts of Penticton and Mrs. Howard Cloz, observe the animal for at least ten minutes. • **July 6:** Mrs. Evelyn Little visiting from Scotland, her sister Mrs. El Campbell of Vancouver and local resident Mrs. Fred Campbell watch in amazement as they watch this creature with a cowlike head and saw-edged coils in Okanagan Lake.

1953 **July 19:** Sgt. and Mrs. N. Hilborn become believers in the space of a few minutes. The local soldier and his wife were fishing all afternoon, moving north toward the yacht club in response to a get-out-of-the-way blast from the ferry's whistle, when they see what looks like a big rope dragging behind the ferry. Realizing it was Ogopogo they watch it follow the ferry for some distance, splashing and cavorting in the lake before making a complete circle back to where it was first seen. • After watching the lake for six years, Mrs. Ernest Pearce, accompanied by her sister, Mrs. Harry Brooks of Winnipeg, finally witnesses the lake monster surface, submerge and then reappear, churning up water as it swims.

1954 **July:** Following an Okanagan Historical Society meeting in Naramata, Bruce Miller and his wife Myra return home along Naramata Road and see a long, sinewy monster in the shallow below. They stop a number of cars and everyone watches the animal for a good hour. • **July 3:** For five minutes, a party of fifteen people including Albert Moore, Mrs. Kellan, Mr. and Mrs. Mel Hudson and Mr. and Mrs. E. Chambers of Vancouver, observe the creature near Trepanier Creek.

1955 - August 29: During a CKOV interview by Edward Boyd of Kelowna held in the Aquatic Dining Room, Ogopogo appears to a large group of people and churns up the calm waters of Okanagan Lake. They all sign a written affidavit.

1956: Nan Dalrymple, a hostess at the Eldorado Arms Hotel, hears a splash coming from the lake, and observes a head and body out of the water. • The second sighting for E. A. Campbell from his lakeside garden is also witnessed by James Campbell of Kelowna and brother-in-law Leslie Campbell of Castlegar.

1957 **July 9:** James Shelly, Bob Derker and Jerry Huffman get to within twenty-five feet (7.6 m) of Ogopogo and see dorsal fins.

1958 **July 19:** Albert Moore observes the animal for the third time from the west shore of the lake and his belief is bolstered. • **Late July:** William Marks sees a swimming object with multiple equidistant protrusions, near Casa Loma Point. • **September 10:** Ogopogo races by as Mrs. W. Walker and Edward Coelen sit in the garden near the lake. It submerges when a motorboat is heard.

1959 **July:** A dark green object with smooth skin and visible head amazes Mr. and Mrs. Albert Block and son Denis near Cameron's Point in Vernon. • **July 17:** Ogopogo follows a cruiser returning to Vernon and two sketches of the head are drawn. Scared but thrilled are Mr. and Mrs. Dick Miller and Mr. and Mrs. Pat Martin and six-year-old son, Murray.

1960 **January 10:** Ogopogo is sighted near a Summerland beach. Mr. and Mrs. Stoyanowski try to alert passing motorists as the animal picks up speed and disappears from view.

1962 **May:** At 5:50 P.M. Ron Nishi and brother Doug, along with friends Allan Miller and Bruce Giggy watch as the lake monster surfaces and quickly submerges as they approach with their boat near Okanagan Centre. • **July:** ninety years after her mother, Mrs. Susan Allison, sighted Ogopogo in 1872, Mrs. Alice Allison Wright and her daughter Mrs. Jim Sisson of Vancouver are alerted to a long black creature with humps, revealing both head and neck, near Trout Creek in Summerland at around 4:00 P.M. • **July 17:** Ogopogo surfaces, churns up water and takes off at an unbelievable speed at 8:00 A.M., north of Squally Point as John and Lisa Schneider and eight-year-old son Frankie are boating. • **July 29:** Thirty parishioners from the Immaculate Conception Church, enjoying a picnic at a south Kelowna beach, are in awe as the creature passes by. Present were James Campbell and children, Leonard and Barbara Campbell, Joseph Ernest, Margaret Cowan and George and Marie Vetter. • **August:** What was first assumed to be a log soon transforms into a lake monster creating a turbulence in what was once shallow water, as museum curator, Ursula Surtees, watches in disbelief. She and her friend Mrs. Tostenson were waiting near Popular Point as their husbands John and Carl were waterskiing. • Thinking it first to be a wave, Mrs. Vic Welder and children Michael and Billy see an unusual creature with two humps move parallel to the beach near West Avenue in Kelowna. • **October:** Leslie Follard, out fishing near Sunset Island, sees a dark green twenty-foot (6 m) creature with a head and three humps moving through the lake just 150 yards (137 m) away. • While working at Sunnyside Ranch near Greenbay in Westbank, Daniel Alexander sees a creature roll over in the water, swim a short distance then submerge.

1963 Seventy-two-year-old Sy Jenkins of Naramata observes a commotion in the lake while fishing. A twenty-foot (6 m) long object travels past his boat into deeper water.

1964 While swimming at Dellcliff Lodge south of Vernon, Alan Hassell, his wife Joan and father William catch a glimpse of Ogopogo moving north.

1965 Jo Driftmier and son Rick run over a large animal while boating in Skaha Lake. It churns up the water, and a large eighteen- to twenty-foot (5.5–6 m) portion comes out in a loop. They see a V-shaped cut on its body oozing some dark liquid which stains the water. • Terry Upton and wife Primrose attempt to record two Indian pictographs painted in red ochre on granite rock between Kelowna and Okanagan Landing. The paintings reveal a creature's head, humped back, short legs and a long neck. • Excited but shaken, Mr. and Mrs. George Hubley and Mr. and Mrs. H. G. Baylis see a monster creating a stir in the lake near Okanagan Landing.

1966 Appreciating the view from the top of Mount Boucherie, Dorothy Gellatly of Westbank and Mrs. Fell of Vancouver are treated to several appearances by the lake monster.

1967 A photo taken by Eric Parmenter of Kelowna reveals a large disturbed area of water in the lake as the animal, first seen on the surface, submerges. • **April:** One quarter of the display at the Boston Museum of Sciences features Ogopogo and includes the Parmenter photo. • **July:** As Brenda Briese of Kelowna is driving a boat towing water skier Brian Bocking, she spots a creature scaring a school of fish off Casa Loma. Mrs. Carl Briese, her mother and Al Bocking watch the animal from the Briese home at Casa Loma. • Fifteen employees at the fish cannery near Naramata are curious as Ogopogo attempts to get into a school of fish. Mr. and Mrs. John Durrant of White Rock watch as Ogopogo appears to spout water. It was reported to have a head like a bucket.

1968   Ken Goodall, recently retired from the air force, is driving with his family looking for work. Looking down on the lake between Peachland and Summerland a long, wide V appears heading north with a wake at least 200 to 300 feet (61–91 m) long. No boats are in sight. • **April:** Four North Vancouver men laying a water line near Poplar Point are interrupted as Ogopogo pays them a visit. Jack Lowe, Victor Berger, Alfred Williamson and Al Francis all become believers. • **July:** Connie Marlow and Lucille Roche, both employees of the Kelowna Chamber of Commerce, see Ogopogo for the first time in the reeds near Okanagan Lake Bridge. • **July 9:** Colonel Stock jokes about catching Ogopogo on his fishing line just as the creature surfaces some fifty yards (46 m) away. Ernest Lording and Mrs. Stock are also in the boat and witness the event just north of Kelowna. • **July 23:** While water-skiing, Sherri Campbell runs into Ogopogo lying motionless on the lake. She panics and falls. Friends Bruce Johnson, Willie Walls, Gwen Johnson and Renee Bliss pick her up and then drive the boat to within five feet (1.5 m) of the monster before it takes off swiftly to the north. • **August:** Art Folden shoots the first 8 mm movie footage of Ogopogo from a high point on Highway 97 between Peachland and Summerland near the Viewpoint. His wife and children witness the event and the film reveals the presence of a very large animal. • **September:** Peter Pearson sees a fifty- to sixty-foot (15–18 m) object lashing water and creating a loud noise on Okanagan Lake from his Lakeview Heights home.

1969   **Spring:** Roy Wignall notices a disturbance on the lake and sees a horse or deer's head. His wife, daughter-in-law and grandson look up just as the animal takes off at high speed and they see three protrusions behind the head. • **August 12:** Doreen Billeau and Connie Marlow, along with other witnesses, watch an unusual eel-like creature just 300 yards (274 m) south of the chamber of commerce office on the west side of Okanagan Lake Bridge. • **August 13:** "A monster, 35 feet long with horns coming out of its head thrashes through the water," according to three fishermen from Edmonds, Washington. Don Fink, Donald Sr. and grandfather Anton Schmidt are startled by this sudden appearance. • **August 22:** As Sam MacDonald and Ed Bell are fishing off the Kelowna Yacht Club, three or more humps suddenly surface two feet above the lake. The part showing is at least eight feet (2.5 m) long in a mirror-calm lake. • **December:** A believer, but never a witness until one early winter afternoon, R. P. Maclean, *Kelowna Daily Courier* publisher, is rewarded when he checks on some frightened mallard ducks and sees three protrusions above the lake's surface. He observes a serpentine animal busy feeding, which then turns slowly at an angle, heading out to deeper water.

1970   **February 22:** Ogopogo makes an early debut near the statue at the base of Bernard Avenue for an undetermined number of witnesses. Most agree that it was forty (12 m) feet long but no head was visible. • **May 22:** Martin and Jo-Anne Firstenburg of Kelowna and Greg Dineta Firstenburg of Michigan are startled when a silvery grey object moves quickly through the lake. • **May 24:** Ogopogo rises from the depths, displaying head and horns just fifty feet (15 m) away from the Boychuck's houseboat as Mrs. Andrew Boychuk and Mrs. Peter Swetc look on in amazement. They scream to alert their husbands and the creature dives. • **May:** A twenty- to twenty-five-foot (6–7.5 m) snakelike creature, light green in color, surfaces as fish scurry from Dick Luca's fishing line. Thoughts of the $5,000 reward prompts Dick to row frantically toward the animal with a lasso. Just at arms reach, reality sets in and he sits quietly observing the animal until it submerges. • **June:** It was 6:15 A.M. Paul Pugliese drives his taxi from Bernard on to Abbott in Kelowna and stops his cab when he notices a lake disturbance. He sees a forty-foot (12 m) long greenish animal with a head like a horse "swimming as large as life." • **June 14:** Bill Long, Brenda, Linda and Robis Repp and Helmut Neufeld see Ogopogo swimming south to Squally Point at 8:55 A.M. • **June 23:** Four teenage girls see Ogopogo from Knox Mountain. • **July 10:** Ogopogo is seen again by Barry Chapman and Richard Lockie near the fish hatchery. • **July 20:** Sudden waves at the west end of the bridge puzzle Eva Menu and Chris Swayze who believe it to be Ogopogo. • **August 21:** Ken Charlish is flagged down by a woman on Lakeside Road in Westbank at 11:30 A.M. who points to Ogopogo just fifty yards (15 m) away. • **October 10:** Something black surfaces in the center of Okanagan Lake. "I saw something lumpy stop," stated Scott Dowle. He and his friend Jerry Banson believe they just saw Ogopogo. • **November 1:** Frightened and breathless, two teenage girls tell the *Courier* staff that Ogopogo chased their motorboat in circles south of the bridge, then followed them closely for ten minutes.

1971 Ogopogo skeptic, Joe Davignon is a convert as the creature interrupts his fishing at the west end of Okanagan Lake bridge and remains visible for ten minutes. The time was 3:00 P.M. • **August 2:** Calgary visitors Mr. and Mrs. Scott Young and Mrs. Blanche Inglis of Summerland observe the antics of Ogopogo.

1973 Mr. and Mrs. Hurd describe an animal with humps as large as tire wheels in the lake off City Park.

1974 **April 29:** Ogopogo is seen once again stalking the Summerland Trout Hatchery by Dr. Wilf Evans, his daughter Claudie and guests Mr. and Mrs. Ed Robinson of Brandon, Manitoba. • **June 12:** A whalelike animal surfaces as Mrs. Gwen Evans, her husband and daughter Glynis drive toward Penticton. • **July:** Barbara Clark experienced a close encounter while swimming at the south end of Okanagan Lake at around 8:00 A.M. when something big and heavy bumped her legs. Making a dash for the raft, she observed an eight-foot-long (2.5 m) animal slowly swim away followed by a forked horizontal tail, much like a whale's, at least four to six feet (1.25–2 m) wide and twelve inches (30 cm) out of the water. • **August:** Three undulating humps move in a northerly direction as Mike and Mary Nolan watch. The animal is described as being twelve to fifteen feet (3.7–4.6 m) in length and traveling at about 2 mph (3 km/h). Neighbor Gweneth Gilmour confirms the sighting.

1975 **July:** An unconfirmed report is made by a local resident and visitor from Calgary who sighted the lake monster.

1976 **April:** A large black object is reported by a Westbank resident moving toward a Kelowna beach north of the Okanagan Lake Bridge. • **May 16:** While scanning the lake through binoculars, Mr. Albert More is startled as a snakelike head surfaces. • **June 30:** Lynda Peters reports a dark brown object creating a massive spraying action before a head and neck emerge a good ten feet (3 m) out of the water at Okanagan Centre around 12:30 P.M. • **July 2:** A creature surfaces near Fintry and moves like a caterpillar with a head and tail visible and is a good forty to fifty feet (12–15 m) long. The dark object seen by Stan Baron of Calgary and Lowney Scown appears to be trying to move the boat and its occupants out of the way. • **July 5:** Mr. and Mrs. Ongman watch a thirty-foot (9 m) animate object surface just 200 feet (61 m) away from their boat near Peachland. It has three greenish humps. • **July 17:** Betty and Harry Staines fishing near Peachland were just fifty feet (15 m) away from a forty-foot-long (12 m) creature, which was enough to make them firm believers. It resembles a long eel, is blackish gray in color with a fin formation down the center. Betty had a close look at the animal through binoculars. • **July 17:** Mabel and Harry Price, along with Marg and Matt Peebles, spot a long dark object with a reptilian head moving through the lake at about 1:30 P.M. from Summerland Hill. • **July 20:** Gabriele and Paul Toiyon take a picture from Calamore Park of a dark brown lake creature as it surfaces, creating a wake as it moves. • **July 22:** It resembled a large reptile, swam in an undulating motion and had two visible humps. Jeffrey and David Sherwin, Make and Paul Hasagawa watch in amazement as it swims across the lake and disappears. Connie McDonald, Marne and Debbie Hammell, Kathleen Young and Gail Dalbourg confirm the sighting as they circle the fifty-foot-long (15 m) creature from their motorboat. Each time they got close the animal would dive under. • **August 3:** Ed and Jillian Fletcher, Gary and Diane Slaughter are out boating and chase a seventy-foot-long (21 m) animal for about ninety minutes and take five good photos. It was dark in color and created a large wake. Gary and Jillian see the head for a few seconds. • **August 9:** The first aerial sighting is by Mr. and Mrs. Glen Reichenbaugh and Mr. and Mrs. Marty Ballam when they see a 20-foot-long (6 m) creature with two black humps leaving a long wake. It slowly submerges. • **August 18:** For three minutes, Mrs. Epperson and a friend watch a dark object with four humps move through the lake near Scottish Cove in Westbank. • **August 23:** Three simultaneous encounters in less than an hour. Sue Kusnieryk sees a dark greenish creature in the center of the lake near City Park. Then Val Gibson sees it about fifty yards (46 m) from shore near Poplar Point thirty minutes later. Jergen Tobias and four friends see it move further north through the lake for one minute. • **August 28:** As Elson Moar turns to pick up a fallen water skier, a large animal surfaces close by for about thirty seconds. • **September 4:** A huge serpentine head surfaces as Lloyd, Ed and Colin Wong are fishing on the south side of Okanagan Lake Bridge. As Ed turns to get a better look he sees a body submerging with waves rolling off its back. They were so shocked that they did not think to use the camera. • **September 12:** Not one, but two Ogopogos, swim toward each other as Mr. and Mrs. Rowden relax at the Peachland government lookout. • Rick Dupperon reports seeing a moving black object 100 feet (30 m) from the Fintry docks. • **September 14:** A twelve-foot (3.7 m) swimming animal is seen on the east side of Okanagan Mission resembling an unusually large snake in a curled-up position. • **October:** At water's edge near City Park, Inez Cooper uses binoculars to see what resembles two logs swimming side by side in the middle of the lake. She speaks of seeing two unidentifiable footprints at Gyro Beach a few months earlier.

1977 **February 5:** Bruce and George Elliott and John McNaughton see three protrusions creating a wake south of Okanagan Lake Bridge. The object submerges and reappears north of the bridge and just 200 yards (183 m) from shore. • Karen Christen sees an object moving through the lake from Okanagan Lake Bridge. • **March 17:** A creature is seen in the lake from a backyard on Manhattan Drive. Susan Cairns and her grandmother believe it was Ogopogo. • **April 23:** Screaming nine-year-old Jamie-Lea Vogelgesang alerts her mother to the presence of a fifty-foot (15 m) creature sticking three feet (1 m) out of the water at the end of a dock at Sarsons Beach in Kelowna. Lillian Vogelgesang counts five darkish green humps at least five feet (1.5 m) wide as the water froths and churns around each. Mrs. Brome who lives next door verifies the object as it took off at high speed across the lake. • **April 24:** Gyro Beach is the scene of the next sighting as Ernie Muir and Donald Major see a thirty-foot (9 m) animal traveling swiftly through the lake just 500 yards (457 m) offshore. • **April 30:** Two black humps surface at Squally Point as Ken Nelson and Bruce Filipenko watch. • **May 9:** For almost an hour, Mrs. Sutton watches a creature cavorting in Gellatly Bay from her home just above. • It's a scary experience for Coralee Plimentos and her mother-in-law as a large object surfaces just 100 feet (30.5 m) from their boat near Green Bay Resort. • **May 18:** Around 6:15 P.M. Dorothy and David Proudfoot see an animate object propelling itself in the lake off Scottish Cove creating a massive wake. They alert Dorothy's mother who is visiting. • **July 1:** Jillian Fletcher and Erin Neely are frightened by the appearance of three humps surfacing off Scottish Cove. • **July 2:** A blackish green object, ten to fifteen feet (3–4.6 m) long surfaces off Okanagan Lake Bridge and is seen by Kevin Shore and Kevin Smith. • **July 3:** Terrified Erin Neely encounters Ogopogo while water skiing and is upset by the wake. Stunned by her fall, she opens her eyes to see the creature pass just in front of her. • **July 6:** While out fishing, Carol Lavigne, Hugh Greer and Russell Berner see a moving object with four humps, near their boat. • **August 8:** A dark scaly "something" rises from a perfectly calm lake off the beach near Manhattan Drive. Valerie Gibson and Jackie Michaud verify the sighting. • **August 14:** Janet and Dale Abbey see a large black object rise six feet (1.8 m) out of the lake while they were swimming off Scottish Cove. A head and part of the body are visible. • Ted Gerk swimming at Kelowna Beach also reports seeing a dark object traveling through the lake. • **August 28:** Darlene and Sonja Kovach are water-skiing when an unidentified swimming object surfaces near them at Summerland. • **September 16:** Sandy Ripple and friend see something in the lake off Coral Beach in Winfield. • **November 5:** While driving on Okanagan Lake Bridge, fifteen carloads of people, including Darryl Hunt, Dawsha Malove and Betty and Harry Staines, observe a creature moving through the water and submerge.

1978 **February 19:** Thirty witnesses are on hand, including Mrs. McAdam of Penticton as a jet-black, fifty-foot-long (15 m) snakelike creature suns itself a short distance from shore near a Penticton campsite. Several humps are seen as it frolics for some time before moving out into deeper water. • **May:** Emil Puffalt, his wife and her family observe a shiny forty-foot (12 m) animal surface and submerge near Okanagan Landing. • **May 20:** An object estimated to be forty feet (12 m) long moves swiftly toward Scottish Cove to the amazement of Linda Robertson and Jackie Frabone. • **May 21:** "It casts a shadow the length of a football field," states Albert and Ethel London who are stunned as Ogopogo remains visible for over an hour while they are fishing off Mission Creek. The forty-foot-long (12 m) animal with three visible humps surfaces about twenty-five feet (7.5 m) away from them and then submerges. • **June 29:** A long dark snakelike form is seen 200 yards (183 m) off Boucherie Resort. Arnold Frank and a visitor agree that it was round with humps. • **August 8:** Alice Blais and friend sight an animal while fishing in Okanagan Lake near Vernon. • **September 11:** While fishing north of Munson Mountain, Larry Warner sees a whitecap moving against the wind. As it gets closer, he sees something large and dark pushing water. It surfaces and submerges only 200 yards (183 m) away. • **September 17:** While exploring the area around Rattlesnake Island, Steve Bakalso, Alan Spilde and diving instructor Len Melnyk observe a large eighty-pound (36 kg) animal pass in front of them at a depth of seventy-five feet (23 m). They are able to see dark caves revealing a rocky inlet some fifteen to sixteen feet (4–5 m) deep. • **October 17:** Bill Steciuk, a car salesman from Kelowna sees an animal with three black humps and a head protrude as it moves underneath Okanagan Lake Bridge. He stops his car and gets out to look. Clem Harrison later confirms the sighting. • **October 24:** Arlene Gaal is checking out Bill Steciuk's sighting and is stunned when something suddenly breaks water creating massive rolling waves similar to a submarine surfacing. Five sequential photos reveal the presence of something long and dark on what was a completely calm lake. • **December 21:** As Mr. and Mrs. Dennis Hanson look from the window of their home on Chute Lake Road bluff, they see something large and black swimming quickly toward Okanagan Lake Bridge. They confirm it to be an unknown animal through binoculars.

1979 **May:** The head and neck is seen by a woman who requests anonymity. • **May 2:** Ontario visitors Al and Betty Kirby watch a grayish white object in the center of Skaha Lake keeping pace with their car which is moving at 55 mph (88.5 km/h). It remained visible for several miles before disappearing. • **May 28:** As something long and dark protrudes from Okanagan Lake near Kinsmen Beach 500 yards (457 m) off shore, Arlene Gaal with daughter Laurie photograph it and note a visible wake coming off its back. The photo gives the appearance of it being the top of the animal's head. **August:** Rick Bachand is water-skiing half a mile (.8 km) from Okanagan Lake Bridge when he sees a log-shaped object in the center of the lake. • **August 20:** Rene hears a *swoosh swoosh* sound and as she looks up three humps rise from the lake very close to her boat. She is near Okanagan Centre. • Chris Clayton takes photographs and an unidentified Alberta man takes movie footage as a large group of people watch the animal frolicking in the lake from Highway 97 near Peachland. • For Frank and Jim Reiger and six-year-old Aurie it is a day not to be forgotten. A large dinosaur-like creature at least twenty tons (18 t) swims alongside their boat. It has four legs, a massive shoulder structure and a tail long or longer than the body. (Author's note: This description bears similarities to the Folden film). • **September 2:** At Okanagan Centre a group of people witness a fifty foot (15 m) animal break water and watch it come to within twenty feet (6 m) of the dock. • **September 4:** Two ladies observe a large swimming object just off of Lakeshore Road. They see a head rise up out of the water twice as it continues on through the lake.

1980 **April 13:** The Shepherd family observe an animal that is at least fifty feet (15 m) long while out fishing. It travels at 15 mph (24 km/h) and John, Bev, Jeanine and Debbie become believers. • **May:** Doug McClelland spots the legendary Ogopogo surfacing early morning just off the *Fintry Queen*. • Gary Sharpe driving with his wife and son along the lake sees turbulence in the water. "We saw an object that looked like a cigar in the water just below. It surfaced like a submarine and then submerged." **August 11:** The Thal film is taken. At least fifty tourists from around British Columbia and Alberta are in awe as Ogopogo performs nonstop for at least forty-five minutes off the beach near Blue Bird Bay Resort (now Monteo Beach). It surfaces and submerges, turning and returning from Okanagan Lake Bridge and back. Two still photos are taken along with an 8-mm movie film shot by Larry Thal of Vancouver. Signed affidavits are obtained from Noel, Angie, Ethel, Stephen and Michael Mellross; Kathleen, Alan, Mark and Samantha Johnson; Pamela, Katherine and Coralee Meier (all of Calgary); Steven Miller of Edmonton and Shana and Jamie Watson of Victoria. • **August 12:** Orm and Edith Pasquill spot a turbulence while out fishing. Suddenly, three humps and part of a dark green body appear as an animal surfaces and submerges while moving around them for at least ten minutes before finally disappearing. • **August 31:** Five people aboard the CKIQ Radio's marine cruiser spot a ripple that continuously changes direction and is about twenty feet (6 m) long. Just below the surface they see what appears to be a dark brown-skinned animal. The wake is so great that it rocks the boat. It is certified by Yvonne Svennson, Tony Klotz, Vila Costigan, Brian Telford and Lisa Klingspon. • **September 4:** Mrs. Marie Carter Kane and sister Marguerite Carter watch a creature with four or five successive humps in the lake from their apartment window on Lakeshore Road in Kelowna. A black head appears to rise around fifteen to twenty feet (4.6–6 m) long. It submerges and surfaces twice, creating a two-foot-high (.6 m) wave. • **October 28:** Arlene

Gaal observes a long dark object in Okanagan Lake while driving near City Park in Kelowna at 1:30 P.M. She stops the car, sees Carol Francey with a camera and asks her to take pictures of the fifty- to seventy-foot (15–21 m) animal as it thrashes about. The animal swims to the center of the lake and slowly northward as the lake returns to its calm. One photo shows the classic long neck sticking straight up attached to a dark body. • Heather Zais watches as her friend slips underwater for a swim, between Bear Creek and Fintry. She observes a fifteen-foot (4.6 m) animal close to where he is swimming, remains very still and sees ridges along its dark back about 3 to 5 inches (7.7–13 cm) high. It gently moves away just before her friend surfaces. The animal was within arms reach.

1981 **January 25:** During the Snowfest Fishing Derby, John Taylor, Claudio Cellini and John Slaughter joke about Ogopogo as they near Rattlesnake Island. A sudden wave and then three humps surface, measuring between fifteen and twenty feet (4.6–6 m) in length. It submerges and surfaces twice, creating a two-foot-high (.6 m) wave. • **February 28:** Randy Nagel of Winfield sees an unusual disturbance in a calm lake near Okanagan Centre. He photographs a spray over twenty feet (6 m) long and at least thirty feet (9 m) high rising from the disturbance and dark shadows are seen below. • Coren Archibald and Lee Varnum, while looking at Okanagan Lake near Westbank, observe two black humps emerge from the water just after a flock of geese take off squawking in fear. The lake was mirror calm. • **June 18:** James Moller and Rober Blasek see a huge fin slowly rise three feet (1 m) out of the water at Sarsons Beach. It was at least four feet (1.25 m) wide and hit the water with such force that it created a whirlpool disturbance. • **July 1:** A third photo is taken by author Arlene Gaal from Westside Road as an object travels at high speed through the lake. No boats are in sight. • **July 24:** Photos are taken by Seattle resident, Sherri Wachlin as she, her father Walter and brother Randy are visited by Ogopogo while fishing off Rattlesnake Island. • **August:** Former Vancouver resident Rick Trembley sees what he believes to be a whale surface while looking out onto the lake from Okanagan Lake Resort across from Okanagan Centre.

1982 A person wishing to remain anonymous reports seeing an object surface and submerge before heading to the center of the lake and disappear from view. • **September 5:** Eugene Boisselle videotapes the antics of an unusual object with black protrusions from the lookout on Knox Mountain. It is observed by his son who watches as it creates a large boiling wake, swims in a circular motion and then changes direction.

1983 **June 7:** "If there's an Ogopogo in the lake, I've just seen it!" Russell and Gloria Butte are amazed as a forty- to-fifty-foot (12–15 m) animal, darkish green with a horselike head and tucked-in ears swims toward their boat and cuts in front just thirty feet (9 m) away, taking off across the lake at a tremendous speed. • **June 7:** Sarah Kirkby confirms the Butte sighting. Sarah and her husband were out in the center of the lake at the same time and saw an object moving very quickly from east to west against the waves. It was dark in color with three humps and moved in an undulating manner. • **June 23:** While preparing to water-ski on the west side of the lake, Lawrence Kolidab, his daughter Darcy, niece Leslie Vandervol of Saskatachewan and Nadeen Hilbolm observe approaching waves and see three or four solid sections above the surface, estimated to be thirty to forty feet (9–12 m) long, moving from east to west. • **July 30:** Michael Berger and Maureen Lisle see a large disturbance in the water and take after it in their twelve-foot (3.7 m) aluminum boat as an incredibly large dark animal with three humps breaks water. "As we got close it broke through the wake and water rolled over its body. By then we were in a panic and turned to get behind it." • **August 26:** Ron Smith spots a dark animal moving quickly through the lake. Three sections are visible at least two feet (.6 m) out of the water, along with a neck and possible tail. • **August 29:** While fishing near the mouth of Mission Creek, Frank Penner is stunned when he sees a fifty- to sixty-foot-long (15–18 m) snakelike animal at least ten to twelve feet (3–3.7 m) wide with a blunt head. He describes it as being dark in color and moving in a snaking or coiling manner. Frank was just 250 yards (229 m) away and states, "I believe what I saw." • **September 3:** Four visitors from Portland Oregon are drawn to a large V-wake stirring up the lake when a black shape surfaces traveling about 3 mph (5 km/h). Edward and Cheri Moore and Douglas and Susan Siewert watch from Chute Lake Road in Naramata until it disappears. They photograph the experience and submit a signed affidavit.

1984 **January 28:** About 4:00 P.M. Yvonne Svennson and Sharon Ross look out over the lake from Westside Road and notice a thirty- to forty-foot-long whitecap just out from Paul's Tomb on the east side. It vanishes and returns, bobs up and down and continues this for a good hour. Yvonne takes three photos and then she and Sharon decide to drive across to Paul's Tomb to get a better look, but when they arrive it had disappeared. • **January:** The Okanagan Similkameen Tourist Association announce a $1 million reward insured by Lloyds of London to anyone who can prove the fabled lake monster, Ogopogo, really exists. No one collects. • **February 18:** Alan Gartrell and Ray Piper see what they first thought was a small boat heading north up the lake from Penticton. It turns and swims toward them. Using binoculars they see a white underside pushing water behind the wake, and fin or winglike thrusts churning the lake. • "Dad, Dad, look over there!" Scott Rose and his father Ray see Ogopogo swimming in a southerly direction, its brown-black head held high with the classic protrusions following as they drove down Brenda Mines Road to Peachland. The head is a good seven feet (2 m) out of the lake remaining that way for at least five minutes. They quickly sketch the details on a napkin. Eleven-year-old Scott says, "I believe what I saw." • **March 23:** "It was something alive. It moved, but I'm not going to say it was Ogopogo," is how Marianne Dunbar describes what she and her son Ris saw while driving along Sunnyside Road on the west side. They observe a rippling, as dark brown humps surface, but no head. Now a confirmed believer, she carries a camera. • **April 5:** While up on Knox Mountain Lookout, Mike Levin and Joe Gaal observe a dark object creating a commotion in the lake below. A section rises out of the water and splashes the surface. It resembles a large log. • **July 4:** Steve watches an anomaly moving toward Penticton at about 30 mph (48 km/h) about 150 feet (46 m) from shore. It moves from an inlet into deeper water. • **July:** David Methedal observes an unusual animal surface near Peachland. • **September 28:** Pauline and Bill Trakalo are startled when a forty-foot-long (12 m) creature accompanied by two other fifteen- to twenty-foot (4.6–6 m) animals move together in a circle and create air bubbles. They remain visible for forty-five minutes off Heritage Park in Peachland. Five other witnesses verify the sighting.

1985   **January:** Voyager Expedition's Rick Bain and Dave Faubert announce a sonar search of Okanagan Lake with a team of fourteen including eight divers in a six-day underwater search planned for July. Should the animal come within 200 feet (61 m) of the surface, divers will attempt to place a tracking transmitter on its back. • **May:** A woman who wishes to remain anonymous was walking her dog beside her lakeshore property late afternoon when Ogopogo surfaces about 300 feet (91 m) offshore creating quite a splash before making his way toward Mission Creek. • John Jansen sees something in the lake while fishing and is sure that it is Ogopogo. • **June 28:** Wallis Bierowski tells media that he photographed an elongated object moving through shallow water from the Delta Hotel in Penticton. Bierowski disappears leaving many unanswered questions. • **July 11:** Mailtruck driver Gwen Griffith while driving home from Penticton, is detoured to Sutherland Road. Coming down the hill facing the lake, she sees a forty-foot (12 m) black object with a greenish hue out in a calm lake. "My grandfather saw Ogopogo while digging graves at the cemetery in the 1940s," writes Griffin. • John Raeside and family are water-skiing by the bridge when they see a large object moving like a whale. • **Summer:** Carol Pattenaude and her boyfriend observe an object moving quickly through the lake leaving a long wake as they drive from Westbank to Peachland. It disappears within minutes.

1986   **July 20:** *Kelowna Daily Courier* editor, Andre Wetjan and Lionel are boating across from Bear Creek Park when they observe a twenty-foot-long (6 m), dark animal with visible humps break water. The animal overtakes their boat and makes a right turn. • **August 14:** Two girls from Vancouver report seeing a twenty-foot-long (6 m) eel-like object off Gellatly Bay in Westbank. • **Summer:** Shona Gates, her children David, Bobby, Jimmy, and Paul and Gordon Portman of Penticton all observe something in the lake while driving. • Donna Sutter and fourteen-year-old Amie, Victoria 10 and Jennifer 8 are two miles south of Peachland. They see an animal close to shore with four visible black humps. It travels north to south creating waves in a moderately calm lake. • **October 27:** Walter Floyd of Kelowna spots a strange and unusual animal in a mirror-calm lake from a steep slope overlooking the lake between Summerland and Peachland. It is eight to ten feet (2.5–3 m) wide and at least twelve feet (3.7 m) long minus the tail, head and neck. It swims slowly for a few minutes then takes off at high speed. Floyd's experience compares to Art Folden's 1968 film.

1987   **May 19/20:** John Kirk, wife Janet, six-year-old son John along with Phyllis Frew of Kelowna see an animal at least forty feet (12 m) long with a reptilian head displaying several black humps from Mission Hill above Okanagan Lake. John videotapes the experience. • **July:** ABC cameraman Michael Tabor and producer David Frank are in Kelowna to shoot *Secrets and Mysteries*. Gerry Frederick, Kelowna Chamber of Commerce manager, takes them out on the lake for some scenic shots. Something surfaces and ABC films an unusual object for about three minutes. • **September:** While Emma Gloer eats breakfast at the Sandcastle Resort overlooking Okanagan Lake she sees an unusual wave. Watching intently she observes a slim "horsey-like head" at one end and two to three protrusions. "Under one of the loops, I saw daylight, it moved at a leisurely pace and then disappeared." • Over ten years Jake Heppner has three sightings of Ogopogo while out fishing. It passes within fifty feet (15 m) of his boat and it resembles a brownish green snake with diamond-shaped squares. "The girth was far more than I could reach around." A frightened Rudy Grunau of Abbotsford screamed for his friend Jake to get him off the lake, when Ogopogo suddenly surfaced. Jake and his friend Harry Pridgeon see what appears to be three animals cavorting in the lake. They were too big to be either fish or waterfowl.

1988: Kelowna Chamber of Commerce tourism vice-president offers a $2,000 reward for the best picture taken in 1988 of the legendary Ogopogo. • **July:** Willis Allsup and his eighteen-year-old daughter, Sheila, of Kelowna see a blackish green object with two large humps about forty feet (12 m) in length, eighteen inches (46 cm) wide with smooth snakelike skin. He takes two pictures before it disappears. • **July 26:** While vacationing at Okanagan Mountain Park, Barbara and Sheldon Rowell of Victoria, B.C., along with Marjorie and Arch McCraig, Jim and Margaret Black, Donald and Francis Beresford and two unidentified ladies from Quebec, watch an unusual animal surface. • **August 28:** Mel Zummack, Natalie and David Dray and Sharon are driving on the road to Fintry Estates looking down onto the lake. They take four pictures of a large animal at least seventy feet (21 m) long. • **September:** Denise and Bill Nahirney, their daughter Lynette, and Mary and Lawrence Kolidab are moving at cruising speed through Okanagan Lake near Okanagan Centre. Three forty-foot-long protrusions surface. The group is stunned when they find Ogopogo just 200 feet (61 m) in front of their boat swimming parallel across the lake. It submerges and surfaces and is visible for about five minutes. • **October 21:** Jim, Myrna and Keren Brandenburg of Delta see three humps about thirteen inches (33 cm) above the water in a mirror-calm lake. The object travels east to west for three minutes and then submerges.

1989 **July 10:** Kelowna seniors, Clem and Joyce Chaplin, are camping at Bear Creek Park. They see a dark green creature with smooth skin and brown spots at the mouth of Bear Creek. An avid fisherman, Clem determines that this is no fish, as the neck width was over fifteen inches (38 cm) wide. • **July 17:** Ken Chaplin along with his father Clem and well-known Kelowna businessman Horst Simpson see something surface in Okanagan Lake near Bear Creek. It appears to be about fifteen feet (4.6 m) long, black in color and swats its tail on the water before diving. Ken videotapes the event. • **July 22:** Arlene Gaal accompanies Ken and Clem Chaplin to Bear Creek to check out the details. At around 8:30 P.M. Gaal is surprised as an animal surfaces just off of the mouth of Bear Creek and heads out to the center of the lake. It turns right and swims toward the log booms. Arlene Gaal takes two photos and Ken Chaplin turns on his video camera as he runs to follow its path. • **July 30** : John Kirk, John Kirk Jr. and Jim and Barbara Clark members of the BCSCC expedition observe an unusual disturbance in the lake near Summerland as a thirty-five-foot-long (10.5 m) animal, three feet (1 m) wide swims north to south about 200 yards (183 m) out. One large hump is visible through a 40X telescope twelve to thirty-six inches (30–91 cm) above water. The skin appeared whalelike. • **August 1:** Near Green Bay aboard the CKIQ Cruiser, John Kirk, his son, along with Blaine Pudwell and Angie Yielding see an animal three feet (1 m) out of water with three to six protrusions visible. No head, but a tail seemed to be flicking water behind it. Frenzied thrashing gave the appearance of perhaps two animals. • **August 26:** At Bertram Creek Park at 7:30 A.M. John Kirk, while climbing up a headland, looks to the lake and sees two extremely large animals. The one in front appears over seventy feet (21 m) long and the second following behind was sixty feet (18 m). One of the creatures arches its body allowing Kirk to see through to the other side. Kirk drives to Sarsons Beach and continues to view the animals from a distance. • **3:30 P.M.** Kirk is now at Greata Ranch area near Peachland. He observes and records a huge six-foot hump in the distance for about forty-five minutes. It reacts to a motorboat and then disappears. Kirk videotapes twenty-five minutes of activity. • **August 29:** Westside Marina. John Kirk, Rob Turnbull, Patricia Plancher and Henry see three 12-inch humps swim right up to Okanagan Lake Bridge and promptly disappear. Fifteen minutes later it swims back north to south 200 yards (183 m) past the bridge. A huge arch rises up four feet (1.25 m). • **August 31:** Letter from Joyce Christie tells of a dark brown object suddenly flipping out of Okanagan Lake, resembling an arm. It sank back down just as fast. Seeing the Chaplin photo she states, "I had nothing to compare it to until now, and it helps to substantiate your convictions." • **September 5:** While crossing Okanagan Lake Bridge at 3:20 P.M. Stella Friedel sees a rise in the water and a long slim animal twenty to thirty feet (6–9 m) out of the water. The head is small and rounded and has a wide smooth-lipped mouth. No ears are visible, but a large dark-brown reddish eye encircled by a band of white could be seen. • **September 15:** Ernie Giroux and his wife Margaret are surprised by a large fifteen-foot (4.6) animal swimming fast, but gracefully, in Okanagan Lake near the mouth of Bear Creek. It had a round head like a football and about two feet (.6 m) of head and body stuck up out of the water. "I've seen a lot of animals swimming in the wild and what we saw was no beaver," said retired big-game hunter, Ernie Giroux. • **September:** Arlene Gaal presents a copy of her book *Ogopogo* to Governor General Madame Sauvé at the offical opening of the therapeutic pool at Kelowna General Hospital. • **November:** The team from *Unsolved Mysteries* arrive to shoot the "Chaplin Story."

1990 **February 4:** At 1:45 P.M. Susan and Michael Filiatrault work their way from

View #6 to View #1 near Bear Creek Park. Looking down toward the lake, they see a thirty- to forty-foot (9–12 m) dark brown object in the water stretched out between two large trees below. Waves roll over it, as it moves slowly to the center of the lake toward Okanagan Lake Bridge. • **March 19:** Graham Merrick of Lethbridge, Alberta, while on an Air B.C. flight sees three brown Ogopogos swim out near a sandbar and head to the center of the lake: one large animal and two smaller ones. He records his sighting and draws a sketch. • **June 29:** Lily Granfield and husband spot something large rise three or four feet (1–1.25 m) out of the lake near Peachland. • **July 17:** Ann Kline and her husband Dick observe an animal swimming in the center of the lake from their Lakeshore Road home in Kelowna while eating breakfast. Ann takes her binoculars and sees a head, body and what looks like a tail out of the water. • **July 17:** One hour and thirty minutes later Bob Pearce and his friend Ron spot a large animal swimming under Okanagan Lake Bridge heading north as they drive down the hill to cross the bridge into Kelowna. • **July 24:** A flotilla of boats including a houseboat head north to search for Ogopogo under the direction of Nippon TV Tokyo. Arlene Gaal together with Japanese reporter Masayuki Tamaki and boat driver Mike Guzzi take off toward the center of the lake near Bear Creek. A sonar reading is recorded at the 350-foot-depth (107 m) mark as a large thirty-foot (9 m) object appears, showing body proportions, and moves across the screen as air bubbles rise up. John Daly and the BCTV crew videotape the event. • **July 24:** At 5:00 P.M. the Nippon crew check out an area near Peachland and the camera crew spots an anomaly in a perfectly calm lake moving toward shore. The object moves swiftly in a circular motion, breaks water and is perhaps feeding. Arlene Gaal, Sheila Pearson, Don Defty of Kelowna and Gan Hanada of Los Angeles also observe the event. • **July 29:** John Kirk Sr., son John Jr., Kenji Chono of Japan and Ken and Andrew Shauntz near Rattlesnake Island see what looks like a peeled log. As they approach, the log takes off toward the eastern shoreline. The creature was just fifty feet (15 m) away from a motorboat, but two people remain unaware. • **July:** A jet black object with a brontosaurus-like head and neck is seen by Paula and Cindy off Campbell Road in Westbank. It moves very slowly in the center of a very calm lake. • **August 1:** Gus is both surprised and frightened by the appearance of a three-foot-high object just thirty-three to forty-nine feet (10–15 m) away on the beach off the Francis Road beach access. His fear sent him running out to the road. When he felt confident enough to return it had disappeared. • **August 9:** Katherine Brunette, her son Gregory and his wife Diane were driving to Summerland. South of Peachland, near Old Antlers Motel, they spot a huge creature swimming toward Penticton about forty yards (36.5 m) from shore. A snakelike head and three humps are visible, and they say it is charcoal in color and thirty to forty feet (9–12 m) long. • **August 12:** Mike and Tina Paskal of Fort McMurray, Alberta, photograph a large animal while boating near Fintry. It rises five feet (1.5 m) out of the water close to the side of the boat. Terrified, Tina drops six-month-old Jamie in the boat. Mike takes photos and then moves his family out as fast as the boat is able to go. • **August:** Natalie Butler, a local high school teacher, and a group of eleven friends observe an unusual animal in Okanagan Lake near Bear Creek. • **October 20:** Canada Post launches the Ogopogo stamp in a presentation to Arlene Gaal, the first in a series of folklore stamps which include the Sasquatch, Loup-Garou and Kraken.

1991 **July 6:** While traveling in a boat about half a mile north of Okanagan Lake Bridge, Arlene Gaal sees a large whalelike dark flipper or appendage rise out of the lake and resubmerge quickly. She compares it to the Thal and Bart footage. • **July 20:** Ron Elies of Calgary, Alberta, observes what looks like a small island just beneath the surface of Okanagan Lake about forty feet (12 m) long and six feet (1.8 m) wide near Peachland. Water was spurting in the air just above it. • **July:** Bob is boating with his two children. His ten-year-old son took his turn to be towed on a dinghy. The boy's screams to "get him off the boat" alerts Bob to turn his head. He sees this large animal coming for his terrified son. He grabs the boy and pulls him in. • **August 5:** Dr. Rod Simmons, a Westbank dentist, his wife Pam and Ed Liggett and his wife are boating across from Peachland near Rattlesnake Island. Ed Liggett notices a disturbance in the lake and alerts the others. Rod grabs his video camera and videotapes a large animate object moving quickly through Okanagan Lake. • **August 8:** Thirty staff and guests at Vernon's Lakeside Marina Hotel outdoor patio lounge see a huge rippling disturbance offshore. It moves rapidly through the lake and a six-foot-tall (1.8 m) black protrusion juts out of the water in an arch. Frothing water and waves three feet (1 m) high churn the water 600 yards (549 m) off shore. • Mary Mckee, owner of Mary's Kitchen in Peachland, sees something in the lake early in the morning and snaps a picture of a dark black object. • **August 21:** While camping at Bear Creek Park, Gloria Fanslau's husband notices whitecaps moving parallel to the shore from south to north as a large shadow appears about twenty-five feet (7.5 m) long with a much smaller shadow along each side six to eight feet (1.8–2.4 m) long. A shiny black body surfaces. It is seen by another family. • **September 20:** Two painters, Bruce Mayes and Brad Virtue, working on the roof of a Naramata home see a dark spot in the lake with a V-shaped wake moving slowly for 100 feet (30 m) before it disappears.

1992 **June 18:** Ken Bart, his wife Janis, son Devin of Regina, Saskatchewan, and his parents Jackie and Ewalt take a boat out on Okanagan Lake for the first time. As they relax to enjoy the scenery through the passage at Rattlesnake Island, Ken videotapes. Suddenly, a large wave appears as large black protrusions leap out. Devin is excited and yells, "Lets race it." • **July:** Ogopogo cruises at top speed from Peachland to Kelowna. The twenty-three-foot (7 m) fiberglass replica is the brainchild of CKIQ news director Mike Guzzi. The structure is submerged in thirty feet (9 m) of water off Paul's Tomb. • **July 24:** Paul DeMara of Delta, British Columbia, videotapes a group of unusual moving objects in the lake from his mother's cottage near Okanagan Centre. His wife Kathy, mother Denise, Donna and Ken Fraser of Kelowna and Daryl Banks and Tracy Robinson of Vancouver watch in awe as a water skier crosses its path. The skier falls as the objects continue on. One animal surfaces , revealing a body, head and neck, then swims away. • **July 26:** Stella Friedel and husband

Carl along with cousins Patricia Rossmiller visiting from Colfax, Washington, and Evelyn Montreuil of Coeur D'Alene, Idaho, stop to enjoy the scenery across from the Chinese Laundry Restaurant in Peachland. Patricia is videotaping when something large and dark in color in the lake flips out of the water creating a disturbance as it moves and swims off to the south. • **October 13:** Burt and Brenda Johnson and Brenda's brother, Roy Rolston, hear and see a large churning in Okanagan Lake near the "Sails" in Kelowna. A long, dark object breaks water and Roy Rolston takes some pictures.

1993   **April 11:** Bill and Pete Penner of Edmonton are relaxing at a picnic table on a beach by Skaha Lake. Conditions are calm, but they notice forty to fifty ducks suddenly disappear before a hump rises gently out of the water, followed by a second one. Water rolls over this twenty-five-foot (7.5 m) black animal with a giraffelike neck and small head. • **July 13:** Craig Fiddler is entertaining friends at home near the Lakeside Marina Hotel when they see something in the water, resembling a serpent, that fits the description of Ogopogo. Fiddler is now a believer. • **August 11:** At 1:50 P.M. Sharon Sylvestor, on her lunch break, sits watching the lake at the back of Southgate Shopping Center in Kelowna when a huge turbulence with white water materializes. A large snakelike animal is swimming southward and Sharon sees dark protrusions rise up. It's seen by another woman and a teenager. "I didn't believe it was happening," Sharon stated. • **August 11:** Chris Barile, his wife and sister-in-law were boating north of Rattlesnake Island when a strong fishy smell rises from the lake just before a huge black animal emerges from the center of churning water about twenty feet (6 m) from the boat. • **August 31:** Lidia Allen, Trudy Towers and Debbie Nielsen were sitting in the picnic area near Bear Creek Park looking over the calm water when a black streak appears in the water about 200 feet (60 m) offshore. They watch the object, which is ten to fifteen feet (3–4.6 m) out of the water, until it disappears. • **August:** A Kelowna woman and her two adult grandchildren observe two dark, smooth humps and a wake from the stern of the *Fintry Queen*. "It looked like a large water snake coming out of the water," states Brenda Massey.

1994   **March:** The Sommer family of Peachland watch as a dark blob moves above the surface across the lake. "It wasn't just a ripple in the water," states Luke Sommer who videotapes the experience and then drives down to Beach Avenue for a better look. • **March 15:** Kevin Berry of Winfield videotapes two objects in Okanagan Lake from his Okanagan Centre home. They each leave a definite V-wake in a mirror-calm lake. One swims off to the right while the other comes further out of the water and then continues to swim toward the northwest. • **May 10:** Ronda Caplan and her friend Michelle Horn see the legendary lake creature in Okanagan Lake three times near Peachland. A big black thing surfaces with whitecaps on top, forty feet (12 m) from shore. It slowy submerges as they watch the animal beneath the water. • **June 20:** Guy Banks and Larry Burton drive over Okanagan Lake Bridge at 6:30 A.M. and see something break water with nothing else in sight. Banks who lived by the water states he never saw anything like what he saw that morning. "It was like something was pushing the water up from beneath the surface." • **July 13:** Darlene Viala, her six-year-old son Billy George, Tammy Duncan, Marilyn Duncan and children Jamie 8, Scott 9 and Laura 10 bring their boat to an abrupt stop when the body of a fifty- to sixty-foot (15–18 m) creature surfaces about twenty feet (6 m) away. The animal had eight to ten fins, no head, but a tail similar to that of a snake was blackish green with skin like a dolphin. The group is traumatized. • **September 13:** Shari McDowal sees something in the lake while driving to Kelowna from Okanagan Lake Resort. She and her husband pull over for a better look. The water bubbled and frothed in a fifty-foot-long area (15 m) of a very calm lake. A large mass could be seen in the center as it moved southeast leaving a long wake. • **September:** Doug Mallo, Delores Keuning, Mary Mckee and Vic Bozowski are startled into disbelief as they watch an object rise and submerge four times as it moves slowly northward from the veranda of Mary's Kitchen in Peachland. It was a gray-greenish black. • **May 12:** Alan Gillette, a California native, begins a one-man, three-month vigil of Okanagan Lake to prove or disprove Ogopogo's existence. He videotapes some unusual experiences, although the animal never surfaces nearby. Alan is convinced that something does break water in Okanagan Lake that cannot be explained. • **June 28:** Brian and Janet Hutchinson of Peachland observe three humps, as well as a head and neck, surface while they are eating a late supper on the deck of their home overlooking Okanagan Lake. Brian sketches the experience. • **August 26:** Anthony Hyde is out boating with his grandchildren and daughter-in-law near Carrs Landing. They all see huge waves at least ten feet (3 m) long rise up and they observe something moving at a good pace. Hyde is certain he saw a snout and face of a reptilelike creature about seventy-five feet (23 m) away from the boat. • **August:** Jack Mieras of Kelowna, his son Jeff and Patrick Morgan of Vancouver are looking out on the lake from Strathcona Park and in the distance see a large black object spouting water as it moves. It submerges, surfaces and turns; two sections, one larger than the other, are visible. Young Jeff says that it looks like a whale. Jack videotapes the event.

1996 **February:** Michael Zaiser, his brother and sister-in-law are hiking in Okanagan Mountain Park overlooking Lake Okanagan. They spot something moving in the water creating an unusual disturbance leaving a long wake. Michael takes five pictures revealing a brownish colored animal out of the water at least forty feet (12 m) long with a long neck, small head and appendage. • **March 15:** Frank Serio and his girlfriend are out for a stroll near the dock between the SS *Sicamous* and SS *Naramata* when they hear two loud splashes and see a large head swimming southward. "It was moving faster than anything I've ever seen swimming in my life," says Serio. • **August 20:** Six people, including a family from Calgary, camping at Bear Creek see a long wave parallel to shore moving around the log booms. A shadow is seen beneath the water and a twenty-foot-long (6 m) animal, dark in color, breaks water.

1997 **April 3:** Two people watch for an hour from City Park in Kelowna as a moving animal surfaces: it is described as being fifty feet (15 m) long and five feet (1.5 m) wide. The lake is mirror calm. • **August:** Valerie West was returning from Rattlesnake Island with three others plus the boat driver. Halfway to Peachland an unusual wave appeared and churned up the lake, there were no boats and the lake was perfectly calm. All thoughts were on Ogopogo. • **September:** Valerie West slowly crosses Okanagan Lake Bridge due to traffic congestion. She observes a wave moving toward the bridge and about thirty feet (9 m) away, three dark protrusions break water, each a few feet apart. • **November 29:** Gary Sorrenson and Terry Horton observe a twenty-five to forty foot (7.5–12 m) object while driving down Terrace Mountain Road near Bear Creek. The object resembled a very long wake until portions of it broke water revealing a swimming animal. They watch it through binoculars and estimate it moving along at trolling speed.

1998 **June 23:** News reports from Vernon tell of Kin Beach resident Doug Alexander observing a series of thirty- to forty-foot (9–12 m) humplike ripples on the water for ten to fifteen minutes at around 5:30 P.M. • **June 27:** Early in the morning, Linda and Walter Bauer, along with their eleven-year-old son Clayton and Bob Burrell, see an unusual object break water in Lake Kalamalka about 150 feet (46 m) from shore. It rises out of the water and swims toward Vernon leaving a visible V-wake. • **July:** Nippon TV Tokyo request the Folden film footage to air in a two-hour special called *World's Mysterious Phenomena* sometime in September to be incorporated with previous footage shot in Okanagan Lake in 1990 and 1991. • **August:** Crew members and guests aboard the *Okanagan Princess* view a large animal on sonar, just sixteen feet (5 m) below the boat. It appears to have body proportions as well as an appendage and long tail.

1999 **April 25:** Pat and Irene Dineen, out for a walk in Peachland, look down at the lake and see an eighty-foot-long (24 m) animal stirring up the waters in what was a very calm lake. Six humps are visible and as it continues to move the Dineens are certain they are seeing more than one animal. • **May 5:** Two Westbank women, Donna and Kathy M. see a large wave materialize in a calm lake creating whitecaps and watch as it moves quickly through the water toward Kelowna. A boat comes by and the disturbance suddenly disappears. • **August:** Once again the crew and captain of the *Okanagan Princess* spot a large animal on sonar, this time it is only eight feet (2.5 m) below the boat and is similar to the object spotted in 1998. They discuss the coincidence of both sonar sightings happening in the same area of the lake just a year apart. • **December 7:** Two women on their way to Kelowna from Penticton see a commotion in the lake as a large animal surfaces below near Rotary Beach. The water appears to be boiling as bubbles and waves stir up the lake. It surfaces and submerges. • **December 8:** THE LAST SIGHTING OF THE CENTURY. Nellie and Stan Bayrack, a retired couple from Westbank, are shopping in downtown Peachland. An Electrolux salesman stops to talk. All are surprised when they see the head and neck of a large animal surface out on the lake. While in conversation, the three watch the animal turn its head in both directions as though scanning its surroundings and then disappear.

2000 **March 9:** THE FIRST SIGHTING OF THE MILLENNIUM. Kevin Berry looks out his bedroom window from his Okanagan Centre home at the lake below and yelled to his family, "It's Ogopogo." His son Jackson, daughter Layana and his brother Roy E. Berry rush to the balcony and observe an aquatic animal swimming quickly through the water from north to south while Kevin readies his video camera. He captures a few seconds of a very large, dark animal swimming and then rolling into the depths below. Kevin took his first videotape March 15, 1994, of two animals swimming side by side. • **July 11:** Two men on motorbikes come down Summerland Hill toward the bluff when they spot two fifteen-foot (4.6 m) humps in the lake just 100 feet (30 m) from shore. Stopping their bikes, they watch in amazement as the waves churn and boil around each protrusion. • **August 22:** Six witnesses, four of whom work for Crown Security were shaken by the appearance of a twelve-foot (3.7 m) animal with front and back flippers, translucent skin, beady eyes and whiskers moving from the dock at Kelowna City Park in a thrusting or caterpillar-like movement toward the *Fintry Queen* on Bernard Avenue. One of the security guards states that she was within three feet (1 m) of the animal's face as it suddenly broke water close to where she was standing. • **August 9 to 23:** Cancer survivor, Daryl Ellis swims the length of Lake Okanagan from Penticton to Vernon. Near Rattlesnake Island he finds himself paced by two animals twenty to thirty feet (6–9 m) long. Wearing goggles his visibility was good. "They were swimming just below me and feeling a bit spooked I swam to the boat and requested a break. Getting back into the water again, there they were." The animals stayed with him for almost two hours. When Ellis neared Okanagan Lake Bridge, a large grayish animal flips out of the water near him and he sees a huge eye, almost the size of a grapefruit, embedded in flesh. It quickly submerges. Daryl Ellis becomes a believer. • **August 28:** As Bill Steciuk and Len Melnyk bring the Search for Ogopogo to a halt, they decide to take one more chance excursion near the mouth of Bellevue Creek. Something at least fifteen feet (4.6 m) long appears on sonar near the twenty-foot-depth (6 m) mark. • **September 4:** A minister of a local church, takes a photo of a long, dark object as it breaks water across from Monteo Resort in Kelowna. • **September 9:** Nippon Television Project 200X Search for Ogopogo picks up a sonar scan near Bear Creek. The object does not register as fish and is close to forty feet (12 m) long. • Andy and his partner Vince are gathering the day's catch of *Mysis* shrimp in early fall and are shocked when an animal close to forty feet (12 m) enters the visual sonar field and breaks through the net leaving a large hole.

2001   **January 16:** CHBC Television weatherman Mike Roberts reveals footage taken that morning by cameraman Colin Macdonald as he was getting a weather related shot for the evening news. Macdonald was standing on the west side of Lake Okanagan parallel to and north of Okanagan Lake Bridge above the Indian cemetery. His camera focused on the lake, he observes and films an animate object swimming at a fast speed through the water leaving a long wake. The lake was glassy calm. The USO was visible for a few minutes and Macdonald managed to get one minute and forty seconds of footage. The dark portion out of the water was estimated at one foot (30 cm) in length and about thirty feet (9 m) out from shore. Macdonald was unable to determine what it could be.